SNEAKY KID AND ITS AFTERMATH

Charles Banaszewski as Brad, David Vining as Harry, in a scene from the ASU production of Finding My Place, *February 2001.*

SNEAKY KID AND ITS AFTERMATH

Ethics and Intimacy in Fieldwork

Harry F. Wolcott

ALTAMIRA
PRESS

A Division of
ROWMAN & LITTLEFIELD PUBLISHERS, INC.
Walnut Creek • Lanham • New York • Oxford

AltaMira Press
A Division of Rowman & Littlefield Publishers, Inc.
1630 North Main Street, #367
Walnut Creek, CA 94596
www.altamirapress.com

Rowman & Littlefield Publishers, Inc.
A Member of the Rowman & Littlefield Publishing Group
4720 Boston Way
Lanham, MD 20706

P.O. Box 317
Oxford OX2 9RU, England

British Library Cataloguing-in-Publication data available.

Library of Congress Cataloging-in-Publication Data

Wolcott, Harry F., 1929–
Sneaky kid and its aftermath : ethics and intimacy in fieldwork /
Harry F. Wolcott.
    p. cm.
Includes bibliographical references and index.
ISBN 0-7591-0311-9 (cloth : alk. paper)
ISBN 0-7591-0312-7 (pbk. : alk. paper)
1. Educational anthropology. 2. Dropouts—United States. I. Title.
LB45 .W65 2002
306.43—dc21   2002003797

PRINTED IN THE UNITED STATES OF AMERICA

∞ The paper used in this publication meets the minimum requirements of American National Standard for Information Sciences—Permanence of Paper for Printed Library Materials, ANSI/NISO Z39.48–1992.

The quote by Norman Cousins on pp. 165–66 is reprinted by permission of *The Saturday Review*, © 1961, General Media International, Inc.

Contents

Foreword

THE Sneaky Kid story has finally become a book on its own. No longer a simple trilogy of professional articles in educational research, it is presented here with an abundance of detail and drama. More questions are answered than many of us would consider decent to ask. The self-conscious analysis of ethnographic text adds appropriate questions of research validity and ethics to the basic question with which the work began: What is "educational adequacy"?

I still value the original article as an example of what I called "morally significant ethnography" when it first appeared 20 years ago, a critique of our popular expectations that schooling will serve all the educational needs of our society. The life history of one 20-year-old homeless youth refutes those expectations. Practicing "food-stamp survival" was Brad's way to avoid the pull toward compliance and dependency in school and work. He was an independent learner, a self-described sneaky kid who could well be seen as "stealing the secrets" of the bureaucracies he confronted.

This book is a critical interpretation of American culture—much like Jules Henry's 1963 *Culture Against Man*—that undermines smug assumptions about our schools and other respected social institutions. Beyond the story of Brad, Harry now tells us how he and his Sneaky Kid articles were received in a courtroom, in professional journals and conventions, and in university seminars. We learn about much more than schools and educational adequacy. The personal and social constructions of mental illness that can treat "making it crazy" as a career choice; the ambiguities of sexual and gender roles; the imperfect constructions of "justice" in our legal institutions—these too are "educational" understandings that are painfully offered in this volume.

How does one introduce Harry adequately to the various audiences that may be attracted to this book? The book is his own self-introduction, and it includes an additional introduction by a creative playwright, Johnny Saldaña. Harry has also been an explicit character in every ethnographic account he has published. No pseudoscientific observer who melts into the woodwork, Harry has always given explicit accounts of his role as a participant with the people and cultures he set out to study. In his first published work, he described teaching in a one-room school in a remote Indian village. His classroom experience was summed up later in a paper, "The Teacher as an Enemy." But he was more than a teacher in the village; he also was a crewmember, a commercial fisherman on the Indian fishing boats in the summer. Entering into the life of the village, he was the complete field anthropologist.

In each succeeding field project, he reveals more of himself than ever before. In the third installment of the Brad story, for instance, he "came out" in one subtle sentence. In the expanded story that follows here, there is nothing subtle about his sexuality. He once thought seriously of writing his own novel or play to delve into the personal issues raised by his "life history" with Brad. Wisely, he let somebody else do that—he had already put himself on the record. Brad, Harry's one-time informant, savagely beat Harry and burned down his home. Harry endured this and subsequent victimization during Brad's arson trial. He survived these traumas by maintaining his anthropological eye and attitude, using his experience as further data for his understanding of American culture. It is an effective strategy for dealing with such anguish.

When speaking to education, Harry delights in the guise of a professional curmudgeon, but he gives himself away as a hopeless romantic in his identity as anthropologist. He takes natural delight in the personal relations of fieldwork that has ranged from an African beer garden to a Northwest Coast Kwakiutl potlatch. He has, however, also made elementary schools and his backyard into dramatic fieldwork locations.

Another indication of his romantic nature is his drive to present a personal drama as legitimate theatre. While archaeologists and cultural anthropologists have made their way onto the popular stage, Harry is the first educational anthropologist I know to get there, his role played by a professional actor. (I wonder whether there will be movie rights?)

When Harry and I came to educational anthropology 40 years ago, there wasn't even such a job title. We've come a long way since we sat together with our mentor, George Spindler, at Stanford. Educational anthropology is now a thriving field. Following Harry's admonition to "heady candor," therefore, I must admit that this preface is not a disinterested endorsement of his work. Harry pursues difficult goals with lively style, provocative scholarship, and admirable collegiality. As I've done before, I recommend him as a colleague.

This is a book I've long encouraged Harry to write because of the importance of the questions about educational adequacy and the necessary distinction between education and schooling. The inadequacy of our institutions of schooling, justice, and welfare is an important expansion of the original agenda.

The book has turned out to be much more than what I expected, while still a powerful cultural critique. We need Harry's insights on critical ethical problems enshrined in our society and in our expectations of schools, courts, welfare offices, prisons, and hospitals.

—JOHN SINGLETON
Professor Emeritus, Education and Anthropology, University of Pittsburgh

Introduction

MY first publication about Brad was in 1983, in an article for the *Anthropology and Education Quarterly*. I had written about him in a report submitted earlier, but the publication in *AEQ* was the first time the story was widely circulated. I subtitled the piece "The Life History of a Sneaky Kid." Subsequently, I used the article zas an example of ethnographic writing to accompany my essay in *Complementary Methods in Educational Research*, which appeared in 1988 and was revised and reissued in 1997.

I wrote two additional articles about Brad, one published in 1987, the other in 1990. In 1994, I had a chance to bring all three articles together under one cover in *Transforming Qualitative Data*, and I began to refer to them collectively as the Brad Trilogy.

So if you have been around a while, you may have come across the Sneaky Kid article before or encountered Brad in the trilogy. If you haven't, not to worry, for I have reproduced here as chapter 1 the Sneaky Kid account as it originally appeared in *AEQ*. (Even if you remember the original Sneaky Kid article, you might want to read it again before proceeding with the rest of the text.) I have also brought you up to speed in the chapters that follow, without the repetition necessary to bring new readers up to date for each part of the trilogy.

If you have already seen the third piece, titled "On Seeking—and Rejecting—Validity," you won't find much additional information about Brad in this account. He had, after all, left my place before the first article appeared, and he came back only once after that. This account deals instead with the *story* of the Brad story. Thus, the title, *Sneaky Kid and Its Aftermath,* is a reference to the written accounts, not to Brad himself. And the story has become the story of the two of us, and involves others as well.

This "story of a story" is incomplete—all stories are—and although you will get several points of view, mine will predominate. So this is Harry's version, and thus it is *a* story, not *the* story. But there is plenty here to serve as food for thought, both on substantive issues and issues of method. Some interpretive remarks will be found in each chapter, since each phase raises new issues to be explored. In a final chapter, I examine some of the important questions the study raises for me.

I am pleased to include the text of the ethnodrama *Finding My Place*. The script offers another way of presenting the Brad story, this one written and produced by Johnny Saldaña, professor of theatre at Arizona State University. Johnny has transformed the story into a play based on the same corpus of material, so the perspective will be similar. If you can visualize as you read, you will be able to see and hear the performance as well. You might save that for your final reading, as I have done by making it the last entry.

Part One

The Sneaky Kid

Chapter One

Adequate Schools and Inadequate Education

The Life History of a Sneaky Kid

"I GUESS if you're going to be here, I need to know something about you, where you're from, and what kind of trouble you're in," I said to the lad, trying not to reveal my uncertainty, surprise, and dismay at his uninvited presence until I could learn more about his circumstances. It wasn't much of an introduction, but it marked the beginning of a dialogue that lasted almost two years from that moment. Brad (a pseudonym, although, as he noted, using his real name wouldn't really matter, since "no one knows who I am anyway") tersely stated his full name; the fact that his parents had "split up" and that his mother was remarried and living in Southern California; his father's local address; and that he was not at present in any trouble because he wasn't "that stupid." He also volunteered that he had spent time in the state's correctional facility for youth, but quickly added, "It wasn't really my fault."

It was not our meeting itself that was a surprise; it was that Brad had been living at this remote spot on my steep and heavily wooded 20-acre homesite on the outskirts of town for almost five weeks. In that time, he had managed to build a 10-by-12-foot cabin made of newly cut sapling logs and roofed with plywood paneling. A couple of weeks earlier, I had stumbled across his original campsite, but I assumed it had been made by some youngster enjoying a bivouac en route to hiking a nearby ridge that afforded a fine view, a popular day hike for townspeople and an occasional overnight adventure for kids. I also found a bow saw, but I thought it had been left by a recent surveying party. Brad had been watching me at the time and later admitted cursing to himself for being careless in leaving tools about.

I did not realize that I had both a new cabin and an unofficial tenant until a neighbor reported that his 8-year-old son claimed not only to have seen but to have spoken to a "hobo" while wandering through my woods. The hobo

3

turned out to be the then–19-year-old youth, slightly stoop-shouldered and of medium build, standing opposite me. And it is his story that I am about to relate.

As intrigued and involved as I eventually became with Brad and his story, my purpose in providing this account transcends the individual case, even though I will tie my remarks closely to it. That purpose is related to my professional interest in anthropology and education and, particularly, in cultural acquisition, drawing upon anthropology both for approach and for perspective in looking at educational issues (see Wolcott 1982). There is no shortage of case study materials about alienated youth.[1] Attention here will be drawn particularly to educationally relevant aspects of this case. Brad's story underscores and dramatizes a critical distinction that anthropologists make between *schooling* and *education* and raises questions about our efforts at education for young people beyond the purview of the schools.[2] Adequate schools may be necessary, but they are not sufficient to ensure an adequate education.

Brad's strategy for coping with his life first impressed me as bold, resourceful, and even romantic, as did his building of a cabin. Faced with jobs he did not want to do (he abhors dishwashing, yet that seemed to be the only work he felt he could get because "those jobs are always open") and expenses he could not afford (renting an apartment, buying and operating a motorcycle), he had chosen to change his lifestyle radically by reducing his cash needs to a minimum. What he could not afford, he would try to do without.

Never before had he done the things he now set out to do. He had never lived in the woods (though he had gone camping), never built a log house (though he had occasionally helped his father in light construction), never thought about a personal inventory of essential items. He had identified the cabin site, hidden from view but with a commanding view of its own, during one of his endless and solitary explorations of streets, roads, and paths in and around the city. The location was near a section of the city where he had once lived as a child. He went deep into a densely wooded area, entering from the east and failing to realize how close he had come to my house on the county road around the west side of the ridge. But he knew he had to be near town. He needed to be where, one way or another, he could pick up the things essential to his anticipated lifestyle. He did not need much, but what he did need—hammer, saw, nails, sleeping bag, stove, cooking utensils, flashlight and lantern, pants and shoes, containers for carrying and storing water—he scrounged, stole, or, occasionally and reluctantly, purchased.

Brad displayed few qualities that would earn him the title of outdoorsman. His tools and equipment were often mislaid or neglected. He proved terrible at tying knots. He cut trees unnecessarily and turned his own trails into slippery troughs of mud. In spite of occasional references to himself as "Jungle Boy," he was basically a city boy making whatever accommodation was necessary to survive inexpensively. His fuel and food came from town; he was totally dependent on the city even though he could not afford to live in it. If his menu gradually became more like that of the woodsman (potatoes, onions, pancakes, melted-cheese sandwiches, eggs, soup, canned tuna, powdered milk, and powdered orange juice), it was because he realized that these items could almost stretch $70 of food stamps into a month's ration. He washed and dried his clothes in coin-operated machines at night at a nearby apartment complex. His battery-operated radio played almost constantly, and he became even more cabin-bound watching a small battery-operated TV set purchased for him by his mother during a brief visit, their first in over two years.

It was not Brad's wont to take leisurely walks in the woods, spend time enjoying sunsets, or listen to birdcalls. He brought what he could find (and carry up steep, narrow trails) of his urban environment with him. Though not very sociable, he calculatingly mismanaged his purchases so that on many days he "had to" bicycle two miles each way to his favorite store to get a pack of cigarettes and perhaps buy a can of beer or smoke a joint in a nearby park. Town was the only direction he traveled. Yet, almost without exception, he returned to his cabin each evening, usually before darkness made the trip hazardous on an unlit bike. The security of having literally created a place all his own lent a critical element of stability to his life. He was proud of what he had built, even though he acknowledged that, were he starting over, his cabin would be "bigger and better in every way." His dreams for improving it never ceased.

For a while he envisioned building a tree house high in a giant Douglas fir nearby. A fearless tree-climber, he attached a high pulley and cable swing so he could trim branches and hoist construction materials. The tree house idea occupied his thoughts for weeks. During that time, he made few improvements on the cabin. The idea of being virtually inaccessible high in a tree proved more romantic than practical, however, and eventually he gave it up, brought his tools back to the cabin, and began work in earnest on improvements that included cutting out a section of wall and adding a lean-to bunk bed. The cable was removed from the tree house site and found its permanent place as a hillside swing with a breathtaking arc amongst the tree-tops on the slope below. Swinging provided a literal as well as figurative high for Brad. Pausing to rest between turns at the strenuous exercise, he volunteered the only positive comment I ever heard him make regarding the future: "I'll still swing like this when I'm 60!"

In brief glimpses, other people's lives often appear idyllic. Brad's Robinson Crusoe–like life had many appealing qualities. He seemed to have freed himself from the trappings of the Establishment, which he saw as a curiously circular and uninviting system that required him to take a job he hated in order to earn enough to provide transportation to and from work, and money for the rent on some cheap place where he would rather not live. He had seen his father work hard, dream even harder, and yet, in Brad's opinion, "get nowhere." Brad was trying to figure out for himself what he wanted in life and whether it was really worth the effort.

I found it hard to argue on behalf of what some menial job would get him. I heard quite well his argument that, lacking in skill or experience, he would probably have to do work at once physically harder and lower-paying than most jobs today. He could be an indefatigable worker, but I think he felt some anxiety about being able to keep up on jobs requiring hours of continuous hard physical labor. An earlier and short-lived job as a tree planter had convinced him that hard work does not ensure success.

A glimpse into Brad's daily life does not dispel the romantic image of his existence. He arose when he wanted and retired when he wanted (although, with the cold, dark, and perennial dampness of the Northwest's winters, and with little to do, he spent so much time in the sack that getting to sleep became increasingly problematic). He could eat when he chose and cook or not as mood—and a rather sparse cupboard—dictated. Food and cigarette needs dominated his schedule of trips to town. A trip to the store, or to see about food stamps (in effect he had no address, so he went to the Welfare Office in person), or to secure other supplies (a tire for the bicycle, fuel for lanterns or the stove, hardware items for the cabin) occurred once or twice a week. And if there was no needed trip, he was free to decide—quite consciously, though rather impulsively, I think—how to spend the day.

Although the cabin was sometimes untidy and utensils were seldom washed before they were used again, Brad kept his person and his clothes clean. He brushed his teeth regularly. He never went to town without "showering," or at least washing his face and hair. In warm weather he underscored the nymphlike nature of his existence by remaining almost, or totally, unclad in the seclusion of his immediate cabin area, though he was excruciatingly self-conscious in public settings. His preference for privacy was highlighted by recollections of his distress at regimented public showering "on procedures" at reform school, and such experiences had made options like joining the armed services something he insisted he would only do if he had to. Brad was, at first glance, a free spirit. He regarded himself that way, too: "I do what I want."

The Cultural Context of a Free Spirit

There is no universal set of things to be desired or events to fill one's days and dreams, just as there is no absolute set of things to be learned (see Wallace 1961b:38). What people learn or want or do or dream about is embedded in particular macro- and microcultural systems.

Brad was aware of many aspects of his "culture" that he felt he could do without, including—up to a point—seeking much involvement within his society, seeming to heed its expectations, or depending on its resources. But he was accustomed to technological innovations and he had been reared in a society where, it seemed to him, virtually *everyone* had everything they needed. Although he saw himself as living figuratively, as well as literally, at the edge of society, he was still society's child. He was free to insist, "I do what I want," but he was not free to do what he wanted. What he had learned to want was a function of his culture, and he drew narrowly and rather predictably from the cultural repertoire of the very society from which he believed he was extricating himself.

Brad needed to cook. An open fire is slow and most impractical on a rainy day. One needs a camp stove in order to cook inside a cabin. And fuel. And then a better stove. Cold water is all right for washing hands but it can be a bit too bracing for washing one's hair or torso, especially when standing outside with the wind blowing. One needs a bigger pan to heat water for bathing. Soap and shampoo. A towel. A new razor. A mirror. A bigger mirror. A foam rubber mattress. A chair. A chaise lounge.

One needs something to look at and listen to. Magazines are a brief diversion, but rock music is essential. One needs a radio. Flashlight batteries are expensive for continual radio listening; a radio operated by an automobile battery would be a better source—and could power a better radio. An automobile battery needs to be recharged. Carrying a battery to town is awkward, and constantly having to pay to have it recharged is expensive. As well as access to a power supply (in my carport), one needs a battery charger. No, this one is rated too low; a bigger one would be better. Luckily not a harsh winter, but a wet one. The dirt floor of the cabin gets muddy; a wood floor is essential. The roof leaks; a heavier grade of plywood and stronger tarpaulin to place over it are necessary. The sleeping bag rips where it got wet; a replacement is needed. Shoes wear out from constant use on the trails; clothes get worn or torn. Flashlights and batteries wear out. Cigarettes (or tobacco), matches, eggs, bread, Tang, Crisco, pancake flour, syrup—supplies get low. An occasional steak helps vary the austere diet.

One needs transportation. A bicycle is essential, as are spare parts to keep it in repair. Now a minor accident: The bicycle is wrecked. No money to buy a new one. Brad "hypes" himself up and sets out to find a replacement. "Buy one? When they're so easy to get? No way!"

The Life History of a Sneaky Kid

Here is the place to let Brad relate something of his life and how he had tried to make sense of, and come to grips with, the world about him.

Ideally, in relating a life history through an ethnographic autobiography, informants tell their stories almost entirely in their own words (e.g., classics such as Leo Simmons's *Sun Chief*, 1942, or Oscar Lewis's *Children of Sanchez*, 1961; see also Brandes 1982). There should be a high ratio of information to explanation in a life story; sometimes there is no explanation or explicit interpretation at all. Time, space, and purpose require me to proceed more directly. I have organized the material around themes suggested by Brad himself, and although I have been faithful to his words as he spoke them, I have tried to select the most cogent excerpts from months of informal conversations and several hours of formal interviews that Brad volunteered expressly for this purpose.[3]

I have given particular attention to aspects of Brad's story that illustrate the two major points of this paper: that education consists of more than schooling, and that we give little systematic attention to the course of a young person's education once he or she is out of school. For these purposes, I have dwelt more on social concerns than on personal or psychological ones. Brad had some hang-ups focused largely on his acceptance of his body and a preoccupation with sexual fantasy as yet unfulfilled—*Portnoy's Complaint* personified. In time (or, more candidly, not quite in time; he sank unexpectedly into a mood of utter despair and abruptly announced he was "hitting the road" because he saw no future where he was), I realized he had some deep-seated emotional hang-ups as well. My concern in this paper, however, is with Brad as a social rather than a psychological being, and thus with personality-in-culture rather than with personality per se.

"In the Chute"

A speaker at the 1981 American Correctional Association meetings was reported in the national press to have used the phrase "in the chute" to describe individuals whose lives seem headed for prison, even though they have not yet arrived there: "People who are 'in the chute,' so to speak, and heading toward us, are beginning that movement down in infancy."

When the ethnography begins, Brad is not yet in the chute. It is not inevitable that he end up in trouble, but he could. Excerpts from his life story suggest how things point that way. Here he recalls a chain of events that started at age 10 with what proved a traumatic event in his life, his parents' divorce:

On the loose. "After my parents got divorced, I was living with my dad. I had quite a bit of freedom. My dad wasn't around. If I didn't want to go to school, I just didn't go. Everybody who knows me now says, 'That guy had the world's record for ditching school.' My dad was at work all day and there was no one to watch me. I was pretty wild. My dad took me to a counseling center at the university; they told me I was 'winning the battles but losing the war.'

"After my dad got remarried, I had no freedom any more. I had a new mother to watch me. I got mad at her a couple of times, so I moved in with her parents. I went to seventh grade for a while and got pretty good grades. Then I went to Southern California to visit my mother. When my dad said he'd have to 'make some arrangements' before I could return, I just stayed there. But I got into a hassle with my stepdad, and I ditched some classes, and suddenly I was on a bus back to Oregon.

"My father had separated again and I moved into some little apartment with him. He wanted me to go to another school, but I said, 'Forget it, man, I'm not going to another school. I'm tired of school.' So I'd just lay around the house—stay up all night, sleep all day.

"Finally I told my mom I'd be a 'good boy,' and she let me move back to Southern California. But I got in another hassle with my stepdad. I ran out of the house and stayed with some friends for a few months. But then the police got in a hassle with me and they said I'd have to go back with my dad or they were going to send me to a correctional institution. The next thing you know, I was back on the bus."

Getting busted. "By then my dad had remarried again. I wasn't ready for another family. I stayed about two days, then I left. I figured any place was better than living there. But they got pissed at me because I kept coming back [breaking into the house] for food, so they called the cops on me. Running away from them, I broke my foot and had to go to the hospital. Then I got sent to reform school. They had a charge against me [contraband], but I think the real reason was that I didn't have any place to go. I was in reform school for eight months."

Second-rate jobs and second-rate apartments. "I finally played their 'baby game' and got out of reform school. They sent me to a halfway house in Portland. I got a job, made some money, got a motorcycle, moved to another place, then that job ended. I got another job with a churchgoing plumber for a while, but I got fired. Then I came back and worked for my dad, but there wasn't nothing to do. And I got in some family hassles. So I got a few jobs and lived in some cheap apartments.

"For a while I was a bum down at the Mission. I'd get something to eat, then I'd go sleep under a truck. My sleeping bag was all I had. I knew winter was coming and I'd have to do something. I saw a guy I knew and he said, 'Hey, I've got a place if you'd like to crash out until you get something going.' So I went there and got a job for about four months washing dishes. Then my mom came up from California to visit and found me an apartment. God, how I hated that place, with people right on the other side of those thin walls who know you're all alone and never have any visitors or anything. I quit washing dishes; they cut me down to such low hours I wasn't making any money anyway. So I just hibernated for the winter."

A new life. "When the rent ran out, I picked up my sleeping bag and the stuff I had and headed for the hills at the edge of town. I found a place that looked like no one had been here for a while, and I set up a tarp for shelter. I decided to take my time and build a place for myself, because I wasn't doing anything anyway. I just kept working on it. I've been here a year and a half now. I've done some odd jobs, but mostly I live on food stamps.

"I used to think about doing something like this when I lived in Portland. I read a book called *How to Live in the Woods on Pennies a Day.* I even tried staying out in the woods a couple of times, but I didn't know exactly what to do. I wasn't thinking about a cabin then. All I knew was that I needed some place to get out of the wind and some place to keep dry. I saw this piece of level ground and knew that if I had tools and nails I could probably put up some walls. As I went along I just figured out what I would need.

"I put up four posts and started dragging logs around till the walls were built. There were plenty of trees around. It took about a week to get the walls. I slept in a wet sleeping bag for a couple of nights, 'cause I didn't have a roof. The first roof was some pieces of paneling that I carried up from some kids' tree fort. I had a dirt floor but I knew I'd have to have a wood floor someday. I knew about plaster because I had worked with it before, so I smeared some on the walls. All that I really needed at first was nails. I got the other stuff I needed from new houses being built nearby."

"Picking up" what was needed. "I got around town quite a bit. Anyplace where there might be something, I'd take a look. If I found anything that I needed, I'd pick it up and take it home. I just started a collection: sleeping bag, radio, plywood for the roof, windows, a stove, lanterns, tools, clothes, water containers, boots. If you took away everything that's stolen, there

wouldn't be much left here. Like the saw. I just walked into a store, grabbed it, put a piece of cloth around it to hide it, and walked out.

"Before I got food stamps, I'd go to the store with my backpack, fill it with steaks and expensive canned food, and just walk out. If anybody saw me, I'd wave at them and keep walking. I didn't have much to lose, I figured. The closest I ever got to being stopped, I had two six-packs of beer and some cooked chicken. The guy in the store had seen me there before. I just waved, but he said, 'Stop right there.' I ran out and grabbed my bike, but he was right behind me. I knew the only thing I could do was drop the merchandise and get out of there with my skin and my bike, and that's what I did. He didn't chase me; he just picked up the bag and shook his head at me."

The bicycle thief. "We lived in the country for about three years while I was growing up. Moving back into town was kinda different. I went pretty wild after moving to town. Me and another kid did a lot of crazy stuff, getting into places and taking things. I'd stay out all night just looking in people's garages. I'd get lots of stuff. My room had all kinds of junk in it. That's when I was living with my dad, and he didn't really notice. He still has an electric pencil-sharpener I stole out of a church. He never knew where I got it.

"Instead of going to school, I'd stay home and work on bikes. We used to steal bikes all the time. We'd get cool frames and put all the hot parts on them. I've stolen lots of bikes—maybe around 50. But I probably shouldn't have never stolen about half of them, they were such junk. I just needed them for transportation."

Being sneaky. "I've always been kind of sneaky, I guess. That's just the way I am. I can't say why. My mom says that when I was a small kid I was always doing something sneaky. Not always—but I *could* be that way. I guess I'm still that way, but it's not exactly the same. It's just the way you think about things.

"I don't like to be sneaky about something I could get in trouble for. But I like to walk quietly so no one will see me. I could get in trouble for something like sneaking in somebody's backyard and taking a rototiller. I did that once. I sold the engine.

"I guess being sneaky means I always try to get away with something. There doesn't have to be any big reason. I used to tell the kid I was hanging around with: 'I don't steal stuff because I need it. I just like to do it for some excitement.'

"Last year I went 'jockey-boxing' with some guys who hang around at the park. That's when you get into people's glove compartments. It was a pretty dead night. One guy wanted a car stereo. He had his tools and everything. So we all took off on bicycles, five of us. I was sort of tagging along and watching them—I didn't really do it. They got into a couple of cars. They got a battery vacuum cleaner and a couple of little things. You go to apartment houses where there's lots of cars and you find the unlocked ones and everybody grabs a car and jumps in and starts scrounging through.

"I've gone through glove compartments before and I probably will again someday if I see a car sitting somewhere just abandoned. But I'm not into it for fun anymore, and it doesn't pay unless you do a lot. Mostly young guys do it.

"I'm still mostly the same, though. I'll take a roll of tape or something from the supermarket. Just stick it in my pants. Or if I saw a knife that was easy to take. That's about it. Oh, I sneak into some nearby apartments to wash my clothes. I pay for the machines, but they are really for the tenants, not for me. And I'll sneak through the woods with a piece of plywood for the cabin."

I don't have to steal, but . . . "I'm not what you'd call a super thief, but I will steal. A super thief makes his living at it; I just get by. I don't have to steal, but it sure makes life a hell of a lot easier. I've always known people who steal stuff. It's no big deal. If you really want something, you have to go around looking for it. I guess I could teach you how to break into your neighbor's house, if you want to. There's lots of ways—just look for a way to get in. It's not that hard to do. I don't know what you'd call it. Risky? Crazy?

"I can be honest. Being honest means that you don't do anything to people that you don't know. I don't like to totally screw somebody. But I'll screw 'em a little bit. You could walk into somebody's garage and take everything they have—maybe $5,000 worth of stuff. Or you could just walk in and grab a chain saw. It's not my main hobby to go around looking for stuff to steal. I might see something, but I wouldn't go out of my way for it."

Breaking and entering. "I remember busting into my second-grade classroom. I went back to the schoolground on the weekend with another kid. We were just looking around outside and I said, 'Hey, look at that fire-escape door—you could pull it open with a knife.' We pulled it open and I went in and I took some money and three or four little cars and a couple of pens. There wasn't anything of value, but the guy with me stocked up on all the pens he could find. We got in trouble for it. That was the first time I broke in anywhere. I don't know why I did it. Maybe too many television shows. I just did it because I could see that you could do it.

"And I've gotten into churches and stores. I've broken into apartment-house recreation rooms a lot, crawling through the windows. And I've broken into a house before.

"I went in one house through the garage door, got inside, and scrounged around the whole house. God, there was so much stuff in that house. I munched a cake, took some liquor, took some cameras. Another time I thought there was nobody home at one house, and I went around to the bathroom window, punched in the screen and made a really good jump to the inside. I walked in the house real quietly. Then I heard somebody walk out the front door, so I split. I didn't have nothin' then; I was looking for anything I could find. I just wanted to go scrounging through drawers to find some money.

"If I ever needed something that bad again and it was total chaos [i.e., desperation], I could do it and I would. It's not my way of life, but I'd steal before I'd ever beg."

Inching closer to the chute. "Just before I started living at the cabin, I kept having it on my mind that I needed some money and could rob a store. It seemed like a pretty easy way to get some cash, but I guess it wasn't a very good idea. I had a BB gun. I could have walked in there like a little Mafia, shot the gun a few times, and said, 'If you don't want those in your face, better give me the money.' There were a couple of stores I was thinking of doing it to.

"I was standing outside one store for about two hours. I just kept thinking about going in there. All of a sudden this cop pulls into the parking lot and kinda checks me out. I thought, 'Oh fuck, if that cop came over here and searched me and found this gun, I'd be shit.' So as soon as he split, I left. And after thinking about it for so long.

"But another time, I really did it. I went into one of those little fast-food stores. I had this hood over my head with a little hole for the mouth. I said to the clerk, 'Open the register.' And she said, 'What! Are you serious?' I knew she wasn't going to open it, and she knew I wasn't about to shoot her. So then I started pushing all the buttons on the cash register, but I didn't know which ones to push. And she came up and pulled the key. Then someone pulled up in front of the store and the signal bell went 'ding, ding.' So I booked.

"Another time I thought about going into a store and telling the cashier to grab the cash tray and pull it out and hand it to me. Or else I was going to wait till near closing time when they go by with a full tray of 20-dollar bills and grab it. Or go into a restaurant right after closing time, like on a Saturday night or something, and just take the whole till. I was going to buy a motorcycle with that. All I needed was $400 to get one.

"If I was ever that hurting, I could probably do it if I had to. It's still a possibility, and it would sure be nice to have some cash. But you wouldn't get much from a little store anyway. I'd be more likely just to walk in and grab a case of beer."

I'm not going to get caught. "I can't straighten out my old bike after that little accident I had the other day, and that means I need another bike. I'll try to find one to steal—that's the easiest way to get one. I should be able to find one for free, and very soon, instead of having to work and spend all that money, money that would be better off spent other places, like reinstating my driver's license.

"The way I do it, I go out in nice neighborhoods and walk around on people's streets and look for open garages, like maybe they just went to the store or to work and didn't close the door. I walk on streets that aren't main streets. Someone might spot me looking around at all these bikes, but even if somebody says something, they can't do anything to you. The cops might come up and question me, but nothing could happen.

"Now, if I was caught on a hot bike . . . but that's almost impossible. If I was caught, they'd probably take me downtown and I'd sit there awhile until I went to court, and who knows what they'd do. Maybe give me six months. They'd keep me right there at the jail. But it's worth the risk, because I'm not going to get caught. I did it too many times. I know it's easy.

"Even if I worked, the only thing I'd be able to buy is an old Schwinn 10-speed. The bike I'm going to get will be brand new. Maybe a Peugeot or a Raleigh. A $400 bike at least. It might not be brand new, but if I could find a way, I'd get a $600 bike, the best one I could find. And I'll do whatever I have to, so no one will recognize it."

Home is the hunter. "I think this will be the last 'bike hunting' trip I'll ever go on . . . probably. I said it *might* be the last one. I could probably do one more. When I get to be 24 or 25, I doubt that I'll be walking around looking for bikes. But if I was 25 and I saw a nice bike, and I was in bad shape and really needed it, I'd get it. I'm not going to steal anything I don't need. Unless it's just sitting there and I can't help it, it's so easy. I'm not really corrupt, but I'm not 'innocent' anymore. I can be trusted, to some people."

"Can I trust you?" I asked.

"Yeah. Pretty much. I dunno. When it comes to small stuff. . . ."

Growing up. "When I was growing up, I was always doing something, but it wasn't that bad. My parents never did take any privileges away or give me another chance. Anytime I did something in California, my mother and stepdad just said, 'Back to Oregon!' They didn't threaten, they just did it. My mom could have figured out something better than sending me back to Oregon all the time. She could have taken away privileges, or made me work around the house. And in Oregon, my dad could have figured a better way than throwing me out of the house. Bad times for me were getting in a hassle with my parents. Then I wouldn't have no place to go, no money or nothin': That happened with all of them at different times."

[By my count, Brad was reared in six households, including a time when he lived with his mother at her sister's home, and when he lived with one stepmother's parents for a while. That fact did not seem as disconcerting to him as the abruptness with which he was dispatched from one household to another.]

"The last time I got kicked out in California, I moved back to Oregon, but I only stayed in the house a couple of days. My stepmom and my dad started telling me I wasn't going to smoke pot anymore, I would have to go to school, I was going to have to stop smoking cigarettes, and other shit like that. I didn't like *anything* about that fucking house. Another reason is that my dad said I couldn't have a motorcycle.

"So I split. I just hung around town, sleeping anywhere I could find. I ripped off a quilt and slept out on a baseball field for a while. I stayed in different places for a couple of weeks. Then I got busted, got sent to reform school; then I got some work and the first thing I did was buy a motorcycle. I was riding without a license or insurance for a while. Even after I got a license, I kept getting tickets, so finally my license got suspended, and my dad took the motorcycle and sold it to pay for the tickets.

"If I had kids, I would just be a closer family. I would be with them more and show that you love them. You could talk to your kids more. And if they do something wrong, you don't go crazy and lose your temper or something."

Getting paid for dropping out. "I've earned some money at odd jobs since I came here, but mostly I live on food stamps. I knew that if I wasn't working and was out of money, food stamps were there. I've been doing it for quite a while. When I was at the Mission I had food stamps. A guy I worked with once told me all you had to do was go down there and tell 'em you're broke, that's what it's there for. I haven't really tried looking for a job. Food stamps are a lot easier. And I'd just be taking a job away from someone who needs it more. Now that I've figured out the kinds of things to buy, I can just about get by each month on $70 for food. If I couldn't get food stamps, I'd get a job. I guess food stamps are society's way of paying me to drop out."

Hiding out from life. "So now I've got this cabin fixed up and it really works good for me. This is better than any apartment I've ever had.

"I guess by living up here I'm sorta hiding out from life. At least I'm hiding from the life I had before I came up here. That's for sure. The life of a dumpy apartment and a cut-rate job. This is a different way of life.

"What would I have been doing for the year and a half in town compared to a year and a half up here? Like, all the work I've done here, none of it has gone for some landlord's pocketbook. I should be able to stay here until I get a good job.

"I like living like this. I think I'd like to be able to know how to live away from electricity and all that."

The romantic Robinson Crusoe aspect of a young man carving out a life in the wilderness, what his mother referred to as "living on a mountaintop in Oregon," is diminished by this fuller account of Brad's lifestyle. Brad would work if he "had to," but he had found that for a while—measured perhaps in years rather than weeks—he did not have to. If he was not hiding out from life, he had at least broken out of what he saw as the futility of holding a cut-rate job in order to live a cut-rate existence.

Brad kept a low profile that served double duty. He had a strong aversion to being "looked at" in settings where he felt he did not "blend in," and his somewhat remote cabin protected him from the eyes of all strangers—including the law. His cabin became his fortress; he expressed concern that he himself might be "ripped off." On sunny weekends, with the likelihood of hikers passing through the woods, he tended to stay near the cabin with an eye toward protecting his motley—but nonetheless precious—collection of tools and utensils, bicycles and parts, and personal belongings. He sometimes padlocked the cabin (though it easily could have been broken into) and always locked his bike when in town if he was going to be any distance from it. Had he been ripped off, he would hardly have called the police to help recover his stolen items; few were his in the first place.

Technically, he was not in trouble with the law, but to some extent the law exerted a constraining influence on him. In his view, to get caught was the worst thing that could happen to him and would have been "stupid" on his part. That tended to circumscribe both the frequency and extent of the illicit activities in which he engaged. But the law also menaced him because of his status as a down-and-outer and as a relatively powerless youth, a youth without resources. The law works on a cash basis. Working for me, Brad earned and saved enough money to purchase an engine for his bicycle in order to circumvent his earlier problems with the motorcycle. He was later to discover, via a traffic violation of over $300 (reduced to $90 with the conventional plea "guilty with explanation"), that a bicycle with an engine on it is deemed a motorized vehicle. Therefore, he was required by law to have a valid operator's license (his was still suspended), a license for the vehicle, and insurance. To make himself legal, he needed about $175 and would continue to face high semiannual insurance premiums. To his way of thinking, that expense got him "nothing," so he preferred to take his chances. Traffic fines were actually a major budget item for him, but his argument remained the same: "I won't get caught again."

Margaret Mead once commented that most Americans would agree that the "worst" thing a child can do is to steal (in MacNeil and Glover 1959). As a "sneaky kid," Brad had already been stealing stuff—little stuff, mostly—for more than half his lifetime. He seemed to be approaching the moment when he either would have to forgo stealing, regarding it as a phase of growing up and doing "crazy things" (jockey-boxing, breaking into the school on weekends, petty shoplifting, stealing bicycles), or step into the "chute" by joining the big leagues. With mask and gun, he had already faced the chute head-on. That event might have ended differently, had someone not called his bluff. With the issuance of repeated traffic fines, the courts themselves could conceivably precipitate a desperate need for quick and easy money.

Worldview: "Getting My Life Together"

The material presented thus far lends ample support for Brad's depiction of himself as a "sneaky kid" exhibiting a number of anti-social and unsociable traits. In the last 10 of his 20 years, Brad's antics often resulted in trouble ("hassles") and paved the way for more trouble than had actually befallen him. (In that regard, it is ironic that being sent to reform school—though on the technically serious charge of "supplying contraband" coupled with "harassment"—was, in his opinion, more a consequence of having "nowhere else to go" than of the offenses themselves.)

From mainstream society's point of view, Brad's story would seem to reflect the enculturation process going awry, a young person growing up apart from, rather than as a part of, the appropriate social system. Brad did not behave "properly" with regard to certain critical dimensions (e.g., respect for other people's property, earning his way); therefore, his almost exemplary behavior in other dimensions (his lack of pretense, his cleanliness, and, particularly, his resourcefulness and self-reliance) was apt to be overlooked. He was not a social asset, and he seemed destined for trouble.

Yet in both word and deed (and here is the advantage of knowing him for two years, rather than depending solely on formal interviews), Brad repeatedly demonstrated how he was more "insider" than "outsider" to the society he felt was paying him to drop out. In numerous ways he revealed a personal worldview not so far out of step with society after all. Adrift he may have been, but he was not without social bearings. The odds may have been against him, but they were not stacked. This was neither a "minority" kid fighting the immediate peril of the ghetto, nor a weak kid, nor a dumb kid, nor an unattractive kid, nor a kid who had not, at some time in his life, felt the security of family. Indeed, somewhere along the way he learned to value security so highly that his pursuit of it provided him an overriding sense of purpose.

Both of Brad's parents had worked all their adult lives and, judging from statements I heard them make, took pride in their efforts. If, as Brad sized it up, they were "not really rich," they were at least comfortable. Perhaps from Brad's point of view they had paid too high a price for what they had, or had given up too much to attain it, but they are the embodiment of the American working class. As Brad expressed it: "My dad's worked all his life so he can sit at a desk and not hold a screwdriver any more. But he just works! He never seems to have any fun."

Absolutely no one, including anthropologists who devote careers to the task, ever learns the totality of a culture. Conversely, no one, including the most marginal or socially isolated of humans, ever escapes the deep imprint of macro- and microcultural systems in which he or she is reared as a member of a family, a community, and a nation. Evidence of that cultural imprinting abounds in Brad's words and actions. I have combed his words and found in his worldview glimmers of hope—if only he does not "get caught doing something stupid" or in some unexpected way get revisited by his past. Though he occasionally makes some deliberate, unsanctioned responses, Brad appears well aware of the "cultural meanings" of his behavior (see Wallace 1961a:135).

If Brad does "make it," it will be largely because of the cultural imprinting of values instilled at some time in that same past. Let me here make the point to which I will return in conclusion: There was no constructive force working effectively on Brad's behalf to guide, direct, encourage, or assist him. He had no sponsor, no support system, virtually no social network. The agencies poised to respond to him would act when and if he made a mistake and got caught. He could not get help without first getting into trouble. The only social agency that exerted a positive educative influence on him was an indirect consequence of the mixed blessing of food stamps, which kept him from having to steal groceries but made it unnecessary for him to work. He had learned to spend his allotment wisely in order to see him through the month.

The following excerpts, selected topically, suggest the extent to which Brad already had acquired a sense of middle-class morality and an ethos of working to achieve material success. They also point to loose strands that remain to be woven together someday, if he is to be bound more securely to the Establishment.

A job—that's all that makes you middle-class. "A job is all that makes you middle-class. If I'm going to have a job, I've got to have a bike that works. I've got to have a roof, I've got to have my clothes washed. And I'd probably need rain gear, too. You can't go into any job in clothes that look like you just came out of a mud hut.

"Even though I've worked for a while at lots of different things, I guess you could say that I've never really held a job. I've worked for my dad awhile—altogether about a year, off and on. I helped him wire houses and do other things in light construction. I scraped paint for a while for one company. I worked for a graveyard for about eight months, for a plumber a while, and I planted trees for a while.

"I wouldn't want to have to put up with a lot of people on a job that didn't make me much money. Like at a check-out counter—that's too many people. I don't want to be in front of that many people. I don't want to be a known part of the community. I don't mind having a job, but I don't like a job where everyone sees you do it. Working with a small crew would be best—the same gang every day. I'd like a job where I'm out and moving. Anything that's not cleaning up after somebody else, where you're not locked up and doing the same thing over and over, and where you can use your head a little, as well as your back.

"My mother said, 'If you had a little job right now, you'd be in heaven.' Yeah, some cash wouldn't hurt, but then I'd have to subtract the $70 I wouldn't get in food stamps, and there might not be a whole hell of a lot left. So I'm living in the hills and I'm not workin'. No car, either. So no girlfriend right now. No big deal.

"If I did have a job, the hardest thing about it would be showing up on time and getting home. Living out here makes a long way to go for any job I might get.

"If you get your life together, it means you don't have to worry so much. You have a little more security. That's what everybody wants. Money—a regular job. A car. You can't have your life together without those two things.

"My life is far better than it was. I've got a place to live and no big problems or worries. I don't worry about where I'm going to sleep or about food. I've got a bike. Got some pot—my homegrown plants are enough now, so I don't have to worry about it, even though it's not very high-class. But you've got to have a car to get to work in the morning and to get home. I can go on living this way, but I can't have a car if I'm going to do it.

"Sometimes my mom sends me clothes, or shampoo, or stuff like that. But if I had a job, I wouldn't need that. She'll help me with a car someday, if she ever thinks I'm financially responsible."

Building my own life. "I'm not in a big hurry with my life. If I can't do super-good, I'll do good enough. I don't think I'll have any big career.

"Maybe in a way I'll always be kind of a survivalist. But I would like to be prepared for when I get to be 50 or 60—if I make it that far—so that I wouldn't need Social Security. I get food stamps, so I guess I'd have to say I'm part of the Establishment. A job would get me more into it.

"Over a period of time I've learned what food to buy and what food not to buy, how to live inexpensively. I get powdered milk, eggs, dry foods in bulk, and stuff like that. Food costs me about $80 per month. I could live on $100 a month for food, cigarettes, fuel, and a few little extras, but not very many, like buying nails, or a window, or parts for a bike. But I don't really need anything. I've got just about everything I need. Except there is a few things more.

"I might stay here a couple of years, unless something drastically comes up. Like, if a beautiful woman says she has a house in town, that would do it, but if not for that, it isn't very likely. I'll have to build my own life.

"I wouldn't mind working. I wouldn't mind driving a street sweeper or something like that, or to buy a $30,000 or $60,000 piece of equipment, and just make money doing stuff for people. You see people all over who have cool jobs. Maybe they just do something around the house like take out washing machines, or they own something or know how to do something that's not really hard labor but it's skilled labor.

"But living this way is a good start for me. I don't have to work my life away just to survive. I can work a little bit, and survive, and do something else."

Being by myself. "At this time of my life it's not really too good to team up with somebody. I've got to get my life together before I can worry about just going out and having a beer or a good time.

"Being by myself doesn't make all that much difference. I guess that I'm sorta a loner. Maybe people say I'm a hermit, but it's not like I live 20 miles out in nowhere.

"I don't want to be alone all my life. I'd like to go camping with somebody on the weekend. Have a car and a cooler of beer and a raft or something. It's nice to have friends to do that with. If I had a car and stuff, I'm sure I could get a few people to go. Without a car, man, shit . . ."

Friends. "A friend is someone you could trust, I suppose. I've had close friends, but I don't have any now. But I have some 'medium' friends. I guess that's anybody who'd smoke a joint with me. And you see some people walking down the street or going to a store or to a pay phone. You just say, 'Hi, what's going on?'

"I know lots of people. Especially from reform school. I've already seen some. They're not friends, though; they're just people you might see to say hello and ask them what they've been up to and ask them how long they did in jail.

"The first time I met one guy I know now, I was pushing my bike and I had my backpack and some beer and I was drinking a beer. I'd never seen him before. He said, 'Hey, wanna smoke a joint?' I said, 'Sure.' So I gave him a couple of beers and we smoked some pot and started talking. I told him I lived up in the hills. I see him around every now and then. He's known me for a year and I talk to him sometimes and joke around. He's sort of a friend.

"I had a few friends in Southern California, but by the time I left there I wasn't too happy with them. I guess my best friend was Tom. I used to ride skateboards with him all day. His older brother used to get pot for us. That's when I think I learned to ride the very best. We always used to try to beat each other out in whatever we did. I was better than him in some things and after a while he got better than me in a couple of things. But I think I was always a little bit more crazier than he was—a little bit wilder on the board."

I've been more places and done more things. "I've lived in a lot of different places. Like going to California. Living out in the country. Living different places in town. Dealing with people. Living at the reform school. Living in Portland. Living here.

"I've definitely had more experiences than some of the people I went to school with, and I've had my ears opened more than they have. In *some* things, I'm wiser than other kids my age.

"I saw a guy a few weeks ago who is the same age as me. He lived in a house behind us when I was in fifth grade. He still lives with his parents in the same place. I think about what he's been doing the last nine years and what I've been doing the last nine years and it's a big difference. He went to high school. Now he works in a gas station, has a motorcycle, and works on his truck. I guess that's all right for him, so long as he's mellow with his parents. That way he can afford a motorcycle.

"But you've got what you've got. It doesn't make any difference what anybody else has. You can't wish you're somebody else. There's no point in it."

Some personal standards. "In the summer I clean up every day. When it starts cooling down, I dunno; sometimes if it's cold, I just wash my head and under my arms. Last winter I'd get a really good shower at least every three days and get by otherwise. But I always wash up before going to town if I'm dirty. I don't want to look like I live in a cabin.

"I don't really care what people on the street think of me. But somebody who knows me, I wouldn't want them to dislike me for any reason.

"And I wouldn't steal from anybody that knew me, if they knew that I took something or had any idea that I might have took it. Whether I liked them or not. I wouldn't steal from anybody I liked, or I thought they were pretty cool. I only steal from people I don't know.

"I don't like stealing from somebody you would really hurt. But anybody that owns a house and three cars and a boat—they're not hurtin'. It's the Law of the Jungle—occasionally people get burned. A lot of people don't, though. As long as they've got fences and they keep all their stuff locked up and don't leave anything laying around, they're all right. The way I see it, 'If you snooze, you lose.'

"If you say you'll do something, you should do it. That's the way people should operate. It pisses me off when somebody doesn't do it. Like, you tell somebody you're going to meet them somewhere, and they don't show up. But giving my word depends on how big of a deal it is; if it's pretty small, it would be no big deal.

"Sure, stealing is immoral. I don't like to screw somebody up for no good reason. But my morals can drop whenever I want.

"I went to Sunday school for a while and to a church kindergarten. I guess I heard all the big lessons—you get the felt board and they pin all the stuff on 'em and cut out all the paper figures: Jesus, Moses. But our family doesn't really think about religion a whole lot. They're moral to a point but they're not fanatics. It's too much to ask. I'd rather go to hell. But any little kid knows what's right and wrong."

Moderation: Getting close enough, going "medium" fast. "One of my friend's older brothers in Southern California was a crazy fucker. He'd get these really potent peyote buttons and grind them up and put them in chocolate milkshakes.

"One time they decided to go out to the runways where the jets were coming in, 'cause they knew somebody who did it before. Planes were coming in continually on that runway. They'd go out there laying right underneath the skid marks, just right under the planes. I never would get that close. Just being out there, after jumping the fence and walking clear out to the runway, is close enough. I never did lie on the runway. . . .

"On the skateboard, I just go medium fast. . . .

"The fun part of skiing is knowing when to slow down. . . .

"When those guys went jockey-boxing, I didn't actually do it with them. I was just tagging along. . . .

"Robbing a store seemed like a pretty easy way to get some cash, but I guess it wasn't a very good idea. . . .

"I don't know why I didn't get into drugs more. I smoke pot, but I've never really cared to take downers and uppers or to shoot up. I don't really need that much. . . .

"I like to smoke pot but I don't think of myself as a pothead. A pothead is somebody who is totally stoned all day long on really good pot, really burned out all the time. I smoke a joint, then smoke a cigarette, and I get high. I just like to catch a buzz. . . .

"If you really get burnt out, your brain's dead. You can get burned out on anything if you do it too much. I don't do it enough to make it a problem. If you take acid you never know who's made it or exactly what's in it. I've taken it before and gotten pretty fried. I don't know if it was bad acid, but it wasn't a very good experience. . . .

"Sometimes when I want to be mellow, I don't say anything. I just shut up. Or somebody can mellow out after a day at work—you come home, smoke a joint, drink a beer—you just sort of melt. . . ."

Putting it all together. "Anything you've ever heard, you just remember and put it all together the best you can. That's good enough for me."

Formal Schooling

I knew little about Brad's schooling when I began to collect life history data from him. By his account he had often been "slow" or "behind the rest of the class." He could read, but he faltered on "big words." He could write, but his spelling and punctuation were not very good. He had trouble recalling number sequences and basic arithmetic facts. ("Lack of practice," he insisted.) In one junior high school he had been placed in "an EH [educationally handicapped] class with the other stonies." As he recalled, "I don't know if I felt I was special or not, but I didn't like those big classes."

Measures of IQ or scholastic achievement did not really matter anymore. Brad was well aware of his capacities and limitations. The degree to which he was "below average" or "behind" in his schoolwork had become, and had been for a long time, purely academic. Schooling for him was over; he was out.

Formal schooling aside, Brad could, for practical purposes, read, write, and do simple arithmetic. The only book he "requisitioned" for his cabin was a dictionary. That alone was incredible. Even more incredibly, he occasionally labored through it to find a word—no easy task for one who has to recite the alphabet aloud in order to locate an entry.

Schooling had played a part in Brad's life, but not the vital part educators like it to play. In 10 years he enrolled in eight schools in two states, ranging from early years at a small country school to a final eight months at a state reformatory, and including attendance at urban elementary, junior high, and senior high schools. I traced his attendance record where he boasted having "the world's record for ditching school." Perhaps it was not the world's record, but following his midyear enrollment in grade five he maintained 77 percent attendance for that year and 46 percent attendance in grade six the year following. He began the term in a new school four different years, and often changed schools once the academic year was under way: "I guess I was in school a lot but I was always in a different school."

In Brad's assessment, school "did what it's supposed to do. You gotta learn to read." He laid no blame, noting only that "maybe school could of did better." He acknowledged that *he* might have done better, too: "I was just never that interested in school. If I knew I had to do something, I'd try a little bit. I could probably have tried harder."

The earliest school experience he could recall was in a church-sponsored kindergarten. Hearing Brad use objectionable language, the teacher threatened to wash out his mouth with soap. At the next occasion when the children were washing their hands, he stuck a bar of soap in his mouth: "I showed the kids around me, 'Hey, no big deal having soap in your mouth.' "

He recalled first grade as a time when "I learned my ABCs and everything. It was kind of neat." Apparently his enthusiasm for schooling stopped there. He could think of no particular class or teacher that he especially liked. His recollection of events associated with subsequent grades involved changes of schools, getting into trouble for his classroom behavior, or skipping school altogether. As early as fourth grade he remembered difficulty "keeping up" with classmates.

By his own assessment Brad did "OK" in school, but he recalled excelling only once: at an art project in clay that was put on display and that his mother still kept. During grade seven his attendance improved and, for one brief term, so did his grades, but he was not really engaged with what was going on and he felt lost in the large classes.

"In those big classes, like, you sit around in a big horseshoe, and you've got a seat four rows back, with just one teacher. Like English class, I'd get there at nine in the morning and put my head down and I'd sleep through the whole class. It was boring, man.

"Another class they tried to get me in was typing. I tried for a little while, but I wasn't even getting close to passing, so I just gave up."

Brad's public schooling ended in Southern California. When he got shunted back to Oregon, he did not enroll in school again, although after being "busted," schooling was his principal activity during his eight months in the reformatory. He felt that he had attended "a couple of pretty good schools" in Southern California during grades 8, 9, and, briefly, 10; but, as usual, the times he remembered were times spent out of class, not in it.

"By the end of school, I was cutting a lot. Like, I didn't need PE [physical education]. Look at this kid—he's been riding bicycles and skateboards all day all his life. I didn't need no PE. I don't need to go out in the sun and play games. I wasn't interested in sports. So I'd go get stoned. I'd take a walk during that class, go kick back in an orange grove, maybe eat an orange, get high, smoke a cigarette, and by the time I'd walk back, it was time for another class. I did it for a long time and never got caught. Anyhow, then I switched schools."

Brad felt that his lack of academic progress cost him extra time in reform school, "so I started to speed up and do the stuff and then I got out." In his assessment, "I was doing ninth-grade work. I probably did some 10th- and 11th-grade stuff, but not a lot."

Although young people seldom return to public schools after serving time, I asked Brad to identify the grade levels to which he might have been assigned had he gone back to school.

"For math, if I went back, I'd just be getting into 10th grade. In reading, I'd be a senior or better. Spelling would be about eighth grade. I can spell good enough. Handwriting, well, you just write the way you write. My writing isn't that bad if I work on it. I don't worry about it that much."

He did recognize limitations in his command of basic school skills. He had "kind of forgotten" the multiplication facts, and he was pretty rusty on subtracting or recalling the alphabet. To be a good speller, he once mused, you've got to "do it a lot," but at reform school he did only "a little bit." His awareness of these limitations is revealed in a letter intended for his mother but later abandoned in favor of a cheerier style:

Hi
if I sit hear and stair
at this pieac of paper
eny longer ill go crazy
I dont think im scaird
of witing just dont like
to remind myself I
need improvment. its
raining alot past
few days but its warm
'n dry inside . . .

Reading was the school skill at which Brad felt most proficient, and his confidence was not shaken by the fact that some words were difficult for him. He said he did not enjoy reading, but he spent hours poring over instruction manuals. My impression was that although his oral reading was halting, he had good comprehension. That was also his own assessment. When, at his father's insistence, he briefly entertained the idea of joining the army, Brad had first to take the General Educational Development exam (for his high school certificate) and then take a test for the army. He felt he passed "pretty high" on the Army test; on some parts of the GED, "like reading and a couple of other ones," he felt he did "super, super good."

Brad once observed philosophically, "The people in college today are probably the ones who didn't sleep when I was in English class." At the same time, school was a closed chapter in his life. Other than to acknowledge that he "might have tried harder," though, he expressed no regrets over school as an opportunity missed. Anticipating that his lack of school skills would prove a barrier to enrollment in any technical training program, he couldn't imagine ever returning to the classroom. And, like most school leavers, he couldn't think of anything that might have been done that would have kept him in school.[4]

Adequate Schools and Inadequate Education: An Interpretation

It might be socially desirable if Brad could read better, write better, do arithmetic better, spell better. With better spelling skills, he would "stare" rather than "stair" at a blank page and perhaps feel less self-conscious about needing "improvment." Considering that he devoted some (although certainly not exclusive) attention to schooling for 10 of his 20 years, he does not do these things very well.

On the other hand, that he can do them as well as he does might also be regarded as a tribute to the public schools. Brad's level of school achievement may be disappointing, but it is not inadequate. He is literate. He did get *something* out of school. True, his performance of the three Rs could be more polished, but the importance of his proficiency with such amenities pales before problems of greater social consequence. Brad's schooling has stopped, but his learning continues apace. Exerting some positive, constructive influence on that learning as it pertains to Brad's enculturation into society presents society's current challenge. That challenge has not been taken up.

Schools can affect the rate and level of academic achievement, but they do not set the course of students' lives. They do not and cannot reach everyone, even though they may ever-so-briefly touch them. Schooling is not everyone's cup of tea. As Brad put it: "I've always liked learning. I just didn't like school."

The implicit distinction Brad himself makes between "learning" and "learning done in school" is critical to the purposes of this writing. In the broad enculturative sense of coming to understand what one needs to know to be competent in the roles one may expect to fulfill, learning is an ongoing process in which each human is engaged throughout a lifetime.[5] In Brad's case, the direction that process was taking seemed to reflect all too well what he felt society expected of him: nothing. He was left largely to his own resources to make sense of his world and create his own life. He endeavored quite self-consciously to "figure things out," but his resolutions often put him at odds with society. What appeared as inevitable conclusions to him were neither inevitable nor necessarily appropriate in terms of community norms.

Maybe we cannot reach him; surely we cannot reach everyone like him. I was astounded to realize that no systematic, constructive effort was being exerted to influence the present course of Brad's life. No agency offered help, direction, or concern, and neither did any of the institutions that ordinarily touch our lives: family, school, work, peer group. If it is naive to regard these influences as invariably positive and constructive, our interactions with them do, nonetheless, contribute to our sense of social self. Brad was, for the most part, out of touch with them all.

If Brad is able to get his life together, it will have to be almost entirely through his own effort. Perhaps his personal style as a loner helped buffer him from peer influences that seemed to me, as a wary adult, as likely to get him into trouble as to guide him on the straight and narrow. That he could find time and space "on a mountaintop in Oregon" rather than on a beach or under a freeway in Southern California seemed to give him an advantage over his fellow street people. His lifestyle was not overly complicated by urban trappings or the quickened pace of city life. He was not crowded or pushed. At the same time, he could neither escape the influence of material wants and creature comforts so prevalent in the society in which he lives, nor deny a deeply felt need to connect with others. As much the loner as he often seemed, even Brad could acknowledge, "There must be a group that I would fit in, somewhere in this town."

He had learned to hunt and gather for his necessities in the aisles of supermarkets, in neighborhood garages, and at residential building sites. He conceded that stealing was wrong, but, among his priorities, necessity (broadly defined to allow for some luxuries as well) took precedence over conformity. He saw no alternative for getting the things he felt he needed but could not afford. Still, he took only what he considered necessary, not everything he could get his hands on. He was not, nor did he see himself ever becoming, a "super thief."

I do not see how society can "teach" Brad to not be sneaky, to not shoplift, to not steal. Most families try to do that. His family wasn't entirely successful, though more of the message seems to have gotten through than one might at first assume.[6] In that regard I find useful the distinction between deviant *acts* and deviant *persons* as suggested by anthropologist Robert Edgerton (1978). In spite of occasional deviant acts, Brad's statements reveal his underlying enculturation into the prevailing ethos of mainstream American society. He was well aware of the meanings of his acts to others. As he noted, "Any little kid knows what's right and wrong." Although he prided himself on having the cunning to survive his "hard life" by whatever means necessary, he staunchly defended his behavior ("I couldn't get by without stealing stuff") as well as himself ("I am not that rotten of a kid!").

There was a foundation on which to build, but there was neither external help, support, nor a modicum of encouragement shaping that process. Was schooling an opportunity in Brad's life, or is it the only directed opportunity he gets? It seems to me there might, and should, be a more concerted effort to exert a positive influence to provide him with reasonable and realistic routes of access back into the cultural mainstream. To have any effect, however, such efforts would have to be in the form of increasing the options available to him, rather than trying to force or mold him in some particular direction. He has already heard the lectures about good citizenship.

The community's best strategy would be to ensure that opportunities exist for a person like Brad to satisfy more of his wants in socially acceptable ways. Fear of getting caught isn't much of a deterrent for someone who thinks he's "too smart" to get caught. Armed robbery is already within the realm of things Brad could, and might, do. With an attitude that "just about everybody, or at least everybody my age, does it" toward behaviors like shoplifting, "ripping things off," burglary, operating a vehicle with a suspended license, and even his preoccupation with obtaining an adequate supply of pot, he could too easily find himself in the chute without realizing that everybody isn't there after all. Having gotten out of mainstream society, he does not see a way back in. Nor is he convinced it is worth the effort to try.

It is convenient, and an old American pastime, to place blame on schools. Questions concerning educational adequacy, when directed toward schools, invite that kind of scapegoating by relating the present inadequacies of youth to prior inadequacies of schools. (See, for example, Levin 1983.) Employing the anthropologist's distinction between schooling and education encourages us to review the full range of efforts the community makes to exert a positive educative influence on lives, not only during the school years, but in the post-school years as well.[7] The problems Brad now poses for society are not a consequence of inadequate schooling. They dramatize the risk we take by restricting our vision of collective educational responsibility to what can be done in school.

One hears arguments that today's youth vacillate between extremes of taking what they want or expecting everything to be handed to them on a silver platter. One finds a bit of each in Brad's thinking. He dreams of pulling off a robbery or suddenly finding himself owning and operating a $60,000 piece of machinery. He expresses reluctance to do work like dishwashing that entails cleaning up after others and where everyone can watch you perform a menial job.

But I wonder if young people like Brad really believe that society owes them something? Perhaps that is an expression of frustration at failing to see how to begin to accumulate resources of their own, comparable to what they perceive everyone else already has. A willingness to defer gratification must come more easily to those who not only have agonized during deferment but have eventually realized some long-awaited reward. Nothing Brad had ever done worked out very well—at least prior to his effort to build both a new cabin and a new lifestyle. He had virtually no sense of deferred gratification: Everything was "now or never."

In a society as materialistic as ours, opportunity is realized essentially with money, rather than with school or work. To Brad, money represented security, and he had limited access to it. That is why food stamps, in an annual amount less than $900, figured so importantly to him. His use of the stamps has left me wondering whether it might be possible to design some governmental agency that would calculatedly confront individuals like Brad in an educative way.

But the educative value of a welfare dole is limited. You cannot "service" people out of poverty, and, as Brad had already discovered, the power of the dole-givers and their labyrinth of regulations is seemingly arbitrary but definitely absolute. Food stamps made a better consumer of him (buying generic brands, buying large quantities, buying staples). But he realized that the first $70 of any month's take-home pay would be money he would otherwise have received free from the food-stamp program. To "earn" his stamps, he had to remain poor.[8] Had he found the second-rate job he so dreaded, part of his earnings would simply have replaced the dole, his other expenses (transportation, clothes, maybe a second-rate apartment) would have increased dramatically, and he would have again been trapped in a second-rate life. Until his food stamps were summarily canceled—after he failed to participate in a ritual midwinter job search during a period of staggering recession and regional unemployment—he did not aggressively seek work. When he finally realized he was destitute and began in earnest to look for work, 38 days passed before he even got turned down for a job. He put in many hours at painting and yard cleanup for me (although he refused to equate working for me with "real work") and reverted to "ripping off" items he felt he needed but could not afford.

I invited Brad's thoughts on what might be done to help people like him. His idea, other than a dream of finding "just the right job" (never fully specified) without ever going to look for it, was of a "day work" program, whereby anyone who needed money could appear at a given time, do a day's work, and promptly receive a day's pay. I'm sure Brad's thoughts turned to the end of the day, when each worker would receive a pay envelope; my own thoughts focused on what one would do with a motley pick-up crew that wouldn't inadvertently make mockery of work itself. Yet implicit in his notion are at least two critical points.

First is a notion of a *right to work*: If (or when) one is willing, one should be able to work and, if in dire need, be paid immediately in cash. Brad found no such right in his life. Although he had been able to find—but not hold—a number of jobs in the past, now he heard only "No Help Wanted" and read only "Not Presently Taking Applications." He was not entirely without social conscience when he observed that if he found a job, he would only be taking it away from someone who needed it more. Brad did not really need a job. And, as he had begun to figure out, no one really needed him. Maybe he was right; maybe $70 in food stamps was society's way of paying him to drop out.

Second is a notion of an overly structured wage and hour system that effectively prices most unskilled and inexperienced workers like Brad out of the job market and requires a full-time commitment from the few it accepts. Brad's material needs were slight. He could have preserved the best elements in his carefree lifestyle by working part-time. However, the labor market does not ordinarily offer such options except for its own convenience. Either you want a job or you do not want a job. But work for its own sake, or holding a job, cast no spell over Brad. He did not look to employment for satisfaction, for meaningful involvement, or for achieving self-respect. Money was the only reason one worked.[9]

School provides opportunity and access for some youth; employment provides it for others. Neither school nor work presently exerted an influence on Brad. He was beyond school, and steady employment was beyond him. Without the effective support of family or friends, and without the involvement of school or work, he was left to his own devices. In his own words, he could not see a way to win and he did not have anything to lose. From mainstream society's point of view, we would be better off if he did.

After so carefully making provision for Brad's schooling, society now leaves his continuing education to chance, and we are indeed taking our chances. But educative adequacy in the lives of young people like Brad is not an issue of schooling. Schools provided him one institutional opportunity; they no longer reached him, and no other agency was trying to. His next institutional "opportunity," like his previous one, may be custodial. If it is, we all lose; Brad will not be the only one who will have to pay.[10]

Summary

"The important thing about the anthropologist's findings," writes Clifford Geertz (1973:23), one of anthropology's more articulate spokespeople, "is their complex specificness, their circumstantiality." Whatever issues anthropologists address, they characteristically begin an account and look for illustration through real events or cases bounded in time and circumstance. The effective story should be "specific and circumstantial," but its relevance in a broader context should be apparent. The story should make a point that transcends its modest origins. The case must be particular, but its implications broad.

Following that tradition, I have related a specific and circumstantial life story to illustrate the necessity of regarding education as more than just schooling, and of pointing out how little we attend to that broader concern. That may seem a roundabout way to address such a complex issue, but it is a way to bring an anthropological perspective to the problem.

Brad's story is unique, but his is not an isolated case. He is one among thousands of young people who simply drift away. His uninvited presence on my 20-acre sanctuary, in search of sanctuary for himself, brought me into contact with a type of youth I do not meet as a college professor. He piqued my anthropological interest with a worldview in many ways strikingly similar to mine, but with a set of coping strategies strikingly different. It is easy for people like me to think of people like Brad as someone else's problem, but for a moment that lingered and became two years, he quite literally brought the problem home to me. I do not find ready answers even in his particular case; I am certainly not ready to say what might, can, or must be done in some broader context.

Little is to be gained from laying blame at the feet of Brad's parents or his teachers, and to do so is to ignore indications of repeated, if not necessarily effective, efforts to help and guide him. Though our extended conversations may have been enlightening to Brad, as they surely were to me, my more direct efforts to help seemed to go awry. In the end, he departed almost as unexpectedly as he had arrived. I am not sure what I think "society" can accomplish for an amorphous "them" when my own well-intended efforts seemed only to demonstrate to Brad that I had my life "together" (his term) in a manner virtually unattainable for himself. The easiest course is to blame Brad, but to do so is to abandon hope and a sense of collective responsibility.

The only certainty I feel is that it is in our common interest to seek ways to provide opportunities intended to exert a continuing and constructive educational influence on the lives of young people like Brad. I do not know whether Brad can or will allow himself to be reached effectively or in time. I do know that from his perspective he saw neither attractive opportunities nor sources of potential help. By his own assessment, he simply did not matter. He was not free of his society, but he had become disconnected from it. Once adrift, nothing seemed to beckon or guide him back.

Because we tend to equate education with schooling, we are inclined to look to the past and ask where schools have gone wrong. Brad's story, in which school played only a minor role, serves as a reminder of the importance of other educative influences in our lives. It also points out how little systematic attention we give to discerning what those influences are, or how we might better use them to augment, complement, and otherwise underwrite the massive efforts we direct at youth during their in-school years. In that broad perspective, our efforts at education appear woefully inadequate in spite of the remarkable accomplishments of our schools. Until I found Brad living in my backyard, however, the problem remained essentially abstract. Now it has confronted me with the "complex specificness" of one young human life.

Notes

Acknowledgments: A portion of the work on which this article is based was performed pursuant to Contract No. NIE-P-81-0271 of the National Institute of Education dealing with issues of educational adequacy under the School Finance Project. Data collection and interpretation are the responsibility of the author. I wish to express my appreciation to W. W. Charters, Jr., Stanley Elam, Barbara Harrison, Bryce Johnson, Malcolm McFee, and Esther O. Tron, as well as to Brad for his critical reading and helpful suggestions with early drafts. The material was first published in the *Anthropology and Education Quarterly,* Volume 14, Number 1, pp. 3–32, copyright by the Council on Anthropology and Education, 1983. It has undergone minor editing.

1. If I found any surprises in reviewing the literature, it was in discovering some remarkable similarities between Brad's story and a groundbreaking classic first pub-

lished three-quarters of a century earlier, Clifford Shaw's *The Jack-Roller: A Delinquent Boy's Own Story* (1930).

2. Meyer Fortes (1938:5) noted the firmly established axiom, "Education in the widest sense is the process by which the cultural heritage is transmitted from generation to generation, and that schooling is therefore only part of it." Melville Herskovits (1948:311) subsequently introduced the encompassing term *enculturation* for referring to education in Fortes's "widest sense." But he retained the term *education,* suggesting that it be restricted to "its ethnological sense of directed learning," a term distinct from and more encompassing than *schooling,* defined as "that aspect of education carried out by specialists." (See also Wallace 1961b.)

3. I have been careful to observe the few conditions Brad imposed on my use of the information. He, in turn, was paid for time spent interviewing and for later reviewing the completed account on which this paper was based. That is not to suggest he was entirely satisfied with my portrayal or my interpretation, but he was satisfied that what I reported was accurate. If only to please me, he even commented that he hoped his story might "help people understand."

4. For example, in the *Oregon Early School Leavers Study* conducted at the time (Oregon Department of Education 1980:16), only one-third of the young people interviewed responded that something might have been done to affect their decision to quit public secondary school.

5. A timely article of the day appeared with the partial title "Chasing the American Dream: Jobs, schools, and employment training programs . . ." (Mann 1982).

6. Brad expressed only resentment toward his father, but he often mentioned his mother's efforts to provide a positive influence. When Brad introduced us, after proudly showing her the cabin during a brief but long-anticipated visit, I asked whether she felt she could exert a guiding influence over him living a thousand miles away. "We've always been a thousand miles apart," she replied, "even when we were under the same roof."

On a different occasion, responding to Brad's announcement that he needed to "find" another bicycle, I asked: "What would your mother think about you stealing a bike? That it's dumb; that it's smart?" "Neither," he replied. "She'd just think that I must have needed it. She wouldn't say anything. She doesn't lecture me about things like that. But she used to cut out everything they printed in the paper about pot and put it on my walls. And she'd talk about brain damage."

7. Although the distinction between education and schooling is sometimes acknowledged, it is not necessarily regarded as having much significance, at least for understanding contemporary society. To illustrate, note in the following excerpt how educator and economist Henry Levin, addressing the topic *Education and Work,* at once recognizes the distinction between education and schooling yet bows to what he describes as the "convention" of equating them:

Although the term education is sometimes used interchangeably with schooling, it is important to note that schooling is not the only form of education. However, schooling represents such a dominant aspect of education in modern societies that the convention of equating education and schooling in the advanced industrialized societies will also be adopted here. [Levin 1982:1]

8.   The irony of the implications and consequences when not working is prerequisite to maintaining a steady income is nicely spelled out in Estroff 1981. See especially chapter 6, "Subsistence Strategies: Employment, Unemployment, and Professional Disability."

9.   Paul Willis (1977) notes in his study of working-class youth that it is this "reign of cash" that precipitates their contact with the world of work. As one of Willis's "lads" explained, "Money is life." Brad's mother expressed a similar view: "Money, not love, makes the world go round."

10.   For a grim scenario, including some discomforting parallels and similarities, see Mailer 1979. The protagonist of Mailer's "true-life novel" makes special note of the impact of reform school on his life (chapter 22). Brad did not reveal the extent of the impact of the same reform school on his own life, but he did include it specifically in his brief inventory of significant experiences. Similarities noted earlier between Brad's account and Shaw's *The Jack-Roller* (1930) seem less pronounced in a subsequently published follow-up, *The Jack-Roller at Seventy* (Snodgrass 1982).

Chapter Two

The Brad Saga Continues

W HAT prompted the writing of the Sneaky Kid article must be traced through both a personal and a professional history. And that history can be encapsulated with a single word: serendipity. Serendipity refers to circumstances of chance that turn into opportunity. One synonym for it is luck. In fieldwork, however, serendipity is not pure luck so much as recognition on the part of a researcher that opportunity has presented itself—should one choose to pursue it.

Serendipity can account for what happened in this case, a coming together of unrelated events. But it is important to acknowledge that this is only in retrospect. In retrospect, I can make happenstance *appear* to form a coherent pattern, to the point that one might marvel at how prescient, how clever I was in all this, at least at the beginning. Better perhaps to look upon these events as fate. But that diminishes the role of human volition, for throughout these events all kinds of people have made all kinds of decisions. It simply would not have been possible to anticipate how the various strands of the story would eventually come together in the way that they have.

Sometime during the summer of 1981, I received a telephone call from Washington. It was out of the blue; there was no reason to anticipate such a call, and no explanation was ever offered as to how I happened to be selected. The caller asked if I was available to participate in a writing project. Congress had appropriated money to address the issue of educational adequacy, in anticipation that increased federal funding might become available for public schools. If money were to be appropriated, there would have to be some defensible basis for distributing it. To accomplish the delicate task of distributing "equalization" money, adequacy itself needed to be defined, or at least agonized over. The quest for that definition was to serve as the starting point for a dialogue.

Except for an occasional solicitation, I do not get many calls from Washington. This particular call was from the Office of Education. I had been involved with aspects of education for the previous 25 years, but this topic seemed one for economists, and I said as much to my caller. "Oh, we already have several economists working on it," she informed me. "What we'd like is a perspective from a sociologist like yourself." Sociology, anthropology—we academics all look alike, I guess.

After giving the matter some thought, I countered with the idea of presenting a case study that might raise issues about just what is meant by the idea of educational adequacy. I have always taken opportunities to demonstrate the contribution anthropology can make to education, and it seemed unlikely that my fellow contributors from economics or school finance (or sociology!) would think to approach the issue through a case study. My plan was to examine the issue not in terms of states or local school districts but by using the perspective of someone we claim to be educating.

Of course it was Brad I had in mind as I made my counterproposal. Had my suggestion been rejected outright, I probably would not have participated, and the Sneaky Kid article might never have been written. What I saw in the assignment was an opportunity—or an excuse?—to do some systematic interviewing with Brad about his life, especially to contrast his schooling with his education. The invitation gave focus to an idea I had been mulling over but had never been able to formalize. It also provided an opportunity to determine whether Brad was willing to be interviewed.

Brad was used to doing odd jobs for me—sometimes when I needed help with a big project, more often when he needed money—and there were always projects that needed doing. I assured him I would pay for his interview time. He seemed agreeable, even intrigued with the idea of telling his story. To my amazement, he even predicted how long it would take to recount his life: 12 hours.

I knew the project as I envisioned it was far more ambitious than what the Office of Education had in mind, but I was interested in Brad's story, and the assignment provided the impetus for going ahead with my research. The stipend was enough to cover my time, to pay Brad, and to meet incidental costs of transcribing and typing.

The assignment also came during the summer, a good time for me. I was not on summer salary and had no other commitments. I was spending my time writing, an activity I was finding increasingly difficult to pursue when classes were in session. I discovered that I not only had to write, consistent with the publish-or-perish ethos of the university, but that I had begun to enjoy writing. This unexpected invitation offered not only an opportunity to pursue a topic of interest but required the submission of a report; *something* would come of it.

I had Brad's approval, the project director's approval, and time to get the project started before the new term began. I had no idea how the interviewing would go, but I was confident that I could get enough of a story to raise an issue about what constitutes educational adequacy. Listening to the tape-recorded interviews, planning what topics to discuss, and looking back over written notes, I did not see much of a story at first other than one of a down-and-out youth who was managing to keep a few steps ahead of the law. But the idea of Brad as a *learner*, one whose schooling had stopped long ago but whose learning continued apace, struck me as a powerful one. I began to see how to put the story together in a way that emphasized the contrast I wished to make between school learning and education. When I finished my type-written draft of the report, I had a substantial case to present in fulfillment of my contract with the Office of Education.

For those readers in high places who might fail to see the connection between a modest case study and the broader issue under examination, I offered an introductory explanation. My paper was, I wrote,

> a way to bring an anthropological perspective to the problem and to under-score that educational adequacy must ultimately be viewed in terms of some humans' judgments of what constitutes "enough" of the "right kind" of edu-cation, either for themselves or, as is more often the case, for others.

The Anthropology of Learning

Here I need to introduce another strand of the story: why I was particularly interested in the topic of schooling versus education, and why I seized the oppor-tunity to conduct a series of interviews with Brad focusing on that subject.

My entry into the teaching profession was made possible by the GI Bill, which for me was made possible by a (mandatory) stint in the United States Army from 1952 to 1954, the period of the Korean conflict. I had neither anticipated nor prepared for a teaching career during undergraduate studies at the University of California, Berkeley. In order to be certified as a classroom teacher, I needed a year of coursework, to be followed by a one-year supervised internship. At that time, once the GI Bill was activated, one had to keep it active through additional study each year if one wished to maintain the bene-fits. I was more or less propelled through a master's degree by having to attend summer school while I continued classroom teaching during the academic year.

After I completed my undergraduate degree at Berkeley, I resolved never to set foot in a classroom again. With a few more years away from classes, however, I discovered that I was fascinated by the teaching/learning process. Like Brad, I realized that I liked learning, I just didn't care much for school.

By the time Stanford University extended an invitation to me to accept a fellowship and pursue studies leading to a doctorate, my views had changed. And now that school and schooling had become my career, I assumed that doctoral studies would open up new avenues for examining teaching and learning, although I was not sure just where they would lead. At the time, I tended to think of teaching and learning as processes linked exclusively with schools and schooling.

It was my good fortune to arrive at Stanford during a period when at least some of the professors there were encouraging graduate students in education to pursue educationally relevant studies outside the School of Education, in addition to completing a major concentration of work within it. I had once thought that psychology would be interesting, but professors at Berkeley and Stanford had been able to convince me otherwise. Sociology seemed a possibility, but the subfield of educational sociology was too school-centered to allow the kind of exploration I felt was being urged on us.

One other alternative was mentioned: joining cultural anthropology to formal education under the direction of a relatively recent joint appointment in education and anthropology, George Spindler. Unfortunately, Professor Spindler was not on campus my first year at Stanford, but Patricia Grinager, who was filling in for him, encouraged me to correspond with him. She painted an exciting picture of the kinds of topics that fell within his purview, including cultural transmission, socialization and enculturation, and education in "primitive" perspective. Spindler was looking at the educational process in societies without schools to gain a perspective on what it is schools are up to.

I was hooked right from the start. My program of studies included a formal Ph.D. minor in cultural anthropology. My dissertation was based on a year's fieldwork as a teacher in a one-room school on a Kwakiutl Indian Reserve in British Columbia, Canada (Wolcott 1964, 1967).

Those of us who "took Spindler" were intrigued with the problems he posed and the literature we reviewed. We seriously doubted that we would be as lucky as he had been to secure joint appointments in education and anthropology, but we felt we were engaging with the kinds of issues that represented the best in graduate study. Nevertheless, our projected dissertation studies failed to impress our more methodologically sophisticated colleagues. We proposed doing "fieldwork," while they pursued more rigorous quantitative study examining more obviously school-relevant and measurable effects.

To our delight and surprise, the interdisciplinary adventure did pay off. We found faculty positions where the education/anthropology combination was looked upon favorably. And our new colleagues and students found our cross-cultural perspective and participant observation approach refreshing.

Ironically, I think our acceptance was due to the methods we brought with us from anthropology. The almost self-conscious absence of method that we had internalized, first as students of anthropology, then as fieldworkers, was gaining recognition as a method in its own right. Our timing was exquisite, although I don't think we appreciated that we were perceived as methodologists of a new genre of research: qualitative methodology.

For the first 15 years following completion of my Ph.D., I was allowed to teach courses offering a cross-cultural perspective, although my real contribution was measured in terms of the graduate training I could offer along the lines of ethnographic or qualitative research. I enjoyed leading students into research via this route and watching how qualitative approaches were catching on, not only in education but in related professional fields. Yet I realized that I was getting further and further from that original driving force—my interest in teaching and learning, especially the latter.

By the late 1960s, what had begun in the '50s as a casual liaison between disciplines had been institutionalized into a formal organization, the Council on Anthropology and Education. The council had its own newsletter that soon became a journal, the *Anthropology and Education Quarterly*. As an area of intellectual pursuit, "anthropology and education" was becoming many things to many people and attempting to be responsive to all of them. It provided an umbrella under which interests in multicultural education, ethnographic research, minority-group concerns, studies of schools as cultures, the educative role of museums, and anthropology as curriculum content were all welcomed.

I felt we needed a single banner that would give coherence to our efforts and help to define our mission. Spindler had suggested years earlier that "cultural transmission" provided that unifying theme. I looked for something broader, something that included cultural transmission but encompassed even more.

Tentatively, I proposed "the anthropology of learning" as that broader scope. I made a pact with myself that, from the day of my fast-approaching 50th birthday, I would make the anthropology of learning the intellectual focus of my teaching and research. That did not preclude my commitment to a cross-cultural perspective or to the doing of ethnography, but it gave focus to those interests by pulling everything together under one label.

My personal resolve, in the form of this epiphany (there, I finally got to use that recently popularized word), was of no dramatic consequence to others. In my teaching and research, it lent focus without calling attention to itself. But I wanted to engage my colleagues with the topic and to test the waters for its unifying effect. I organized a symposium under the auspices of the Council on Anthropology and Education on the topic "The Anthropology of Learning," to be presented at the meeting of the American Anthropological

Association in December 1980. (Coincidentally, that was the year that Brad had found his way to my place, some eight months earlier.)

I found willing participants for a symposium presentation and a follow-up special issue of *AEQ*, including George and Louise Spindler, Solon Kimball, Jean Lave, Judith Hansen, and Frederick Erickson. But I worried that the symposium might mark the endpoint of an idea rather than the birth of one. After the symposium, I approached Fred with a question for which I had no answer: "I would like to pursue this topic of the anthropology of learning. Can you suggest how I might operationalize it into a researchable topic to be studied from an anthropological perspective?"

Fred's succinct answer set the course for what follows. "First of all, get yourself a learner." Voilà! I had a learner—and a seemingly ideal one at that.

Back to Brad/Back to the Brad Chronicles

Pursuing the anthropology of learning was not one of the considerations on my mind the day I first confronted Brad. What I had to do before answering his direct question, "Can I stay?" was weigh the risk of allowing him to remain against the consequences of sending him away. "Reform school" rested uneasily on my mind, and his sullen demeanor offered but a poor second. Yet, as he had already been living on my property for the previous five weeks and had managed to construct a cabin without being detected, I could hardly insist that he was proving to be a nuisance. In any case, what he had achieved seemed too little to keep him there. I assumed he would soon move on. Like a too-clever lawyer, I told him only that I would not insist that he leave. If someday I regretted my decision, I could always argue that I had not really given permission for him to stay, I had only not denied it. Stay he did. For more than two years.

It may seem strange that Brad could build a cabin without my realizing it. Had a neighbor's boy not met up with him on a back trail, it might have been even longer before I found him or his cabin. But the back acreage of the property is separated from the front—where my house is located—by a steep slope. On the occasions when I hiked up there, I tended to follow a circuitous route that took me around the perimeter of the property rather than through its interior. My wanderings tended to skirt the site Brad had chosen. He was also initially careful to leave no hint of a trail to his new homesite. Brad had discovered the site coming from the other side of the mountain. That gave him the nearest road access and also took him past houses where he could fill the plastic containers he carried up to the cabin. (Water was his scarcest commodity. Even after I helped him locate a source of running water closer to his cabin, he had a long haul.) I did recall hearing sounds of occasional hammering during the time he was constructing the cabin, but there were several new homes being built not too far distant, and there was enough echo from that construction that it did not occur to me the sounds might be originating on my own property.

After I discovered Brad, there was not much need to infringe on his privacy. He continued to reach his cabin from the back, and I seldom caught even a glimpse of him. Occasionally I made the trip up to see him if there were jobs to do and I needed some help. He was a splendid worker, the more physical the task the better. I paid him at the end of each workday if he needed cash. Our first big project was running a crude boundary line around the entire 20 acres and clearing brush along it.

Brad arrived in April 1980. I had accepted an invitation to teach a semester at Arizona State University as a visiting professor beginning the following August. I was away the next five months, returning only for a short visit at Thanksgiving. My partner, Norman, remained at home, and his teaching duties began late that summer. During October, while Norman was at school one day, the house was burglarized. I have always suspected that Brad was somehow connected with the burglary, probably having tipped someone off that the house was not occupied during the day. He may not have taken an active role except for helping himself to some "little stuff." My suspicion is related to some Polaroid photos that he had taken of himself in the buff, which he he later showed me—one of the things missing after the burglary was a Polaroid camera. We never saw the camera again, but it would have been difficult to explain the photos. Brad never mentioned the break-in and I never asked about it directly. Later, we could ask him to keep an eye on the house when we were going to be away, and there were no more break-ins.

A major project facing me following my return from the semester at Arizona State was to run a new waterline to the house from a spring, my main water source. The old line was badly corroded, and in places it was so close to the surface that the pipe sometimes froze in winter. I sought bids from contractors who could dig a line with a backhoe, though no one was very excited about the job, especially on the steep slope immediately below the holding tank. Brad joined these bidding exercises whenever he heard us. After one contractor departed, he surprised me by making a bid of his own. He said he could dig the trench by hand, it would cost much less to have him do it, and he would not leave the mess that a large machine would make.

We had no idea how long it would take to dig the trench, but Brad's argument that a man-made ditch would not leave a big scar was a compelling one. However, I had reservations about getting involved in a way that could easily lead to a misunderstanding. If he did not complete the job and I had to hire out the work, what would I owe him for his part of it?

We estimated the distance at about 600 feet. I offered him 10 cents a foot for whatever he dug, which gave him promise of $60. He was satisfied with that. I reasoned that I could write off whatever he earned if I later had to call someone to complete the work with a backhoe. But I also offered an incentive. If he completed the ditch all the way to the house, I would pay him $100. And if he helped me lay in plastic pipe and bury it, I would double that figure. By late that same afternoon he had already begun to dig the line down the steepest part of the slope.

The job proved perfect for him. He could work when he wanted for as long as he wanted. The digging did not go quickly, but he kept at it. When he encountered rock outcroppings or unexpected obstacles, I lent a hand. In working together I began to get a sense of who he was and the set of experiences that comprised his view of his recent years.

As the project grew near completion, Brad told me that he had been eyeing a small gasoline engine for sale that could be mounted on a bicycle to motorize it. It cost $230, and he would have "almost enough" to afford it. I figured I could cover the extra cost as a bonus for a job well done. On the morning he dropped by to pick up his pay, I surprised him with an amount sufficient to pay for the engine. He immediately struck off for town to purchase it.

His motorized bike was not powerful enough to get him up the steep grade from town without a lot of extra pumping, but it brought him a great deal of satisfaction until keeping it in repair became impossible. He also managed to get a traffic ticket for riding a motorized vehicle on the sidewalk, and his court appearance—he'd hoped to get the expensive fine waived—unearthed a long-standing contempt of court charge from a failure to appear for a citation years earlier.

His motorized bicycle also changed his travel routes, for now it was more efficient to travel the road that led past my house and to store his bike in my carport. That meant that I saw him much more often, and I knew whether he was at the cabin by whether or not a bicycle was present. (He managed to get broken bikes up to the cabin for repairs but kept a working one on hand in the carport.) Seeing him more often, I was also beginning to piece together parts of his story. When the invitation came to write about educational adequacy, I saw the opportunity to be more systematic in my inquiry.

As Brad and I worked and talked together during the waterline project, I realized that I was becoming fascinated with him personally, as well as with the independence of spirit that had intrigued me from the moment I met him. By this time, he had been living at the cabin for a year. He was no longer the scrawny lad I had encountered a year earlier. We could talk of intimate matters, and I realized that his interest in his own sexuality was arousing some sexual interest of my own. He presented a number of provocative situations and topics. One evening at the cabin, I finally made an overtly sexual advance that he did not turn down. I say "finally" because some time later Brad asked me what had taken me so long: Why hadn't I made such a move earlier?

Once school resumed that fall, my schedule allowed me to work at home two and sometimes three days a week. After some episodes at the cabin, we developed a new pattern that gave Brad added benefits and me some highly anticipated diversion from hours spent writing or preparing for classes. Usually by prearrangement, Brad would appear at the door about midmorning, a bag of laundry in hand. He would head straight for the washing machine, first throwing in his dirty laundry, then stripping naked and tossing in the clothes he was wearing. I followed appreciatively as he headed upstairs for a long shower and then into bed. He was the willing but passive partner. We were both satisfied and literally spent before the session ended. Clean up, put damp clothes in the dryer, have lunch and a visit, and he was off to town or back up the hill to the cabin, depending largely on the weather.

Sex with Brad was an absolute delight. I have no way of telling whether he was as stimulated as I was, but there is no faking an erection, and he was always there with his. I was highly stimulated by his youthful body. The chemistry between us was exquisite.

It is curious how Brad repressed any indication of overt sexuality, guarding the idea that he felt he was constantly preoccupied with sex, for he was so daring in other ways. But once we developed a sexual relationship, there were many more things we could talk about, especially his concerns about masturbating and that he felt he was "hard" most of the time. The latter lament fell on deaf ears to someone 30 years his senior, but in any of our conversations about sex I tried to be casual and forthright, if anything but disinterested.

I asked him once, "Brad, we're both consenting adults, right?" "Yeah," came the reply, "but you're more consenting than I am." I took that to mean that I was the prime mover, and I think Brad wanted it that way, consistent with his denial of himself as any sort of "sex fiend." I marveled at the irony of a guy who could shoplift shoes or a sleeping bag or food or tools, but who had to ask for a condom so he could "see how one worked." He once remarked, "I can drop my morals whenever I want," but somehow he needed to keep his sexual interests closeted. He did not discuss any prior sexual exploits, though I wondered if some of the things that he reported happening to guys he knew were really stories about himself. There was little question in my mind that whatever experiences he'd had were limited to other males, reform school a not unlikely setting. He did say that he had "always been susceptible to older guys," but he defined neither "older" nor "susceptible." I could have answered that I have always been susceptible to younger ones.

I was also infatuated with Brad in a protective way, wanting to try to exert some sense of stability and be a constructive force in his life. "Son and lover" sums it up nicely, though, of course, in his mind he was neither. I did not fully realize it at the time, but it was exhilarating to be in a relationship with someone whose life was totally uncomplicated by any other relationship.

If anything, it was my relationship with my partner, Norman, that complicated things. I was, and remain to this day, in a stable relationship with Norman, but by then our relationship had been going for 13 years, and our passion was subdued. Norman had had an aversion to Brad from the beginning, and it was fueled when he learned that Brad and I were having sex. I still loved, and love, Norman, but I had become infatuated with Brad as well. Brad realized that Norman and I were in a longtime relationship and observed how that made it easy to be around us. I believe he was referring to his feeling that, had there been a woman in the house, he would have felt ill at ease. On the other hand, Brad's advice was to not let Norman in on our new relationship. I was trying not to exclude Norman or to keep anything from him, but it probably would have been better to have followed Brad's inclination, even if Norman had suspected something. If Norman was cool toward Brad from the outset, he was cooler still in his new knowledge.

Our society's glee at labeling people as homosexual, as gay or lesbian, does a huge disservice to anyone and everyone who feels some attraction for members of the same sex, particularly those who feel shame for having such feelings and ambivalence about having to hide them. The labels tend to put people in boxes from which it can be impossible to escape. Too many people are afraid to reveal their ambivalence. I believe that if we did not push the labels so hard, we would not create a problem for so many who are tormented by their ambivalence. Many, perhaps most, young people go through a stage where their physical attraction is to someone of the same sex. Some of us remain essentially at that stage or return to it after experiencing "normal" (i.e., approved) sexual relations.

Brad was still in that early stage: too anti-social to find any other opportunity but, I think, indeterminate as to future preferences. Our relationship was highly sexual and obviously homosexual, but it did not chart his future course. That would depend, I felt, on happenstance—the people whom he would meet up with. Clearly I was not his dream partner, but I was the only person with whom he talked about such things, and we could, and did, for months, turn each other on.

I would ultimately describe my relationship with Brad as a caring one, on both sides. I tried to be as fair and consistent with him as I could in our every interaction. I laid as few conditions on his tenancy as possible, what he could and could not do on my property. Threat of fire was one such consideration.

Brad's cabin was nestled among tall Douglas fir trees. I worried constantly about his makeshift chimney arrangements.

A cable he attached high in a tree that allowed him to swing out above the treetops below was another liability. As long as he was the only one who swung on it, I was not worried. When he developed a small social network and began having occasional visitors, I felt the risk of someone falling from the cable was too great. As the property owner, the person ultimately liable, I reluctantly had to insist that it be taken down. Even more reluctantly, he did finally remove it.

I was also unenthused when I discovered a little garden he was managing, well hidden by berry vines, in which he had started several marijuana plants. The rural areas of western Oregon had become (and remain) popular for such ventures. Although I think Brad's goal was to grow marijuana only for his own enjoyment, I hated the thought of him getting in more trouble, especially if his efforts put me in jeopardy. As I recall, a hot summer put him out of business anyway, for his young plants needed more attentive care than he gave.

Yet, in spite of my having at times to "lay down the law," and his own fierce temper, he never refused to comply with what I took to be reasonable requests. He never threatened. He cussed me out only once, when I would not advance him money at the beginning of a weekend. (That rule was easy: Work first, then pay.) As far as I was concerned, I was up for sainthood in the patience I exercised with him, and he must have felt the same way in his behavior toward me. I enjoyed having him along when I ran errands, yet his company was sometimes awkward. If he stopped to use a toilet along the way, he was likely to come back with pockets stuffed with toilet paper. Having lunch one day at a McDonald's, I noticed that the salt and pepper shakers that had been at our table only minutes before were no longer present. Sure enough, they were already in his pocket. "But I just gave you large salt and pepper shakers for barbecuing, both filled," I reminded him. "Oh, yeah," he acknowledged, and returned the ones he had lifted. Old habits die hard.

He also took risks for me. Under some circumstances he felt uncomfortable riding in my car when he might be seen by someone he knew. ("Hey, Brad, who was that old guy you were riding with?") But there were other times when he was perfectly comfortable accompanying me, such as to the campus. One day he attended one of my classes. He helped with major projects and even suggested things that needed doing around the place. I asked if he thought he could top a couple of tall trees that were blocking the winter sun from the house. Fearless climber that he was, he took on the task. On another day, without even asking, he topped a tree across the road that blocked the view of the Coast Range. I am reminded of these exploits because more than 20 years later, those trees still attest to his climbing ability.

The months following the beginning of our relationship were probably Brad's best. As for me, the relationship simply nurtured my fascination with everything about him. I was away again during part of that second summer, teaching a summer session in Alaska and then traveling with Norman in Japan. Brad had his life in control and even found part-time summer employment. One seemingly perfect job was baling hay on a ranch some miles distant. Brad didn't mind the hard work, but as there was no way to contact him, he showed up for work on days they were not going to bale, didn't show up on days they were, and soon exhausted the patience of everyone concerned. This included his own, because of the long and frequently futile bicycle ride involved. I knew a manager at a local McDonald's, but Brad wouldn't consider the possibility of another long bike ride for the wages involved. There seemed no hope for a regular income. But, as Brad viewed it, there was no need for one, either.

The call from Washington came late in the second summer. It provided the rationale for investigating Brad's life in a systematic way, with the added dividend that our new intimacy would, should, and could help me learn about and understand him. I felt I could attain a greater depth with this study than I ever had before. I was deeply interested in his story, but I did not think of him as a "research subject." Anthropologists do not customarily think of the people with whom they work as subjects or informants, anyway. In this case, I tended to think of Brad and Brad's story as two separate events. I did, however, hope to capture a glimpse of someone else's lifestyle, someone who might as easily have turned up in another person's backyard as in mine.

Brad's Decline

As we headed into the rainy season—with its prospect of gloomy days and muddy trails—and Brad's second winter at the cabin, a gradual and, at first, almost undetectable mood change came over him.

I seriously doubt that there was a precipitating physical event. The only such possible culprit might have been an overdose of psilocybin mushrooms (the hallucinogenic Liberty Caps) some kids had collected and brought him in a paper bag. That evening he reported that he consumed the entire bagful. He described himself as really "going wild." I note this only because he told me about it. I have never been able to ascertain the effects of the mushroom or what would constitute an overdose.

I am more inclined to think that he was simply hardwired for mental disorder and/or had been traumatized as a youth by an abusive father. However, this is also conjecture. The *fact* is that, in his last few months at the cabin, I watched as he became increasingly distraught and disorganized. It seemed ironic that as his physical circumstances stabilized and improved his mental condition began to deteriorate. He became preoccupied with the idea of finding something dramatic to change his life, to open the way to some new experience. He expressed increasing dissatisfaction with his present circumstances and future prospects. He spent most of the lengthening hours of darkness in his sleeping bag, and, of course, he complained that he could not sleep.

After one particularly long and boring week, he resolved to force himself out of his mood by forcing himself out of the cabin. He planned to seek out some new involvement bright and early the following Monday. On the evening before the day marked for his emancipation, the region was covered with an unusual blanket of snow. Determined as he was to turn a new leaf, he trudged down the hill in the snow. He was soaked and in disarray by the time he reached the house. He took that as another sign that everything was going against him.

He considered his possible alternatives, but they were few. He began to describe symptoms of mental stress and anguish, eventually talking about a "sledgehammer to the brain" that was disordering his thoughts. I let him talk out what he could, but talking was producing no relief. Each day seemed to bring a new set of frustrations in which accomplishments were minimized and problems magnified.

An impending and once eagerly anticipated 21st birthday that would mark the completion of two full years "on the mountain" found him instead growing despondent and increasingly preoccupied with events and people largely the creation of his imagination. Recently he had found what he described as "the best job I ever had," working as an occasional helper for a young man who lived about half a mile away and who contracted as an independent gardener-landscaper. Yet after a few weeks of off-again, on-again work, he convinced himself that he was no longer wanted on the job, and he stopped reporting for duty. Following several days of aimless wandering and musing, he announced abruptly (but after what appeared to have been an agonizing decision): "I'm hitting the road. Something's gotta happen. There's nothing for me here." "Something's gotta happen" became his motto, but nothing was happening. And that, it seems, was driving him crazy.

I had always anticipated his departure with mixed feelings, although I never doubted that he would leave someday. Under the present circumstances, I did not feel it wise for him to give up all that he had done to make his life manageable and stable. But he was not to be deterred. He began to sort all that he had collected at the cabin into two piles, one for "junk," the other for things to be boxed and carted down to a crawl space under my house, to which he had access. The day came when he was finally ready to say goodbye, that he would be gone in the morning. It was not without a tear in his eye, but I was sure he meant it.

Later that evening Brad returned to the house, driven there in a pickup truck by the young man for whom he had been working. Norman and I were entertaining guests that evening. By the time I realized what was going on, Brad had loaded into the truck everything he had so carefully spent the past week storing, He dismissed me sullenly. "These are my things. I can take them if I want." And off they drove.

I learned later that the next morning, Brad's former employer drove him to a local pawnshop, where he picked up a few dollars for some of the items in his collection. Then he dropped Brad off at the interstate.

Given his mental state of the past few weeks, and especially the last few days, I was not surprised to find the cabin in disarray. At some distance from the cabin, he had also made a huge pile of his discarded junk. It amounted to another pickup load that subsequently had to be carted away.

After Brad's departure, I, too, sank into a deep depression. His absence might have been sufficient explanation, a genuine sense of loss of someone whom I cared about. Under the circumstances, my grief was greatly complicated by the mental state he was in, reflected in the sudden turn in which the tearful farewell of the afternoon became the angry turning away only a few hours later the same evening.

Coping with Brad's Departure

Writing is what I do, and it has become a way I cope with problems. I began jotting brief notes, then developing them more fully to describe all the avenues that Brad had explored as a way out of the morass he felt himself to be in. This time, however, there were no tape-recorded comments from Brad himself, no way to document how everything looked from his perspective. The account would have to stop with Brad's abrupt departure, an unfinished and unsettling story. In time, that writing became the second piece in the Brad Trilogy, although when I began I had no particular audience or publication in mind. I was, in fact, still wondering what, if anything, could be done with the original Sneaky Kid piece.

I wanted to try to piece together what I had understood and could learn from these recent events. What struck me was how different the alternatives Brad had considered were from the alternatives that I would have considered under similar circumstances. I had been at the university almost 20 years by then, and there had been times when I gave serious thought to whether, and how, I might change my own situation. My thoughts at such times ranged from a change of place at one extreme to a change of occupation at the other. The satisfactions of academic life are not without considerable cost of their own. But my focus would have been on career, the work I do.

Brad wrestled his discontent with alternatives that seemed to focus on cultural survival, with no thought to the kind of work he would do. My title for the second writing, "Life's Not Working," had a double meaning. Brad's life was not oriented around the work he did, but neither did he seem to have his life together. Hardly surprising that, from my anthropological perspective, I would make a distinction that put a cultural spin on events, which I relayed through the subtitle "Cultural Alternatives to Career Alternatives." Let me turn to that part of the story. I present it here in much-abridged form from the article, as it is not necessary in this retelling to repeat the original Sneaky Kid story.

Last Days at the Cabin: Looking Back

Brad's abrupt announcement, "I'm leaving," caught me by surprise in spite of the distraught behavior he had been exhibiting for weeks. Knowing his impulsive nature, and aware that he had been preoccupied with the decision to leave but probably had given little thought to where he would go or what he would do, I urged him to postpone his departure for a few days while he considered his alternatives. Reluctantly, he agreed.

There were several things I hoped might be accomplished by a delay. First, I wanted Brad to have time to renege, if his thoughts of departing were merely an ill-considered whim. Although he had stated more than once his intent to stay at the cabin "as long as two years," and two full years had come to a close just 10 days earlier, this was the first time he had actually mentioned leaving. I also suddenly realized that, in spite of our sometimes uneasy relationship in resolving what he could and could not do as an unofficial tenant, I would greatly miss this unexpected intruder into my life and thought.

Third, although I had harbored little doubt that Brad would leave someday, I felt grave reservation about seeing him depart just then. His recent behavior had become uncharacteristically frenetic. I had asked earlier whether he thought talking to a counselor at a local mental-health office would help, and I felt he might be willing to go there now. Acknowledging his own concern, he conceded that he "might try talking to them," although he insisted that it wouldn't really help.

Fourth, if some new precipitating event had occurred in Brad's wide wanderings or limited social contacts during the previous few days, there had not been time to talk it out. Over the course of two years we had communicated with what seemed a good deal of candor. If something specific was bothering him, I hoped he would be able to talk about it eventually.

Fifth, if Brad was going to leave, here was an opportune time for him to take stock of his options and review what he hoped to accomplish. I suspected that he would identify fewer options than he really had, and I thought I might help him go over his choices. "After all," I argued, "once you get to the freeway, at least you have to decide whether you'll head north or south."

"South," Brad replied, without a pause. Then he added, "Yeah, staying awhile will give me time to get my story, too." If you're going to be hitchhiking, it seems, people want to know why you are traveling. You've got to be ready for them. Deep inside my customarily reticent young friend lurked a ready storyteller.

Cultural Alternatives to Career Alternatives

Here are the options that Brad considered as he set out, deliberately and self-consciously, to take the next major step in his life. Some of them were considered explicitly during the ensuing five days before he "hit the road." Others had been pondered over the course of the preceding months. I have tried to portray these options in the way he perceived them, although the explicit labels are mine. Wherever possible, I have expanded the discussion to include related thoughts Brad had shared during earlier conversations.

Join Up

For Brad, the idea of enlisting was not new, but neither was it his own. More than four years earlier, his father had "encouraged" him to join the Army, to the point of virtually insisting on it. Brad took and passed the necessary paper tests, including the GED exam, attesting to his acquisition of basic literacy. Spending the night in a Portland hotel as a guest of the government, prior to undergoing the routines of the regional military processing station, he had second thoughts. In the morning, he was gone. His view since that time was that he would go into the military only if drafted; he would never volunteer.

Now, on impulse, but also older, stronger, and wiser, he was willing to reconsider enlistment. He imposed only one condition: They had to accept him immediately. Like a flash, with the new stipulation in mind, he was off to the local recruiting station, only to discover, to his surprise, that the U.S. Army had a minimum waiting time of six months, the Navy even longer. Only the Marines offered the prospect of quick processing. Brad made a formal appointment with a Marine recruiter for the following day, elated by easy questions during a screening interview and bolstered by an overheard comment that seemed intended for his ears: "That looks like officer material."

Back at the Marine recruiting office next day, the military option suddenly vanished. High school graduates were preferred; 10th grade was the absolute minimum, at least without the delay of undergoing an entire battery of tests. The GED level was no longer sufficient. At reform school, his last school of record, Brad had been classified a ninth grader. School had failed him one more time! Eventually, the reasons that had gotten him into reform school would probably have been subject to review as well, but at this point, his lack of formal schooling was enough. Brad was not acceptable.

Stay Put

"If you just had a job now, you'd be all set," Brad's mother told him during her visit six months earlier. Even without a job or close friends, however, he did seem to have succeeded in getting his life together. In a rare display of contentment, he once summarized his circumstances with the observation, "For me, it's great." He had found a "perfect job" as a landscape gardener's helper. He voiced little objection to the facts that the job demanded hard work, had more days off than on, was slow to pay, and, as often happens to people who must take such jobs if they want to work at all, part of each hour's earnings were withheld—without receipt—for purported tax purposes. Nevertheless, it provided the prospect of at least part-time work. Brad also liked the young man he worked for: "I can relate to him," he reported, in the argot of his generation.

When Brad failed to show up for work for several days, his employer made a special trip to the cabin to see what was wrong and to disabuse Brad of his illusion that he was no longer wanted on the job. But it was too late: As he had done before, Brad had decided to run away. For once, he was not in trouble with anyone else; this time the trouble was within. Nonetheless, the dearly gained lifestyle and security of the cabin were not enough to hold him.

Be Crazy

The months immediately prior to Brad's 21st birthday became a time of emotional stress and increasing anguish. His wanderings in town seemed to lack their earlier purposefulness, and his activities at the cabin often appeared aimless and repetitive. On dreary, rainy days, he sometimes sat for hours gazing into the flames of his woodstove, interrupting his reveries only to roll a cigarette or a joint, or to prepare a snack. Not only was it an exceedingly difficult time for him (his food stamps had been summarily cut off, job searches seemed futile, and he was penniless), but he also began to brood over his "hard life" and things that seemed forever beyond his reach: a job, a car, friends, a girlfriend.

With the approach of spring, the weather gradually improved and, with his new part-time job, so did Brad's luck. But his outlook did not. Momentary highs—several consecutive days of work; payday and the purchase of a new cookstove; the birthday itself, which did get celebrated—were eroded by days of brooding. He reported distant "voices," usually approving and just within Brad's hearing ("Boy, look at that guy—how strong he is—I wouldn't want to mess with him"), along with occasional headaches that became an incessant "sledgehammer to the brain."

For at least a year I had noticed Brad's tendency to be preoccupied with one—and only one—major purpose or idea at a time, seeming almost to get stuck on any problem until it was resolved. I hoped—but with a rapidly diminishing basis for such hope—that his persistent state of mental turmoil centered on some new and unresolved question. I also broached the idea that perhaps we could—and should—find someone for him to talk to, someone who might provide more help than my patient listening now seemed to accomplish. I doubted that Brad would be receptive to the idea, and he was not, but I blamed part of the problem on my seeming inability to find some way to help him.

He did not appear to take offense at my concern about his mental state; rather, he seemed eager to draw me into his self-diagnosis. On my own, anonymously, I contacted the local mental-health office to learn what resources were available either to me or to Brad, should we want to use them. Having overcome my own reluctance to consider getting professional help for him (was I stigmatizing him?), I inquired how I could ever hope to get an even more reluctant youth to talk to a counselor. I received what seemed reasonable advice that subsequently proved effective: "You might ask whether the things bothering him seem to be making him uncomfortable. Maybe we can get him some help so he won't feel so uncomfortable."

Brad operated at, or near, a level of constant mental discomfort during the days leading up to his decision to leave. He was so distraught on the day he first announced the decision that he agreed to a telephone conversation with a counselor. But his guarded revelations on the phone provided little basis for anything more than encouraging him to come in for a longer consultation. Brad took the unsatisfactory exchange as proof that counselors "don't do anything but talk."

Two days later, following the crushing announcement that his education did not satisfy the required minimum for joining the Marines, Brad was so distraught that he agreed—or at least acquiesced—to my suggestion that now might be the time to talk to someone at the mental-health agency.

Responding to my urgent tone, a counselor set an appointment for that afternoon. After a short consultation, Brad was asked to return the following morning to meet with a staff doctor. As we drove away, Brad reviewed the kinds of questions he had been asked. "Dumb questions," he related, like, " 'Do you know what day of the week it is?' 'Today's date?' 'What month?' " Brad knew it was Wednesday and probably still April; cabin life does not give priority to such information. He said that the two options offered him were to receive outpatient attention (their preferred alternative) or to commit himself to a mental institution until he could "get things straightened out." He was adamantly opposed to medication and outpatient care, but he seemed intrigued with going to a mental hospital where he would be clean, comfortable, and cared for. "Hmmm," he mused aloud as we drove home, "Crazy Brad." In that moment, a new plan seemed to be forming in his mind.

The next morning, in order to catch a ride to town with me to keep his appointment, Brad appeared at the house bright and early, but his demeanor was anything but bright. He had neither washed his face nor combed his hair, and I wondered whether he had slept. He summed up his strategy in one sentence: "I'll tell them whatever I have to tell them to make them think I'm crazy." He appeared convincing enough as Crazy Brad that I wondered whether I would see him again that day after I dropped him off. It seemed thinkable that he might get them to commit him straightaway.

Returning home that afternoon, I set out immediately on the steep trail to the cabin to see whether Brad was there. He was. And what had been the outcome of his visit to the mental-health office, I asked? "They wouldn't help me," he announced, and the subject was dropped. But when I inquired later, I learned that he had been offered help. Brad himself had experienced a change of heart. He was not ready to be Crazy Brad after all. As if to punctuate his decision, he "acquired" a new sleeping bag and backpack along the way back to the cabin. He seemed lighthearted, although with the actuality of his departure now virtually assured, his ambivalence was even more apparent. He announced that he might start hitchhiking that very evening.

Brad did not deny that he was still experiencing a great deal of mental turmoil. He assured me he would find a mental-health clinic or seek out a halfway house if he needed help.

Suicide

I am reluctant to include suicide among Brad's alternatives; I am also reluctant to ignore it. My intuitive sense was that Brad was not a suicide risk. Even if it was at the outermost periphery of alternatives for him, however, it was not entirely unthinkable. For many youth, middle-class whites as well as young people (males especially) in certain ethnic groups, suicide offers a patterned response for coping with the unmanageable. But I think Brad's style was to run rather than to give up.

From my conservative, middle-aged perspective, Brad was an impulsive risk-taker. He liked to impress me with stories of street drugs he had tried, and of dangerous (or at least foolish) things he had done, ranging from driving a motorcycle 115 miles an hour to creeping with companions out on the runway of a busy Southern California airport at night, when jets were landing. His high-climbing and high-swinging antics in the towering firs near the cabin were enough to convince me of his daring. But I also came to appreciate that he was not as foolhardy as he sometimes appeared.

I never felt that this risk-taking reflected suicidal tendencies. At the time of his greatest stress, there was not the slightest hint that "ending it all" was an option he was considering. Nevertheless, he did use the phrase, "I'd kill myself first," to underscore circumstances that to him seemed beyond the pale. And on one occasion, finally talking through a problem that had weighed heavily upon him, he confided, "I even thought of pulling myself up by a rope, and when you came up here looking for me, you'd be staring at my feet swinging from a tree."

Welfare

Brad had observed, "Food stamps are society's way of paying me to drop out." He was first-generation welfare. I doubt that either of his parents had ever sought it. Most likely they would have dealt with an emergency in some other way should an occasion arise where welfare was an option. For some people, seeking welfare is virtually unthinkable. Brad held strong feelings against begging. As he said—and did—"I'd steal before I'd ever beg." But welfare was different.

Even at 19, Brad had been down and out often enough that he saw welfare—particularly food stamps—as one of his rights, albeit a capriciously or conditionally given one. He also knew he could count on handouts any time in a big city. All he had to do was to locate its missions or meal stations, something he had done before. In Brad's experience, it was all right to go for a free meal if you needed one, but in general you were better off keeping to yourself. A mission handout was a last resort: Missions were places where too many people congregated, and they were not Brad's kind of people. In addition, you had to "pray for your supper" (i.e., attend a worship service before you would be served a meal). That type of charity was the emergency solution. Brad preferred government welfare.

Getting Locked Up

In three days of pondering, Brad's options seemed at first to widen, only to narrow again to his original idea of leaving. Adamant in his feeling that he had to move on (thus eliminating the idea of remaining at the cabin), his two most attractive long-term alternatives appeared to be the institutional ones that had now been ruled out: military enlistment or mental hospital.

Although from my perspective the two options are strikingly different, to Brad they shared common and appealing properties—regular meals; a warm, dry place to sleep; clothing; opportunity to keep oneself and one's clothes washed; things to do (e.g., watch television all day, which seemed OK to him), and people to do them with. Those favorable elements compensated for some obvious drawbacks—regimentation, everyone telling you what to do, large groups of people, lack of privacy or autonomy. The military rejected Brad, at least on his "now or never" terms; he, in turn, rejected institutionalization in a mental hospital. One additional institution remained a possibility: jail, leading perhaps to time in prison. Brad had no qualms about going to jail; he had been there before and had no fear of it. Even prison was not unthinkable to someone who had already spent the better part of a year in reform school.

My inclination is to focus on differences among institutions; Brad tended to see their similarities. From his perspective, jail had certain attractions over other institutions, provided one wasn't in for anything too serious. Going to jail offers a chance to clean up, to sleep, and to be fed. And one is not likely to remain as long as might be required in the army or in a mental hospital. In Brad's view, born of experience, "They have to let you out sometime."

With jail as his most likely risk if he were simply to return to the idea of "moving on," living by his own resourcefulness and cunning, that plan surfaced again not only as a good alternative but as the only realistic one for a young man in a hurry to be on his way but with no particular place to go. The ease with which he acquired a new sleeping bag and backpack for his anticipated travels served to reassure him that his shoplifting skills—seldom used in the past year—remained intact for the adventure ahead. As always, he would take only what he needed. He emphatically explained that he was not a "super thief" who made a living by stealing; he was merely resourceful in obtaining necessary items he could not otherwise afford. He could get by. A few days in jail would be the most likely consequence of getting caught at petty theft, and that would be a mixed blessing.

Hustling

Brad's overall strategy was simply to "see what happens and not worry too much about it." On the streets, he would remain alert to whatever possibilities came up. Dealing drugs, for example—particularly to younger kids, just as older kids had sold drugs to him—was a likely possibility.

Brad also recognized a new sexuality and physical prowess in himself, only recently having outgrown an adolescent agony over what he had regarded as his youthful puniness. This was another expressed reason for deciding to take to the woods and live by himself, a topic broached only after months of discussing less personal issues. He now remarked casually about the possibility of marketing his body. His ideal sex-for-hire scenario was, predictably, to have a "beautiful woman" offer him a ride and immediately take him home, where he would enjoy the good life as a handsome young consort.

Brad recognized that at his age and with his physique he was attractive to males as well, and the idea of easy money and no work had its appeal. Along certain well-known boulevards of the metropolitan areas where Brad was headed, "San Francisco, maybe even as far south as Los Angeles," young males regularly hustled customers under the guise of hustling rides. Brad had caught glimpses of the hustler's role in exposés on television; perhaps he had experienced them firsthand on the streets of the larger cities where he had lived or traveled.

There was no moral issue at stake: "I can drop my morals whenever I want." The risk of acquiring a sexually transmitted disease seemed not to be a consideration, and in 1982 there was no talk of AIDS. To my relief, Brad said he "doubted" that he would try it—but the issue was largely academic until a real occasion or real need presented itself. One had to be open to any possibility. After all, if he got to Hollywood, he might end up as a rock star or a hustler. I preferred to think that his chances at either were unlikely.

Going Home

Brad's world was confined essentially to the West Coast, from Portland to Southern California. I asked whether he would return to the community where he had spent several years as a youth and where his mother resided. Expressing feelings of deep alienation from both parents, he insisted that he had no intention of going near his mother's home, reminding me that he was neither welcome nor allowed in his stepfather's house. Brad seemed to regard his departure from the cabin more like leaving home than returning there. More than once while growing up he had run away from both his parents' homes. Once again he was resolving his problems by running away, but this time it was from a literal as well as a figurative home—and life—of his own making.

Brad's feelings of utter rootlessness were evident in a new and poignant concern he expressed during the brief period when he was contemplating enlisting: "When everyone else goes home on leave, like at Christmas, I won't have any place to go." I reminded him that the cabin would still be standing, and that he could return there. Or to my home, if in the semi-stoicism of the peacetime military he had grown used to such creature comforts as hot and cold running water.

Hitting the Road

Underscoring that the cabin did now represent home, Brad sorted through his assortment of tools, parts, and utensils, carrying rubbish to a somewhat accessible pick-up point and storing valued items in cartons packed safely in my basement. Then, moments before his departure, he changed his mind. In the bizarre fashion that had come to characterize his behavior, he began sorting through his stored possessions, looking for anything that might bring a few dollars at a pawnshop. (I hadn't realized our town had a pawnshop.) Then he was off.

Almost from the moment Brad left, I expected either to see him reappear at the cabin—hale, hearty, and resigned, if not content, with his lot—or to receive a long-distance telephone call from (or about) him, informing me that he was in serious trouble. Instead, more than two months after he departed, I received a call from his mother. By a circuitous route that had included "waking up in Phoenix," hustling on the boulevards of West Hollywood ("The things they made him do!" his mother exclaimed), and spending several days in jail in a suburb of Los Angeles on a shoplifting charge, and following a series of increasingly frequent collect calls from localities throughout Southern California that gave his mother her first hint of Brad's current mental state, he had finally gone home.

Initially Brad's mother rented a hotel room for him, but she reported that as she listened to him drift between fact and fancy in relating recent events in his life, she realized that Brad was home to stay. She rented a small trailer where he could live, and discussed with him the idea of seeking professional help. Shortly after arriving home Brad voluntarily committed himself to the county mental institution for 16 days, but a steadfast refusal to join therapy groups or regularly take medication left everyone, Brad included, feeling that institutionalization was not likely to be any more helpful than it was necessary. In response to a letter I sent in care of his mother, Brad telephoned me once from the institution. Our conversation seemed forced and aimless. He concluded by saying, "Send me money."

Distraught and perhaps burdened by feelings of guilt, for several weeks Brad's mother cooked and delivered a hot meal to him daily, did his laundry, and resumed the mothering role she had given up years earlier. Dissuaded by a mental-health worker (as well as Brad's stepfather, who insisted that Brad was not all that helpless), she subsequently reduced her visits to about three a week.

As soon as he was formally diagnosed as a mental-health patient—and thus a disabled member within society rather than a renegade from it—Brad became eligible not only for welfare benefits but also for additional SSI (Supplemental Security Income) payments. In his mother's opinion, given Brad's moodiness, constant daydreaming, and short attention span, it seemed unlikely that he would ever be able to hold a job. She resigned herself to the fact that he was "insane" (her term) and to the likelihood that she would have to look after him the rest of his life.

Although Brad purportedly started taking an antidepressant and, in his mother's words (and in her meaning of them, rather than in Brad's), eventually became "mellow," he continued to refuse counseling or attend voluntary vocational-therapy sessions. She said he occasionally rode his bicycle, mostly sat in his little trailer listening to rock music, and was leading what she described as a "very boring life."

Perhaps it was boring. It appeared so to his mother. It sounded incredibly boring to me when I reflected on the energy and sense of accomplishment once demonstrated by a fiercely independent youth, who now waited for the government to send him money and for his mother to bring his supper and wash his clothes. But from Brad's perspective, compared to the lifetime he could envision as a dishwasher, tree planter, or day laborer, life may have been no less boring as he was living it. He would be the first to admit it was easier. As he once said at the cabin: "I don't have to work my life away just to survive."

Some Concluding Comments to "Life's Not Working"

I felt I needed to situate this part of the Brad story in some broader context. It was some time before I even recognized that the options that Brad had considered were not vocational ones, not even the military option. A phrase circulating in academic circles at the time was the "school/work nexus" (see, for example, Ginzberg 1980). It seemed to me that Brad's way of looking at things did not lock school and work into an inevitable sequence, but placed them at one end of a continuum, with what I have here termed "cultural alternatives" at the other.

The school/work nexus represents neither realistic alternatives nor the full range of alternatives as perceived by all. For many youths, school represents their first task-related failure. A neat and orderly progression from school success to work success is broken at the first step. Brad failed at school (or, stated more accurately, school and Brad repeatedly failed each other) and seemed now to have failed at work. He had taken a roundabout way to locate himself in a world in which he had achieved a modicum of security and control.

I certainly had not sought Brad out as part of a systematic effort to explore cultural alternatives. That opportunity arose in the course of events of Brad's life, the result of an unanticipated (though perhaps impending) crisis that precipitated an explicit review and choice of a course of action. The anthropologist in me was reluctant to dismiss Brad as (1) an isolated case, of (2) an alienated dropout, who (3) began exhibiting psychotic tendencies and therefore could not do what all normal people do, which is (4) hold a job. There were other possible interpretations—cultural ones—that invited examination of the social circumstances of such a case. I concluded the article by suggesting a few of them. Here is the essence of the interpretation I offered at the time.

Reflecting on the Brad Story, 1983–84

First, it is difficult for those of us reared under a strict ethos of the propriety of work, and who have in turn subscribed to that ethos in the ordering of our own lives, to fathom that all individuals capable of doing so would not choose either to work or to occupy themselves with some moral equivalent of work. We need to recognize our own deep-seated and unexamined assumptions regarding the inviolability of work. The dignity we romantically associate with work is not equally apparent in each of the jobs that comprises the workforce. Unschooled young people appear well aware of the distinction. Brad could get jobs, but they did not lead to careers.

My role as an educator is ipso facto evidence of my having bought into the work ethic. The same holds true of any of the formal role-occupiers with whom a young person like Brad comes in contact: welfare worker, psychiatric counselor, personnel manager, police officer, probation officer, employed staff member at an unemployment office. Brad's formal encounters were held entirely among the comfortable and diligent, the standard-bearers of mainstream American society. They surrounded him in every official role to serve simultaneously as his judges, teachers, counselors, and benefactors. They provide living testimony to the fact that the system works because it works for them.

But a dominant ethos is not a universal one. Brad stood not so much in opposition to the work ethos as disengaged from it. He did not seek his identity in work any more than he had sought it earlier at school. He had tailored his hopes and ambitions. He had a keen sense of what, for him, constituted the essentials; obtaining them provided his driving force. His attention was on what he needed, rather than on what he might become. Survival was his challenge and his work, and he worked full-time at it. But work for its own sake cast no compelling spell over him. It was no more than a ready trap back into the second-class life he had already tried and rejected.

Second, Brad's case reveals a far stronger institutional pull in our society than I had been aware of, a pull toward compliance and dependency. The case also illustrates both how powerful and how few are any institutional alternatives. By his assessment, the three "total institutions" that beckoned—the military, jail, or a mental institution—provided roughly the same amenities in exchange for a full-time commitment. Second-order institutional support—welfare, outpatient mental-health services, meals at some mission—required less commitment but offered less in return.

I do not look to these institutions to provide alternative ways to order my life, and perhaps that is why it astounded me to hear Brad review them in his inventory of possible resolutions for his. It proved even more astounding to recognize how limited his choices were, and the social cost of making them. The commitments are not casual. To me, each of his choices represents what I would take to be, at best, an interruption in life's work. To Brad, they represented genuine options.

I have sensed a growing disenchantment with the dominance of the role that work plays in many lives, some lessening of the dignity or pride once associated with it, more tolerance for people who retire early even if they are not technologically displaced or under doctor's orders. As the prospect of having a career seems less and less likely for the younger generation, the ideal of career is disappearing. Still, I assume that gainful employment will continue to reflect an American core value, one of the realities of contemporary life. We should probably be attending more closely to providing institutional options both to help individuals like Brad find their way and to deal more directly with the social fact that we do not need—and cannot accommodate—every able-bodied person in the workforce. One would think that we could come up with more creative primary institutional options than jail, mental institutions, or a reluctant stint in the armed forces.

Rather than foster alternatives that build or nurture institutional dependence, perhaps we should examine the ways we currently provide secondary institutional support. With Brad's problems conveniently medicalized, he received two government checks, one (welfare) rewarding his acknowledged dependency, the other (SSI) rewarding his acknowledged incompetence. During his years at the cabin, Brad was able to live on far less, maintaining his independence through the modest subsidy of food stamps that neither encouraged continued dependence nor (initially) punished him for it. Coincidence or not, it was in the weeks immediately after his food stamps were cut off that Brad began to show the first signs of the stress that eventually consumed him. He needed immediate financial help; instead, he received an appointment for a hearing scheduled for Christmas Eve.

Then, with his newfound and medically validated social status as "mentally disabled," he became eligible for subsidies that might last a lifetime of not working.

Third and last, I want to comment on the totally unexpected alternative that Brad followed, an alternative that anthropologist Sue Estroff (1981) described as "making it crazy" in her study with that title. I am inclined to think that Brad chose the crazy route, not in the sense that he elected mental disorder, but in the sense that he opted to play the crazy card to the hilt. Viewed not only as a psychological response but also as a social solution that simultaneously resolved several important problems in his life, he could hardly have chosen better.

I do not suggest that Brad was faking a psychosis. He was rapidly losing touch with reality during his last few weeks at the cabin, and he steadfastly ignored my suggestions of ways to test whether the things he had begun to hear and to believe were true. Nevertheless, there were important cultural dimensions in the resolution of his problems.

Much as I agreed that enlisting in the military offered Brad a possible option, I breathed a sigh of relief when the Marines turned him down. Given his mental state and his natural antipathy toward being ordered about, I doubted that he was ready for the psychological abuse of initiation into the military, even though he would have reveled—and excelled—in its physical rigors.

Similarly, a customary wariness that had served him well on the streets seemed to have escalated into a dysfunctional paranoia. Whatever actually occurred during his brief escapade as a street hustler, Brad subsequently confided to his mother that he was being followed, and that the "Hollywood Mafia" was after him. The streets had become too dangerous. It was time to go home.

Originally, Brad dismissed the idea of going home. As part of his asser-
tion of independence, he prided himself on not having (and therefore not
being dependent upon) a home or family he could turn to, faltering in his pose
of self-reliance only at the realization that even Marines go home at Christmas. Because he had been banished from the home of his stepfather as a result
of past unruly behavior, all his mother could have done by way of a home-
coming would have been to "go out for pizza" and give him money or buy
him clothes. She had steadfastly refused his demands for a car or another
motorcycle until he could demonstrate responsibility. Showing up jobless and
penniless would hardly have provided a basis for appeal on that decision.

But turning up as a son deeply disturbed and obviously in need of help
provided a point of entrée that made it all right for him to go home, all right
for his mother to assume responsibility for caring for him, all right for him to
cast aside all thoughts of a job, all right to accept a new status as a helpless
dependent—all the very antithesis of the qualities on which he had so prided
himself the previous two years. The physiological basis was there; social circumstances called for everyone to play it to the max.

With Brad-the-social-problem now reinterpreted as Brad-the-medical-
problem, the state was willing to assume the economic burden and provide
the professional help that Brad could not find earlier. The only condition
attached to his new status was that he continue to be crazy, or, more accurately, to act crazy enough to be convincing. That became his work. It is relatively permanent, relatively secure; it requires only physical presence, not
physical effort. One can, more or less, choose one's own hours. The role
requires a certain amount of acquiescence but tolerates a great deal of aberra-
tion as well. Indeed, as Estroff (1981:190) points out, it is important not to
become too compliant or too cooperative.

There is some sacrifice of self-esteem, but as one may remain in relative
isolation, the loss of self-esteem is probably no greater than one would experience in many demeaning jobs. The only thing one must be careful to do is
to demonstrate continuing inadequacy at some—but not all—social roles,
especially work. As Estroff (1981:189) noted in what she identified as "Rules
for Making It Crazy," it is all right to "try new things, like working, every
once in a while," but you must assume you are going to fail. And when you
do, you offer it as proof to yourself and those around you that you are sick and
cannot manage. Brad had been rehearsing appropriate behaviors for years.

In anthropological fashion, Estroff (1981:171) explored paradoxes in the
lives of American psychiatric clients, focusing particularly on the seductive
pull of income-maintenance programs that "may perpetuate the crazy life not
only by making it attractive as a source of income but also by rewarding the

continuation of inadequacy demonstrated by not working." Estroff concluded with a broad generalization amply demonstrated in Brad's case:

> Being a full-time crazy person is becoming an occupation among a certain population in our midst. If we as a society continue to subsidize this career, I do not think it humane or justifiable to persist in negatively perceiving those who take us up on the offer and become employed in this way. [1981:255–56]

Given the slightest hint that an individual has been professionally diagnosed as mentally disturbed, there is the likelihood that the individual will then be regarded only in those terms. Like the label "homosexuality," this becomes what can be called a "master status" that overshadows all other roles one plays. I ran the risk that my efforts to present a study illustrating a range of cultural alternatives could be dismissed on the grounds that crazy people do crazy things, and the case demonstrates nothing more.

I argue that the case does illustrate something more: that school and work are not the only alternatives, that the school/work nexus is not the only nexus, and that the realistic alternatives for eking out a living—that is, for sheer survival—as today's youth perceive them, vary considerably from the ideal world we like to think has been created for them. Schools and social agencies oriented to a world of a-job-for-everyone-and-everyone-in-a-job may address a majority of the population and a majority of the problems posed by transition into adulthood. But they do not address everyone. That is the message, or at least the reminder, of this case.

Against such alternatives as being in jail, joining the military out of desperation, or holding a menial job—and taking into account the dependable income he now "earned"—Brad opted for what seemed, at the moment, to be society's best offer. I did not envy his solution to the dilemma presented by the school/work nexus. Nor, apparently, did he envy mine.

Chapter Three

The Return

IF I had doubts about whether there was a story that could be developed from the original interviews as I first began organizing and writing my material, they had disappeared by the time I completed a working draft. There was a story, and I now had a draft to share. I invited several colleagues to review the manuscript for me. I asked Brad to do the same. I submitted an initial draft to the School Finance Project, received some good editorial suggestions to incorporate in the final version—along with gracious thanks from the project officer—and thereby fulfilled my part of Contract No. NIE-P-81-0271.

But that, it seems apparent in retrospect, was to be the final destiny of Brad's story and of my case study contrasting schooling and education. I never heard another word about my contribution. From anyone. Two decades have passed. I rather doubt that I ever will!

What happened, or, more realistically, why had nothing happened? I can only guess. Congress handled the problem of "educational adequacy" by throwing money at it, which seems to be the way Congress handles most problems. Had educational adequacy suddenly become a red-hot issue that year or the next, Congress could have called attention to its good efforts to be responsive to the issue.

But educational adequacy did not become a red-hot issue that year. Educational adequacy simply smolders, year after year. There were more pressing fires to tend. The only real concern was that the Government Accounting Office, the official watchdog on Congressional spending, would eventually want to know that the money allocated for the report was used (and used up) as Congress had directed. The money allocated for commissioning an inquiry had to be spent, in spite of the fact that there was no point to it, no interest in it, and no audience for the report. My contribution, with its original title, "Adequate School and Inadequate Education: An Anthropological Perspective," was destined not to breathe life into a national concern but to put it to rest.

Assuming an Editorship

Among other events of 1981, and unrelated to Brad's arrival on my property the year prior, I was asked to serve as the next editor of the *Anthropology and Education Quarterly*. My tenure was to begin with volume 14, the spring issue of 1983.

I had been thinking about revising the Brad piece for publication, especially as I realized that nothing was ever going to happen to it in its original form. But initially I did not even entertain the idea of publishing it in the journal I was now editing. Not that I did not think the piece was of publishable quality. I was struck with the power of Brad's story and the perspective it lent to putting schooling itself into a broader cultural context. My concern lay elsewhere—that academic editors don't usually publish their own articles. But why shouldn't they? I decided to ask my three predecessors for an opinion: Would it be acceptable for me to publish the rewritten Brad piece in the first issue of *AEQ* under my editorship?

John Singleton, founding editor of *AEQ*, was not only in enthusiastic support but offered to write an introduction to both my article and my editorship. I accepted his offer. I am forever grateful for the way he explained the position it reflected on the anthropological contribution to education. He also interpreted what he called my "unorthodox way" of proclaiming my editorship, putting forth something controversial as an opening statement to "demonstrate responsible scholarly and moral concerns in promoting the anthropological study of education" (Singleton 1983:2).

My bold move might also be seen as an instance of publish *and* perish. Editor Charles Harrington, my immediate predecessor, thought it a bad idea to publish in one's own journal, regardless of the merits of the piece. On principle alone, he advised against it. My hope for a weak vote of support (two out of three) lay with former editor John Chilcott. The vote was weaker than I had hoped: Chilcott was ambivalent as to what I should do. He would not offer a decisive opinion.

But by this time the question was moot. I was down to the wire and needed the article to fill the journal. I published it with John Singleton's endorsement as an introduction. I do not recall receiving any negative reaction about publishing in a journal under my own direction. Singleton's introduction may have fended off any dissenters, or, if there were any, I may have conveniently forgotten.

The body of the account remained as originally submitted in my report. I gave it a new subtitle, "The Life History of a Sneaky Kid," as I did not have to remind readers of the *Anthropology and Education Quarterly* that the article would offer an anthropological perspective.[1] I eliminated my original introductory comments and went directly to the case, as I urge others to do when presenting their studies. I reserved my commentary for the conclusion, putting the case in a broader perspective than one requiring a quick fix in the schools. That was the idea we were endeavoring to develop in taking an anthropological perspective on education. I noted in my conclusion:

> The problems Brad now poses for society are not a consequence of inadequate schooling. They dramatize the risk we take by restricting our vision of collective educational responsibility to what can be done in school. [Wolcott 1983:26]

I have never been modest about the power of the Sneaky Kid piece, never modest about it as a model of an anthropological contribution to education, never modest about it as an example of the use of the anthropological life history method, or of how much can be said in a journal-length article. I have personally seen to its being published three more times, once in a collection of essays that included 11 of my previously published articles, *Transforming Qualitative Data* (Wolcott 1994), and twice in a publication of the American Educational Research Association, *Complementary Methods for Research in Education* (Jaeger 1988, 1997).

I should note that except for *Transforming Qualitative Data,* there were no royalties associated with these publications—fame without fortune. Brad had departed before I even faced the decision about whether to publish the Sneaky Kid article in my first issue of *AEQ.* Another dozen years passed before the three Brad pieces appeared together to become the Brad Trilogy. I doubt that Brad was ever aware of them, for the articles appeared in professional publications quite unlikely to draw his attention. But I think he would be satisfied that his account has remained the way he first saw it in 1981. Since that time, I have made only minor editorial changes.

I recall one critic's reaction to my disclosure that I had *edited* the original interview material into the sequence as presented in the Sneaky Kid account. I should have been more explicit about what I did. Anyone familiar with life history data, or with interview data of any kind, should have understood that it would be a rare informant who could sit down and spin off a coherent, compelling life story from start to finish without interruption. Brad offered his account in little vignettes, staccato-like, usually unconnected with what had gone before. I did a great deal of rearranging and ordering the material under suitable categories. But that was all I meant by "editing with a heavy hand."

My organization of the material was also influenced by the assignment that drove it initially, which was to consider the issue of educational adequacy.

To accomplish that, I decided to relate something of Brad's personal history and to superimpose his school experience. I was scrupulously faithful to his language and to his words and sentences. It was the arrangement of topics that was mine. The important test for me was Brad's reaction to the account. His only expressed concern was with the image that he felt might be portrayed to hypothetical peers of his own.

By the time the Sneaky Kid article actually appeared in print, Brad was long gone, and I had begun working on the sequel, "Life's Not Working." In that writing, the questions I was left with seemed to get further and further ahead of my data. I had little additional information to work with except for Brad's anguish surrounding his sudden decision to leave and the events prompted by that decision. But I had gained new insight into Brad's worldview as a result of his self-conscious introspection regarding his prospects for the future. An examination of those alternatives became the focus for the new writing, with heavy emphasis on the activities of a single week in contrast to my earlier effort to encapsulate Brad's whole life in fewer than 30 pages.

I had no particular audience in mind for the second piece, not even a clear idea of whether I was preparing a publishable article or simply trying to see what sense I could make out of a series of events so unexpected and unsatisfying. My perspective, however, is always cultural. Although I did not attempt to write especially for an anthropologically oriented audience, and had no intention of slipping another of my own articles into *AEQ* while I was still editor, I pressed heavily on cultural analysis. I wanted to see what insight my professional orientation could offer to my personal one for thinking through issues that had begun to occupy a great deal of my thought.

Neither did the account I was preparing seem a likely candidate for a psychological journal (nowhere near rigorous enough), nor a pedagogical one (implications for the classroom were not all that clear). But these factors were not a primary concern. The Brad story was becoming increasingly personal and conjectural. I wrote because I felt compelled to do so, to try, quite literally, to figure things out on paper.

More by default than by design, the writing offered about equal parts description, analysis, and interpretation, with analysis given a heavier role as I endeavored to make do with the meager additional data at hand. As noted in the article itself, only reluctantly did I raise the issue of sanity. I raised it as reluctantly as I had embraced it myself while interacting with Brad during his final weeks at the cabin. Initially I resisted the idea for both our sakes, his for negative stereotypes that questions of sanity call forth, mine for the realization that, if Brad was crazy, my efforts to describe and understand his social behavior might be rendered largely inconsequential.

The writing did have a cathartic effect on me. And it helped move the Brad story forward, although it was doubtful that anyone would discover it as a sequel. It was so delayed in publication that by the time of its release, the story had entered a dramatic new phase. I could only append a telling footnote that, just as several readers of early drafts had predicted, Brad did return.

Brad Returns

Another phone call came from Southern California, this one with an ominous message. I received the call while working at home one morning in October 1984. It had been almost two and a half years since Brad had left. I wasn't paying close attention; it sounded suspiciously like a telephone solicitation. Later, I could not remember the caller's name, what mental-health organization she was with or her role in it, or the exact text of her message. But it went something like this, once she established who I was and that I did indeed know someone named Brad:

> He has been making threats against you. He says he is coming up to Oregon to get you and burn down your house. We are required by law to report such threats.

I've always wondered when and how one might use the word *incredulous*. Here is my opportunity: The term aptly describes my initial reaction. Another telephone call out of the blue shaping the course of the Brad story, this time with a threat to my property and my life. The stern tone of the woman's voice assured me that this was no prank. The brief message was all she intended to say and perhaps all she knew. "What am I supposed to do?" I asked. "I don't know," came the reply. "Just be careful—be very, very careful."

It had been more than two years since there had been any telephone calls from or about Brad. The first had been from his mother after his return to Southern California. She had been anxious for any details I could fill in as to why he was acting the way he was. Then I got a couple of calls from Brad himself during a brief period when, at her urging, he voluntarily committed himself in a county mental-health facility in San Diego. I had sent Brad letters that went unanswered, and cards on two birthdays following his departure, enclosing a check with the amount of his age in dollars. I thought that enclosing a check seemed a pretty crafty way to find out whether the cards were received, even if I could not get him to answer my letters. The checks were never cashed.

I was more successful at corresponding with his mother, at least at first. One such exchange will help to fill in some details of what had been happening during the months immediately after his return to Southern California. The following letter was written December 15, 1982:

> Dear Harry,
>
> Brad is certainly out in left field. He is on 30 mg of Navane a day. It is not making him sane but he is not hearing voices in his head any more. He still has "Lucy" [his imaginary girlfriend] and the "Hollywood people" in his head. He is in Los Angeles today looking for Lucy. He has an appointment tomorrow morning for a Forensic examination at the courthouse. There is going to be a conservatorship hearing at the county courthouse. I am hoping a conservator will be appointed so that someone else besides myself can deal with his money. He gets SSI and lives in a small trailer a few miles from me.
>
> I was seeing him daily but Mental Health thought it best he not depend on me so much. Now I see him 3 times a week. Brad will not go to any type of therapy. He is not capable of work unless the employer could understand his problems. His attention span is very short. All he thinks of is Lucy. He leads a very boring existence. He rides his bike and a skateboard and listens to music all day.
>
> I am returning your last letter to Brad. Every time he gets a letter it upsets him so I didn't give him the last one. He tells me that he does not want any of his school records made available to you and I have to respect his wishes on that matter.
>
> He has told me of some abnormal and disgusting events that happened on the mountain between the two of you and in my opinion it may have driven Brad off the deep end. He basically knows right from wrong. I think that is why Lucy appeared on the scene.
>
> I don't know what will ever become of Brad. He will probably be insane the rest of his life, and will outlive all of us.

I sent my answer two weeks later:

> January 1, 1983
>
> It was a great relief to hear from you and about Brad. At least now he's taking some medicine. At your last report, he wouldn't even do that. Wish you could get him into therapy. If mental health won't work, I wonder if you could get him interested in a counselor (psychiatrist or at least an MD specialist) who could talk to him about sex and sex hang-ups. He carries around a crushing burden of concerns about his sexuality. (One of his last ideas around here was that his father was going around telling everyone that Brad was impotent.) It might be that he'd be willing to go for a physical

and some medical counseling about sex where he won't do it on purely mental grounds. It seems imperative to me that he get psychiatric help.

On that score, I'm not sure that harsh judgments about "abnormal and disgusting events" are much help to him, either. The enlightened view these days is that what happens between consenting adults is their business, and the view is shared by everyone from psychiatrists and most clergy to Dear Abby. Why Brad is so eager to burden others—you, especially—is a mystery to me, but your interpretation of those events makes the burden what it is. Whether that was just a passing stage in his life or not, I don't know. I think it will largely depend on who he meets up with. Lucy, as his idealized and totally unrealizable romance, probably leaves him more open to males. Don't heap more guilt on him. Lucy herself may be largely invented to please you, but Lucy is also a great convenience to Brad because she provides a rationale for going and doing what he wants. She has proven a splendid invention!

I feel a deep attachment for Brad. Maybe he happened along at a time in my life when I needed someone like him, a strange combination of son and lover. But I happened along in his life when he needed someone desperately, too. My only regret is that I didn't realize that need for so long. My "therapy" was listening and, at times, a firm hug. Until I hugged him I didn't realize how totally beyond reach he had gotten, and by then he'd already been here for 11 lonely months. In the second year he really made progress, including physical growth (even growing out of his stoop-shouldered slouch), a stable life, even a "sometimes" job. He also earned well over $1,000 working for me. Why he "blew" at the end I don't know—there just wasn't time to find out between his Monday announcement that he was leaving and his Friday departure. I have a second regret: that I didn't try to stop him from going. I really thought he'd take off for a month or so, realize that he did have things "together" here, and then return. In a sense, I've been waiting for him to come back ever since then. He goes out looking for Lucy and I go up the hill looking for him. I guess it is catching.

If he does ever want to come back, I'd want him to, of course. He'd have to have a source of income. That could be in working for me, but it would be better if he had some regular income and worked only to supplement it. Matters of money were problems for us. I never advanced him money (but he could work for cash anytime, so I figured I was keeping him secure but not dependent). But I'd also insist he have therapy—and maybe I'd even be able to get away with it (i.e., that he would agree and follow through with it). I could be—and was—pretty firm with him. We both worked to make the relationship work. That's where it was different from family.

I doubt that this is a *better* place for him, but it is *a* place. Matter of fact, if Brad ever just packs up and leaves there, you probably should call me, for my guess is that this is his "other place." He always said he thought he'd stay here two years, and that's exactly what he did. You can listen for clues if he plans another move. If he "reaches his limit" there, I suspect he'll return here.

I'm sorry he doesn't want the school records looked at. My hunch was that agency after agency tested him and diagnosed problems but no one ever really *did* anything. Unless Brad changes his mind, I'll never know. If I did know, I could raise some critical issues that might make programs more effective today. If Brad sees that as prying, after all we shared and talked about, then it only shows how far we've gotten out of touch. And I guess if you won't relay my letters, or at least my greetings, there's nothing I can do about it.

I'll continue to count on you to keep me informed. I'd like to write him and will even enclose another letter to him. You can read it and decide whether to give it to him. At a moment's notice, I'd fly down to talk to him, or talk to him on the phone. I can't imagine ever stopping caring about him or thinking of him. He taught me a lot more about life than I taught him. Please keep me informed.

Brad never did write, and the letter above was the last one I received from his mother. I did think about him often, and I hoped an occasional letter from me would somehow prompt a response, but it never did. Attending a meeting in San Diego gave me an opportunity to try to see him firsthand, but I had no address for him. When I telephoned, his stepfather said that Brad did not want to see me. His mother's letter had already informed me that Brad's imaginary girlfriend Lucy, to whom he began making reference just before departing from the cabin, was still in the picture, along with a new concern that he was being stalked by what he referred to as "the Hollywood Mafia." What had seemed only traces of delusional thinking when he departed had apparently become a full-blown psychosis, though I had a hard time agreeing with his mother that he was "insane."

Subsequently I was criticized for having been so persistent in my efforts to reach Brad, and for attempting to leave the lines of communication open if he chose to contact me. But I had a much different view of how things might be headed, worries that began the moment he told me he planned to leave the cabin. He had no money, and no destination in mind except that he definitely did not intend to return home to his mother. In his mental state at that time, I could not imagine him getting or holding a job, which pretty well limited his survival options to sexual hustling or stealing. By the time he left, he had already explored and rejected the idea of getting help. And for the entire two previous years he had expounded on how he was not welcome in either parent's home.

How he got by in the two months between his departure and when he showed up at his mother's home I will never know, except for a few hints that he probably got into some "rough trade," finally got arrested for shoplifting (food), and arrived at his mother's doorstep "tired, broke, and dirty," at which time she promptly ensconced him in a hotel until she found a small trailer for rent in a local trailer park. It was a relief to know where he was, that he was under some kind of outpatient mental-health care, that he had some regular income, and that his mother visited him three times a week. But, basically, everybody seemed to be doing for him what they had always done, which was to do the least necessary to get him out of the way.

It had seemed so much better while he was at the cabin. Some time later, his mother produced a letter he had written to her while still at the cabin and just before he entered his depressed mental state. (She said that she "saves everything." She is the source of these letters.)

> Making it throw the winter up hear is worth it to be hear in the summer. I can [can't?] wait till summer I know it will be the best one I'v ever had I can hardly beleve the way I have fellt lattly its just like I'm not a kid eny more I can do whatever I want I want to keep riting but I cant think of eny thing els to say

From the telephone warning I received, it was clear that he was alive but not well. How I wished then, and wish today, I could go back and reconstruct what had taken place in his mind between our tearful farewell on the afternoon of his departure and the hostile revamping of his plans and reversal of attitude later that same evening.

It was clear that Brad was still under some kind of mental-health care and in outpatient status. That was all I knew. It did not change anything I had written in the Sneaky Kid report, which had already been put to rest, or in the Sneaky Kid article, scheduled for publication. As for what to do about the warning I had received in the telephone call, I was at a total loss, other than to follow ordinary precautions to be careful—be very, very careful.

The Fire

I was the first one home at about 5:30 p.m. on the evening of November 8, 1984. Norman had not yet returned. Nothing seemed amiss as I drove around the house and parked in back. I noticed that the basement light was on, but thought that Norman had forgotten to turn it off, as he frequently did on dark mornings. Only later did I remember that I had checked the basement light myself that day before I exited through the back door. I unlocked the door, then the key-locked deadbolt, and stepped into the house.

I was struck immediately by two things. The first was the strong smell of stove oil. An oil furnace, fed from a 500-gallon tank on the hillside above, heated the house. My guess, from the looks of things and the overpowering smell of fuel, was that the furnace had blown up and wreaked the havoc I saw. The second thing that struck me was a 2-by-4, or some similar wood object. I fell to the floor. From behind stepped Brad, hitting and kicking and screaming: "You fucker, I'm going to kill you. I'm going to kill you. I'm going to tie you up and leave you in the house and set the house on fire."

For a moment I could not discern who my attacker was. I asked: "Is that you, Brad? What are you doing this to me for? Why don't you run away, get away from here? This is crazy!"

"I *am* crazy," came his reply. "I'm going to kill you, burn the house down, tie you up. You hate me."

"Why are you doing this? You know I love you. I loved you when you were here and I still love you."

"No you don't, you hate me. I'm going to kill you."

Still on the floor, I defended myself as best I could, but I was in no position to fight off my assailant, who was towering above me and striking me repeatedly.

Knowing that Norman and I arrived home separately, Brad's plan as later recounted had been to tie each of us up and then set fire to the house. It was never quite clear whether he planned for us to be in the house or outside. It was in his best interest to insist later that he never intended to kill us.

In the frenzy of his assault, Brad failed to hear Norman's car drive into the carport about 15 minutes after I arrived, or to hear Norman coming up the stairs from the basement. I tried to warn Norman. "Run!" I shouted. Norman misinterpreted my command as a message to hurry. He ran up the stairs, stepped into the surreal scene, and recognized Brad immediately. "I know who you are."

Norman was barely through the door. It was critical that he get out of the house rather than make a futile effort to restrain Brad or free me. I shouted for him to go for the police. "And the fire department," I added, for Brad's intentions were obvious. Norman's arrival surprised and upset Brad's plan to deal with us one at a time. Brad checked an impulse to try to chase Norman. That momentary distraction provided the opportunity for me to escape through the back door, while Norman exited out the basement door into the carport.

We learned later that Brad had broken into the house about noon that day. He used my chain saw to cut holes in the ceiling and roof to create a draft. He also ran a hose from the fuel tank down to the house, through which he siphoned 500 gallons of fuel oil onto the floors (the tank had been refilled for winter only days before). When he was ready to ignite the fire, he emptied a can of gasoline on the oil-soaked carpet, stepped outside, and threw a match; the house exploded into flame. The arson inspector later reported that it was the hottest fire he had ever investigated, estimated to have exceeded 1,980 degrees Fahrenheit as indicated by the absence of any residue of copper wiring. Even my old wood-burning kitchen stove—a relic, but a working one—melted in the heat. The ashes in the rubble remained hot for days.

We all ran. Norman ran to a neighbor's house, where the head of household became so flustered he couldn't manage to dial 911. I ran to another neighbor's house for help, but, alas, as Norman had already discovered, that neighbor was not home. I hid from sight as I heard Brad come running past. He went to the house of another neighbor, someone who had befriended him while he was living at the cabin. That neighbor had occasionally visited him and sometimes used the swing. Brad asked if he could use the telephone to call for a taxi. The neighbor could see the flames from my burning house as Brad ranted crazily about what he had done. Brad boasted, "I really got him good," but he insisted that I was left "bleeding and standing" as a result of a fight. He added: "Next time I'll tar and feather him. I'll hike in from the back so no one can see me. . . . Harry ruined my life. Now Lucy won't have anything to do with me and I can't be a movie star."

He also mentioned the swing, a strange subject to bring up under such emotional circumstances. I know how he enjoyed using the swing—he described swinging as a sort of high for him. I took out extra insurance, fearing that a fall from it could be serious. When Brad ignored my request to keep others off it, I first suggested, then insisted, that he remove the cable. This was probably our biggest clash of wills, but eventually he did take it down. With the house ablaze in the distance, he now reflected nonchalantly, "With the house burned, maybe I can put the swing back up."

Brad's clothes and shoes were drenched in fuel oil. To get him out of the house as quickly as possible, the neighbor offered to take him into town. He drove Brad to the address where he had been staying, then went immediately to notify the police. Brad was waiting when the police arrived. He was in custody within a couple of hours.

In the 20 years that I lived at the house, the county road that passes in front of it had gradually been transformed from a dusty gravel road with a few cars per hour to a busy thoroughfare for peri-urban dwellers who had found that "little place in the country" minutes from downtown. After Brad went running past, I reemerged onto the road in hopes of flagging a passing car and getting help. I do not ever remember a quieter night, full moon not yet visible. No traffic, no sounds, not even the distant wail of the ambulance or fire engine I was expecting to hear, only the sound of flames already beginning to engulf the outside walls of the house. It was eerie indeed to realize that all of Norman's and my worldly possessions were about to disappear, and that we ourselves had narrowly escaped with our lives.

It would have been pointless to try to save the house. When the firemen arrived, I warned them that the flames had been enhanced with 500 gallons of fuel oil. They monitored nearby trees to ensure that the fire would not spread into the surrounding forest. I was quickly popped into an ambulance in a state of semi-shock. I remained in the hospital for two days after the cuts on my head were stitched up in the emergency room. It was six months before I got the last of the splinters out of my hands from fending off the assault.

For Norman and me, the fire ended one era and ushered in another: a period devoted to police investigations, psychological assessments, preparations for a trial that did not begin for five months, a series of temporary relocations, and the gradual replacing of a lifetime's accumulation of items as we needed them. The only clothes I had were those I was wearing, and even they were confiscated as blood- and fuel-soaked evidence. We had to reconstruct all our records and work up a detailed inventory for losses that exceeded $300,000. Friends took us in, then we became long-term motel residents and, finally, house sitters for faculty on leave. We began rebuilding our lives.

Our respective teaching assignments kept us anchored in reality. Norman returned immediately to teaching. In spite of being hospitalized, I did not miss any classes, for I was scheduled for an out-of-town meeting during the week after the fire. I had recently acquired my parents' pristine 1963 Mercury and, of course, lost it in the fire. I still had (and have) my faithful 1966 Chevrolet Impala, which I had parked in back away from the house. A friend loaned Norman a car. I recall a secretary remarking one day soon after the fire how I seemed to wear a new shirt and tie every time I met my classes. We laughed as we both realized why I suddenly had become such a fashion plate.

Notes

1. Were I writing the account today, I would use the phrase "life story" rather than "life history." Narrative categories were not as nuanced at the time. For a discussion of the difference, see, for example, Peacock and Holland 1993; Plummer 2001; Reed-Danahay 2001. Writing at the time, Stanley Brandes also suggested the label "ethnographic autobiography" for a life story *as told to an anthropologist* (Brandes 1982).

Chapter Four

Out

B Y the time the fire was completely out, so was I. Crazy or not, there had to be some motive for the attack and arson. They were not random acts of violence against a random victim. Brad had come back seeking revenge, and the nature of our relationship needed to be adjusted accordingly. So did the time and severity of Brad's breakdown. So, too, did estimates of his emotional stability and mental age and, especially, his vulnerability to the advances of an older man. The former ranged from average ("In the normal range," stated an examining psychologist; "He could be anything he wants," stated another) to having "the mental abilities of a 10- or 12-year-old, which Harry picked up on to take advantage of the situation," according to his mother.

Brad was initially charged with attempted murder. He gave a voluntary taped interview the morning after the fire, during which he confessed to the arson and assault. But by the time a court-appointed lawyer got to him, his plea was changed to one of insanity. Meanwhile, the strategists in the district attorney's office dropped the attempted murder charge as "too hard to prove." Their job is to get convictions, and they reasoned that a murder charge wasn't going to be necessary to get a conviction for crimes already confessed.

As the defense's position unfurled, it seemed they were intent on showing that I not only forced myself on Brad, but that in so doing I had contributed to his mental breakdown, perhaps even caused it. If, to many minds, that stretched the limits of imagination, it was nonetheless quite clear—and the world needed to know—that I was to be identified as homosexual. It was necessary to identify Norman as a homosexual as well, though most of the attention was on the relationship between Brad and me. Brad's sexual orientation and prior experiences never became an issue; mine were presented to portray Brad as a youthful victim rather than a willing partner.

The crimes were committed—and the case tried—essentially against me and my property. Norman was more than simply an unwitting victim, but there was no need to incriminate him when the relationship between Brad and me was clearly at issue. As a public school teacher, Norman's career was more at risk than my own as a university professor, as his work put him in daily contact with children. One of the few times we felt a sense of relief was when a courageous school superintendent reaffirmed her support for Norman: "If no children are involved, then this is a personal matter and does not concern us." Would that there had been more like her at the time. (Would that there were more like her today!)

This was the early 1980s, and it had not been many years since the American Psychiatric Association had formally established (by narrow vote!) that homosexuality is not a mental disorder. That was 1973, to be exact (Kirk and Kutchings 1992; Luhrmann 2000). If homosexuality is no longer viewed in most quarters today as abnormal and immoral, it is not necessarily accepted as normal even among those who congratulate themselves on their tolerance for diversity. Furthermore, the argument went, Norman and I were teachers and therefore could and should be held to higher standards of morality. What Brad had done was reprehensible, but in some quarters it was clear that we were reprehensible too, perhaps even more so. As with the early public reaction to AIDS, how many were thinking that we had gotten what we deserved?

The assistant district attorney assigned to prosecute the case—henceforth referred to here as "the prosecutor" (quite aptly, I might note)—made it clear early on that he did not approve of our lifestyle. Among "the boys" at the D.A.'s office, we learned that the case was casually referred to as "the two fag fire." (The chair of the local Right to Privacy Committee, herself an attorney, quickly put a stop to that!) This did not mean, the prosecutor assured us, that he would not work for a conviction. Indeed, in defense of his own self-righteousness, he told us:

> At least I'm right up front with you. You know how I stand on this. Anyway, I don't consider this a sex case. Brad was above the age of consent. If he had any problems, he should have settled it then, not now.

In his closing remarks, the prosecutor underscored the impartiality of our justice system: "This is not a case about homosexuals. . . . They too, according to our system of law, are entitled to equal justice." If what we got was justice, then in comparable circumstances I'd opt for wisdom next time.

Trial dates were set and reset as the legal process lumbered through negotiations and differing psychiatric assessments that would eventually determine where Brad was to be sent. It took five months for the case to come to trial. We were relieved that the court finally was convened, but I got a rude shock when I realized I was going to be the individual actually on trial. If nothing else, the defense wanted to show that *I* was responsible for what had happened. It was also a shock to learn that, as victims, neither Norman nor I would be allowed in the courtroom except when we were giving testimony. Brad's parents—father, mother, and stepfather—who, for once, had rallied on Brad's behalf, were to be treated the same: They were not privy to trial proceedings except when testifying.

The court-appointed defense counsel did not let Brad take the witness stand. Although Brad might have put forward a convincing argument for why he did what he insisted he "had to do," his ramblings were unpredictable, invariably mixing fact with fancy. He would not have fared well under cross-examination from an overzealous prosecutor.

Ostensibly, Brad was on trial as to whether he had committed the crimes for which he had been formally charged in a grand jury hearing: arson, assault, and burglary (breaking and entering). He had to be tried for these offenses because he had pleaded not guilty. Of course, he had already confessed, so there was no question of his guilt. But under the skillful tutelage of counsel, he had pleaded not guilty by reason of insanity. That shifted the point of law to whether or not he was in control of his actions, which, in courtroom jargon, was a question of whether or not he could "conform" his behavior. State law held that if his behavior was deemed anti-social, then the insanity plea would not hold up. If, however, he was also under such psychological stress that he did not know what he was doing, he could be eligible for psychiatric care in the state hospital rather than placement in the penitentiary. The trial really hinged on how Brad was to be sentenced: patient or prisoner.

Quite predictably, the psychiatrist engaged by the defense argued on behalf of the insanity plea. The prosecution sought a second opinion, either to confirm the first one (and thus skip the trial and go directly to sentencing) or to argue a different view: that although Brad did exhibit symptoms of chronic paranoid schizophrenia—an issue on which there was complete agreement— he had been demonstrating anti-social behavior throughout his life. The methodical way Brad had gone about the arson and assault, something he told the police he had been planning for a year and a half, suggested that although he was doing something he "had to do," and something he acknowledged as being in violation of the law, he was in control. He was doing something crazy, something he recognized as wrong, but he wasn't going about it in a crazy way. Brad had once said to me, "I'm not that rotten of a kid." In short, that was the question the jury was asked to decide. They decided with the prosecutor that he was.

But there was also a moral issue to be aired, something to be entered into the deliberations to cloud the proceedings without having a direct bearing on the case or outcome. Although the judge termed the misdeeds an "enormous" crime, and a case-hardened and upwardly mobile prosecutor conceded it was all "painful and tragic," and it was further acknowledged that Brad remained a danger to society and out of control, there was a lingering notion that the victim (me) had indeed "gotten what he deserved," not only because he was homosexual, but also because he had engaged Brad in a homosexual relationship, whether Brad was willing or not.

Homosexuality itself was tacitly on trial, something inherently wrong that could be introduced to enlist sympathy for the accused and antipathy toward the victim(s). Ubiquitous courtroom watchers offered early verdicts to that effect. Indeed, the nature of the sexual relationship, presented as unwanted, even repugnant, on behalf of the younger man, provided some justification for the revenge he had wreaked. Revenge for wrongs, whether real or imagined, is not a defense, but it does provide a motive. Brad's defense needed that. Why not plant and nurture the idea that the homosexual relationship may have not only aggravated but triggered the mental breakdown? One of the psychiatrists quickly put that idea to rest. Paranoid schizophrenia, which was the accepted diagnosis among everyone who rendered a psychological assessment of Brad, "comes on slowly, usually with no precipitating events." Yet the thought that I had—or might possibly have—induced it is one of those ideas that, once introduced, can never be bottled up again. What if, what if?

Brad did not take the witness stand, but he did volunteer a succinct version of his life story to a custody officer on the day he was to be arraigned, a statement later introduced into testimony:

> I beat up a faggot and burned his house down. I was dropped on my head when I was little and I had a crack in my head. I went to the woods and built a house and along came this faggot and told me I was good looking like a model or movie star. Then this faggot wanted to fuck me in the rear. So I let him. Then I got mad and I beat up this faggot and burned his house down.

Brief as this statement is, it helps explain Brad's rationale for his return and for his subsequent actions. In spite of its brevity, it also reveals a great deal of information (and misinformation) and helps explain the strategy for the defense:

• Brad confesses to the assault and arson, as he has done all along.

- He returns to a theme mentioned repeatedly during the last months at the cabin, that as a child he had been dropped on his head ("by his father," he usually noted), and the fall had caused his mental problems.

- He had consented to the sex. Only later did Brad express misgivings about it.

- His delusions about being a model or movie star were gradually working their way backward in time to become part of a seduction. (Originally they were an element of Brad's delusions, fantasies that did not begin until a couple of months prior to his departure.)

- Everything stays in the singular: The hostility is directed at me; Norman is not introduced into Brad's recounting of the story.

Getting the Help You Need Versus Getting What You Deserve

Reliving this part of the account only heightens my sense of sadness at the course of events and my anger at the way the trial was mishandled. But it does reveal aspects of our justice system and fundamental issues that cannot be resolved through research. They represent differences in outlook or human values, and differences in what is considered relevant evidence.

The issue to be decided in court, as the legal system defined it, was whether Brad needed to be punished or helped. These positions were reflected in resolving the case on the question of whether Brad could "conform" his behavior, an ironic criterion to apply to someone who had spent so much of his life in rebellion. Did Brad understand that what he was doing was wrong?

The fact that he had been plotting his revenge for so long, so patiently, supported the thesis that he knew what he was doing was wrong, in spite of the fact that he felt he had to do it, and knowing he would have to suffer the likely consequences. As a psychiatric issue, the question boiled down to whether he acted solely on the basis of mental defect or whether he also exhibited anti-social tendencies indicative of an underlying personality disorder. (For literature on male schizophrenia and anti-social personality disorder, see, for example, Tengström, Hodgins, and Kullgren 2001.)

That homosexual behavior itself could also be put on trial was something of an extra bonus, a dividend on the investment our society makes in maintaining a moral order through court actions. Although as victim I was not technically on trial, I discovered that I needed to protect myself against both the attorneys for the defense and prosecution: the defense because he was so intent on maligning me (thus making Brad's actions appear "justified," even if wrong), the prosecutor because he was so single-mindedly focused on getting a conviction. The thought of Brad being sent to prison depressed me far more than the thought of him hustling on the streets. Brad himself recognized the physical threat of a sentence to prison: "Send me to the hospital. Otherwise they'll fuck me in the ass."

Based on somewhat conflicting assessments by two psychiatrists, the attorney I hired to protect me from both the prosecutor and the defense suggested making one last effort to forgo the trial and opt for treatment. On the basis of the two psychiatric assessments, my attorney addressed a letter to the prosecutor urging that Brad be sent to the state mental hospital, acknowledging that he was suffering from mental disease and defect and would benefit from a stay there, versus the risk of what might happen to him in prison. Under then-current sentencing standards and parole procedures, it was quite likely that he would spend even more time in the mental hospital, since his release would require psychiatric review. And he would undoubtedly receive superior treatment for his mental problems there. As my attorney reminded the district attorney:

> Mr. Wolcott does want you to be aware that he is not vindictive in regard to Brad. He has no personal vendetta or personal commitment to see him sent to the state penitentiary. He wanted you to be aware that if you were to choose to follow the report of the first examining psychiatrist in stipulating that Brad was operating under a mental disease or defect, he would be supportive of that decision.

The prosecuting attorney simply could not, or would not, accept the mental defense plea. He and the psychiatrist he selected for a second opinion shared a hard-line (but not irresponsible) view that the insanity plea was overused to get people "off" for criminal behavior. He felt that Brad was fully able to conform his behavior and should serve time in prison. In his view, and in spite of general agreement about Brad's disordered mental state, he viewed Brad as a criminal case, not a mental one: Brad was crazy, yes, but he was not *that* crazy.

On the day the trial was finally to begin, my daily horoscope in the local newspaper said: "A legal matter is settled out of court." How I hoped for another phone call! But it was not to be. A trial began that dragged on for the next two and a half weeks. By the end of it, everyone was fed up with everyone else. I learned later that the jury—who, deep down, may not have had any more sympathy for me as the victim than for Brad as the accused— was shocked at the treatment I had received at the hands of the court. They received their final instructions at 3 p.m. on a Friday afternoon and were determined to reach a verdict before returning home that evening. They rejected the insanity plea—unanimously. Brad was returned to the county jail to await sentencing. That took two more months, while more reports were written and screening materials assembled in a pre-sentencing investigation.

Brad received what seemed a harsh sentence: 20 years. But it was imposed with no minimum. Skeptics argued that he might be released after three years, less time off for the eight months he had already spent in jail. After the suspense and agony of the trial, and now fully aware of Brad's delusional state and how I had become mixed up in it, I was as distressed by the fact that he might be out in less than two and a half years as by the fact that he had been sent to the penitentiary in the first place. The one person who seemed to find any satisfaction in the outcome was the prosecutor, who summarized, "Only three words really mattered: 'Guilty, guilty, guilty.' "

Learning How to Be a Witness

Failing in efforts to ward off the trial and have Brad sent to the state mental hospital, my private attorney offered advice on how to be a witness. I thought the advice not unlike what we tell students preparing to engage in fieldwork, except for the dramatic difference that field researchers are responsible for the ultimate interpretation of the information they gather, whereas witnesses serve only as informants for an explanation in a trial in which others do the interpreting. Interpretation is central to both, with the keen distinction that various interpretations are presented and argued before judge and/or jury in a trial, whereas researchers customarily offer their interpretations singly, one to a case.

In that one regard, qualitative researchers might benefit from an approach that entertains multiple theories, interpretations, or explanations, rather than an approach that looks so single-mindedly for one, a point I have argued elsewhere (Wolcott 2001). On the other hand, the rules of evidence and of procedure followed in court, as exhibited in this case, astounded me for the way they restrict evidence and argument, eliminate considerations of context, and provoke endless argument about procedure, in efforts that seemed to facilitate the (eventual) arrival at apparently crisp decisions to hopelessly complex issues. I am committed to the notion that human behavior is overdetermined: There are always a multiplicity of causes and motives for what we do, how we speak and act. There was no such tolerance of ambiguity in the court. Lots of aimless wandering, little room for context.

The advice I received:

- Don't try to help anybody. Tell the truth. Be direct and succinct. Don't provide more information than asked for. (Recall Sergeant Friday's line from radio days: "Just the facts!")

- Listen to the question. Don't tune out. Force yourself to get the question clearly in mind. If necessary, ask to have it repeated. "I don't understand what you mean by . . ."

- Have your answer clearly in mind. Answer the question. Prevent runaway answers or wandering, especially during cross-examination.

- Be alert for questions or statements that are partially true, partially false. If that is the case, just say, "I can't answer."

- Truth is the only way to proceed. Even when it's harmful, put it out there.

- Let the questioner finish before formulating your answer.

- Don't let yourself be interrupted. If necessary, say, "Excuse me, I haven't completed my answer."

- Retain composure. Don't get angry, show hostility, or allow yourself to get to a point where you can't control your answer.

- Let your testimony stand as given. Its "meaning" is up to someone else.

- Don't feel a need to fill silences with talk. Use silence effectively.

- Remember that all measurement is approximate: dates, times, places. Indicate when you are estimating. Be as accurate as you can and emphasize when you are giving estimates.

- You don't have to answer argumentative questions or abusive ones: "Didn't you know . . . ?" "Didn't you realize . . . ?" Or: "Which one of you is telling the truth?"

- Remember that the state is bringing the charges. You are there to provide information. Don't be dragged into the conflict; don't give the defense any ammunition. Be straightforward.

The advice was good, although I wasn't very good about following all of it. I certainly did get angry. I'm still angry. That anger serves as a source of energy for delving again into this aspect of the story. As a witness I found myself to be both victim and victimized. Under oath and asked to tell what had happened, I did not get more than a couple of sentences into the story when the defense rose to object to "hearsay." The judge muttered "sustained," and I realized that I was not going to be allowed to tell my version of "the truth, the whole truth" at all.

I remember getting muddled by the proceedings more than once. On one occasion when the prosecutor (ostensibly on *my* side) raised an objection on my behalf that was sustained, I misunderstood and answered the question anyway. No one in the courtroom had the decency to inform me that I did not have to answer.

On another occasion, the defense wanted to probe into details of my sex life. The prosecutor accused him of being on a "fishing expedition" and argued that the question should not be allowed. The judge agreed, then allowed a "little" fishing expedition anyway. The circumstances are familiar but were seized upon by the defense to condemn my infidelity, for although the nature of Norman's and my relationship was deemed abhorrent, I was also condemned for violating it. The defense hastened to interpret:

> Harry and Norman are essentially married. But Harry has gotten involved with Brad with or without Norman's consent. He gets Norman involved. Norman has a good reputation as a teacher who is caring about kids. But Harry and Norman have a real gap between professed ideals of helping people and exploiting Brad, sexually and professionally.

I wanted to explain that I had a caring and stable but no longer particularly sexual relationship with Norman and a caring and sexual but not particularly stable relationship with Brad. That not-unheard-of "best of both worlds" approach made me fodder for the defense. (I'll admit to personal satisfaction in the knowledge that the defense had not been successful in maintaining a "normal" married relationship of his own.)

The defense asked whether it had been my assessment that Brad had not experienced much love in his life. He insisted that should have told me he was vulnerable. I responded that it told me Brad was lonely, unconnected. I had to remind counsel that Brad and I talked about virtually everything; sex was neither the basis of our relationship nor the focal point of it. But because our relationship had a sexual element to it, that element was represented as dominating every other aspect. Could anyone really believe that for an entire two years, or for the few months that included a sexual relationship, we did nothing else except fool around? That's certainly the impression one would have received from a visit to the courtroom. The defense was allowed to probe intimate details of Brad's and my physical relationship, following which the prosecutor reminded the jury of how they had been made to listen to "nauseating details."

It's all "adversarial," I was reminded. Truer words were never spoken. I came away with no respect for the courts. No doubt things could be worse, but I had always assumed the system to be much better.

Notes from the Trial

We were advised in advance that we would not be allowed in the courtroom except when we were testifying. However, it was suggested that we could ask someone to sit in on the proceedings and take notes for us. I asked a close friend (who had also been a student in my graduate classes on ethnography) to cover the trial. We referred to her as "Sam" during the trial, and the district attorney never did figure out that Sam was a woman. Apparently the trial sparked community interest as well; there were always others present to observe the courtroom antics, and a reporter from the local newspaper was usually present.

Through Sam's exquisite notes, I can offer some insight into the trial proceedings. I have had to comb through those notes, something I have been reluctant to do for the past 16 years. The comments were recorded verbatim to the extent possible. Sam does not take shorthand, but the notes are extensive and she filled in extra detail whenever there was a break in the proceedings. I regard the notes as highly reliable in terms of what was recorded, without claiming that they are complete. Sam was asked to get as much detail as possible, with an emphasis on verbatim data rather than paraphrasing in summary fashion. Future fieldworkers take note: Firsthand quotes are far more powerful than secondhand summaries.

Not until this writing did I learn that an appeal had been filed after the trial and thus, at public expense, a typed copy had been prepared from the court reporters' (there had been 11 in all) transcripts. The complete record, a public document, was available for my viewing at the office of the State Supreme Court in the capital. It ran to 1,588 pages. Had the trial not been appealed, the cost of having it transcribed at current rates would have been almost $4,000! As it was, I could obtain copies of pages I wanted at 25¢ per page, or $397 for the entire document. Sam's notes are better contextualized, but they are not the word-by-word transcript of the reporters. I have drawn from both sources. I remain more impressed than ever by the accuracy of Sam's reporting.

The fact that I commissioned the notes reveals something of my research orientation and my effort to distance myself sufficiently to see the trial in broader perspective. Although it was by no means a welcome opportunity, I felt that the trial would provide a chance to observe another social system at work. Perhaps it could even lead to extending the Sneaky Kid story, although this was not the direction I would ever have imagined the account would lead. At the least, my perspective allowed me to distance myself from events too close at hand.

But the trial was, and remains, a personal horror story that pitted me against Brad explicitly, and implicitly pitted society against me. That is why I later proposed the title "Finding My Place" for recounting the Brad story. I wanted not only to describe how Brad happened onto the property and into a personal relationship with me, but also to show how, in the end, "society," through the courts, found a way to put *me* in *my* place as well.

Sentence First, Verdict Afterwards

The Queen in Lewis Carroll's *Alice's Adventures in Wonderland* voiced a discomforting idea for expediting legal proceedings: Sentence first, verdict afterwards! We could have seen far more dispatch in this trial. The judge reminded counsel at one point, "This is a trial about arson, not a trial about homosexuality." But I had not realized the extent to which the trial had begun the process of putting me in my place from the very outset, through comments made to which I was not privy at the time.

The process proved particularly onerous during voir dire, the selection of jurors through questions ostensibly designed to assess their competence to hear the case. In reviewing Sam's notes, I realized that although jurors supposedly were being examined for their impartiality, they were being carefully coached through what might be described as tacit instruction. While being queried about their ability to remain open and fair-minded, they were informed with phrases like "even if the victim is a homosexual . . .," or told that even if Brad was recognized as having a "mental defect," it nonetheless might be shown that he exhibited sufficient control that insanity would not hold as a defense. By the time the trial formally began, jurors had been warned, advised, coached, informed, questioned, or instructed on several important points.

This part of the trial contains a note in the official transcript, "VOIR DIRE OF JURY reported but not transcribed," presumably because it would have added unnecessary expense (another day and a half of transcription) irrelevant to the appeal. Yet I found Sam's notes of this part of the proceedings exceedingly rich, especially for making the point about the implicit messages the jury was receiving as to what was ahead and how, as good citizens, they ought to be thinking about it:

1. **Homosexuality** was to be a central concern, though, of course, not something to be decided. It was specifically mentioned more than two dozen times in addressing prospective jurors, conveyed through such questions as:
   a. Do you ever come across homosexual people in your daily activities? Do you know any homosexual people?
   b. Can you set aside your personal feelings about homosexual relationships?
   c. You will hear that the defendant was in a homosexual relationship. Will that be difficult to hear? Would that prejudice you?
   d. The defendant and victims are all homosexual. Are you OK with that?
   e. You may feel that Harry got what's coming to him because he is homosexual. Can you put that aside, because he's still a victim, nonetheless?
   f. Because a person is a homosexual, is it OK to burn his house down?

2. Brad did have a **mental problem**. The prosecutor needed to separate Brad's mental state at the time of the crime from a history of anti-social behavior. He reminded prospective jurors that they were to determine guilt, not say what they thought should be done with Brad.
   a. Have you ever heard of paranoid schizophrenia? Do you have any preconceived notions about it? [The defense subsequently described paranoid schizophrenia as "disordered thinking; excessively fearful."]
   b. Brad has a delusional system. His attorney will employ a "mental disease and defect" defense, attempting to show that Brad "lacked substantial capacity to conform to the law" and "could not appreciate what was wrong or was unable to control himself."
   c. Harry is involved in Brad's mind in a delusional system.

3. The trial will be **unpleasant**.
   a. You will hear explicit, nauseating sexual testimony.
   b. Are you willing to listen to sexual details? [Acceptable answer: I may not like the details, but I think I can be fair].

4. There is an **age difference** between the victim and the defendant, who was 19 at the time. [Brad was 20, but the age "error" communicated to jurors effectively portrayed him as a teenager.]
   a. Will the age difference cause a problem for you?
   b. Brad is referred to as "the boy." The Sneaky Kid article is mentioned in an offhand reference as " 'Sneaky Boy,' or something like that."
   c. Brad was seduced by an older, more experienced homosexual man. Will that cause a problem for you?

d. If you seduce a troubled *boy*, you can cause him serious problems.

e. [Addressed to the juror who was later elected foreman:] You have a 19-year-old. Will that affect your deciding about Brad's consenting relationship with Harry? [Implied: Is your own 19-year-old *really* capable of giving consent?]

Indeed, the defense so overdid references to Brad's youth that after his closing argument, the prosecutor included a comment to the effect of, "How many times did the defense call Brad a 'boy' or a 'kid' during his closing argument? Twenty-three is what I came up with. If he is a boy or kid, he is in the wrong courtroom. We try adults around here. . . . The reason for doing that is pretty apparent. It is trying to get your sympathy for him. . . ."

5. Harry has acted in an **unethical** and unprofessional way:

a. There may be a question of Harry's credibility, his intellectual dishonesty in writing and publishing an article about Brad. Will you have any problem in considering this? [There is no real question here, just slipping in some prejudicial material.]

b. Can you say that you won't let the fact that these two homosexual men [Harry and Norman] are teachers influence your determination of the case?

c. [Addressed to a potential juror serving as a school board member in a local school district:] Harry's article ["Sneaky Kid"] is critical of schools. Is that a problem for you?

d. The prosecutor refers to the Sneaky Kid article as "an article about Brad's stealing" [e.g., Harry provides a life story that disparages the informant].

Typical of what seemed to be "approved" or "expected" answers were responses such as, "I think I can hear the case objectively," "I don't have any preconceived notions," and "I'm willing to listen." In my experience, a kind of unofficial contest develops at trials like this, in which prospective jurors willing or eager to hear a particular case strive to give approved answers affirming their fair-mindedness. I had not realized how the questions (pseudoquestions?) addressed to them individually served to instruct the entire group of potential jurors.

Anyone who had worked with Norman or me was quickly excluded, including one teacher who had taught at the same school with Norman, and on whose doctoral committee I was serving at the university.[1] One kind heart was dismissed for answering that "everybody deserves a second chance."

Lawyer intuition led to other dismissals. By the time the impaneling was concluded, the defense had, as the prosecutor complained aloud, already started to present his case. In truth, they both had given jurors a substantial preview of where they intended to go with it.

Insights and Reactions to the Trial

Prior to the trial, I had not realized that the hostility that Brad expressed at the final moment of his departure was the *only* emotion he ever again expressed toward me. At the time he left, I interpreted his comment as nothing more than an explanation as to why he was removing things he had spent all week storing in my basement: "I've had a vision. You'll be gone, and my things aren't safe."

I had no way of appreciating the depth or origins of his anger. They were not relayed in his few telephone calls. He never wrote, as he had promised and as I always hoped he might. I learned that at first he tore up letters sent to him. Then his mother stopped passing them along, which probably explains why the birthday checks were not cashed. During the trial, his mother made a point of expressing her annoyance that I kept trying to reach Brad when I (supposedly) "knew" how much he resented me and resented hearing from me. The only thing Brad said to me in the courtroom, spoken as I exited one afternoon, was, "Why don't you admit you hate me?," returning to the theme he had repeated at the time of the fire.

"Why did you continue to write to him?" I was asked. I answered that a substantial portion of his life, and almost all of his adult life to that point, had been spent at my place. I felt strongly that those had been the best years of his life, not the worst. Although I couldn't imagine exactly how we would ever re-create the way things had been, I didn't want to abandon him if he wanted to return. Further, Brad and his mother both said they would keep in touch. No one said not to write. His mother seemed to think he'd return to Eugene. I thought so, too. Was it too much to want to know how he was or to try to get in touch with him?

If those efforts to reach him were a mistake, it is a mistake I would make again under similar circumstances. I presumed, correctly, that Brad was not going to be welcomed back into the home of his mother and stepfather. Given the angry outburst in his final departure, I felt that I should be the one to keep the way open if he needed someday to return to the cabin and take up where he had left off. I had no way of gauging the extent of his mental stress. All I knew of his formal diagnosis was his mother's succinct summary that he was now "insane." I underestimated the depth of his psychosis. Most certainly

I overestimated the regard he now held for me or any positive feelings he had about the two years he had spent at the cabin. But I did want him to understand that he hadn't completely closed off the opportunity to return.

Although I missed him terribly, it was also the Brad of better times I thought of, not the tormented individual of his final days at the cabin. Realistically, I couldn't imagine how we would ever get things back on an even keel. But I wasn't about to abandon him, as everyone seemed to have done in the past. Big mistake? Or just hope, springing eternal?

Only after departing did Brad introduce hatred into his perception of our relationship. There was no evidence that it existed prior to that moment. Subsequently, he claimed that it was I who hated him because he had cut down trees to build his cabin. That would have dated back to our first meeting. At that time, I was far more impressed with the shelter he had constructed than with the sapling trees he had cut to build it. There were so many similar trees that I never found where a single one had been cut. Brad never expressed anything stronger than annoyance when I asked him to do or not to do something. The instance I reported earlier of taking down the cable for the swing was as touchy as our interactions ever got. His insistence, "You hate me," came as a complete surprise during the attack. I felt I was probably taking a big risk to counter with "I don't hate you. I love you." But I wanted him to hear those words, although I realized that the way things were going, during those moments before Norman arrived, they might have been the last words I would ever speak.

Brad's father did not earn high marks during trial proceedings. Under oath, he was asked, "Do you love your son?" "Yes, very much," was the reply. But he was reminded of an incident between them at the cabin when Brad had struck his father several times while shouting repeatedly, "I hate you, I hate you." Brad often stated that he thought his father was "a total asshole." His father had to acknowledge Brad's outward expression of hate, yet insisted, "Yes, but I think he loves me." I wonder if my own logic was about as realistic, except that Brad insisted all along that it was I who hated him!

In trying to explain the basis of his delusional state, Brad always mentioned having been dropped on his head by his father when quite small, that he was unconscious and had to be taken to the hospital. He said skull X-rays showed a "hairline crack" and that he could still feel the ridge. He attributed his psychological disorders to this injury and he blamed his mental condition on the fall, although subsequent medical examinations never confirmed any physical evidence. During the trial, his mother also related a story of when Brad's father had picked him up and was headed down the lane on the farm where they were living, saying he was going to drown Brad, then about age seven, in the river. The only thing that stopped him, she reported, was her screaming that he would go to jail. Brad had not forgotten that incident.

Brad's father was portrayed as ineffectual and inconsistent as a parent, a person who found little joy or success in efforts to raise his recalcitrant son. Brad's mother reported that Brad never wanted to do anything with his father and that he resented anything his father liked. The fact that Brad's father had abused his mother, even while she was pregnant with Brad's older sister, was another part of the picture that surfaced during his mother's testimony. The beatings, coupled with Brad's father's financial problems and infidelity, provided the basis for their breakup. Hearing that Brad's own life had been a problem one, a business associate of his father's reflected: "I'm not surprised. The apple doesn't fall far from the tree."

As a result of the trial, I also learned that about two years after he had left the cabin, Brad was involved in a major accident. Skateboarding late at night, reportedly on his way to a McDonald's for a midnight snack, he was struck by an automobile and sustained serious injuries. He suffered a broken back; multiple fractures of one leg; head injuries; and skin burns on his face, chest, and stomach. He spent five weeks in the hospital and underwent two surgeries on his leg. Through X-rays he was found to have an unstable break in his upper back that required further surgery. He was in a body cast for about four months, and also in a leg cast. For a while he was cared for at home by his mother. She noted that during his long recovery, he had a lot of time to brood about his past, instead of working out his frustrations as he usually did through physical activities like riding his bicycle or skateboarding. She stated: "His relationship with Harry had been eating away at him during the previous couple of months to the point where he could no longer face it. Everything had to come to a head in the way it did." And she added, "There was no way I could have stopped it!"

His mother's interpretation of the relationship that developed between Brad and me may have played a pivotal role. In order to get back into her good graces, he may have had to absolve himself of any compliance in the relationship, to become the person put upon rather than a consenting, willing partner. I saw it as difficult (nay, impossible) for her to accept that aspect of Brad's behavior. Perhaps more disconcerting still, the prosecutor conjectured, Brad's sense of guilt became more intense after his mother learned of the relationship.

Brad's sexual orientation remained (and remains) a matter of conjecture. Everyone had an opinion that fit the case as they sought to portray or interpret it. Needless to say, I was not portrayed as a loving, caring person, nor was Brad ever portrayed as a willing sex partner or as someone who might have craved male affection that he had never experienced. The most sympathy our relationship ever received was when one of the psychiatrists allowed, however reluctantly, "Maybe it was voluntary at first." But even he quickly amended his answer: "Maybe that is how Brad paid the rent. And maybe he couldn't effectively say no." Brad paid no rent, and he effectively said no whenever he wasn't in the mood. Wish someone had asked! But, then, I wasn't even able to get the prosecutor to refer to our relationship as a "sexual" one rather than as a "homosexual" one.

The second psychiatrist was asked if there was anything in the psychological assessment data (MMPI) to show a homosexual orientation. He explained that sexual orientation cannot be diagnosed from the MMPI. The questioner then asked, "Is Brad someone who would *initiate* sexual behavior?" The answer was: "I only have Brad's opinions on that. To probe deeper would require special testing." Phrased again: "The question is whether Brad would take the initiative." Answer: "I don't think he's an aggressive homosexual *or* heterosexual."

I agree with that assessment. I also agree with the opinion rendered that "having homosexual relations, voluntary or not, doesn't make you a homosexual," although I would want to modify the declaration to read, "doesn't *necessarily* make you a homosexual." What was curious from my point of view was that, although I acknowledged having had sex with females as well as with males, I was branded "homosexual" for purposes of the trial. And Brad, who affirmed in a pre-sentence hearing that he had never had sex with a woman, was described informally as "bisexual, if anything." If anything? For a trial that was "not about homosexuality," a great deal of time was spent addressing that nonissue. Had the court found it as convenient to label Brad a homosexual as they did me, we could have spent a lot less time delving into a subject that the trial was "not about." Instead, in closing, I had to hear the defense state, this time in my presence:

> The only reason Harry let Brad stay was because of the sexual possibility. . . .
> Harry seeks help for Brad, but it's help with a hook . . . to get him well to
> continue the sex. Get well here, where I am, where the sex is.

Getting Help for Brad

"Getting help for Brad" came up frequently as a topic, although it was usually noted by its absence. I can't help wondering how much less serious the consequences might have been had Brad's mother reacted differently when he decided to reveal the sexual dimension of our relationship. What if she had said something like, "Well, at least you're having sex with *somebody*. And somebody who seems to care a lot about you. And you're apparently enjoying it!" What then?

But in looking back, there were all kinds of opportunities missed to help Brad, even getting him adequate legal counsel. As more than one observer noted, "That defense attorney really did him a disservice." Right up to the night before the fire, no one took responsibility upon themselves to intercede in Brad's stated plan to "get Harry and burn his house down."

Brad's mother had been instructed to contact the psychologist immediately if Brad gave any indication of leaving town. Instead, she drove him to the bus station and telephoned his father to inform him that Brad was on his way to Oregon. If Brad's father was not likely to notify the police, he might at least have called me. He was asked at the trial why he hadn't done so. Brad's father answered that he was "too disturbed." Instead he lodged Brad in a motel and reportedly told the manager, "Let me know if he goes out."

His father later telephoned a former employee and asked whether Brad could stay there for the next few days, because his new wife objected to having Brad stay in their house. She, in turn, called an attorney to ask whether they should call the police, but received no satisfactory advice. His wife "also might have wanted to call the police," Brad's father testified, but he claimed to have been so distraught that he "pulled the phone out of the wall so she could not call." He said he did not believe that Brad would attack me, but he was worried. "With hindsight," he noted, "I would have done a lot of things differently."

The former employee in whose home Brad spent his second night in town was also hesitant to call the police, but reported that he did feel he ought to warn me. Unfortunately, he had understood my name as "Wilcox." He could find no match between name and address. He did call Brad's father to tell him about the threats, but reported that he did not really believe that in a confrontation Brad would do anything so serious. Brad had not confided his plans to him. In retrospect, everyone testified that they *should* have done things differently.

"When the Experts Disagree . . ."

I recall, from undergraduate days, examining the proposition "When the experts disagree, the layman can hold no positive views." Yet the trial, after days and days of haranguing, eventually turned on a single point of disagreement between two psychiatrists: Can a person be labeled both paranoid schizophrenic and anti-social? Does one diagnosis rule out the other? The proposition I learned in school had to be turned on its head. Because the experts disagreed, lay jurors were called on to render an ultimate decision that hinged on a topic on which they were eminently unqualified.

The psychiatrist for the defense argued that when paranoid schizophrenia is diagnosed, then anti-social behavior is disqualified. He summed up his testimony this way:

> In Brad's mind, Harry was interfering in his life with Lucy. He projected all that onto Harry. How can you blame Harry for all that was going on in Brad's life? You can't. Brad couldn't separate things out; everything becomes a product of his delusions. While recovering in the hospital, Brad decides to retaliate against Harry, but even if he had ended Harry's life, the delusions wouldn't have stopped. . . . Paranoid schizophrenic people feel justified in what they are doing. It's part of the craziness.

The prosecutor, acting the role of devil's advocate (or possibly by virtue of actually being one), posed an opening question to "his" psychiatrist this way: "The case before us today is a case of a paranoid schizophrenic who is nonetheless being held responsible for his crimes. How can that be?"

The psychiatrist responded: "Paranoid schizophrenics still have a capacity to live their lives. The laws have changed; the mentally ill have retained all their rights because they do retain their capacity to reason, in spite of the mental illness."

Question: "Because in some cases mentally ill people are not necessarily irresponsible?"

Answer: "Emphatically I can say [confirm] that . . . paranoid schizophrenia and anti-social personality are two distinct mental disorders. An individual doesn't *usually* have both. But my opinion is that Brad *does* have both. . . . The crime was the product of a lifestyle of disregard for the property of others. Brad's anti-social behavior is not due to his paranoid schizophrenia. The majority of paranoid schizophrenics don't commit anti-social acts unless it is the product of delusions. Brad's delusions were beliefs based on his homosexual relations, which added to his anger. He felt used in the relationship and that he lost things—like Lucy, his Hollywood career—because of it."

Rose-Colored Glasses

In his closing comments, the prosecutor did finally concede that "Harry probably did harbor a very deep-seated affection for Brad." It appeared, he stated, that I had viewed the relationship with Brad "through rose-colored glasses." On reflection, I would have to agree. One can, after all, see with rose-colored glasses; things are not distorted, they simply aren't as harsh. The prosecutor might have stopped there, but that was not his style. He added:

> Mr. Wolcott, ladies and gentlemen of the jury, is a fool. And, like they say, there's no fool like an old fool.

The prosecutor reminded jurors once more, and they probably did need reminding: "This is not a case about homosexuality. Everyone's entitled to their own choice of lifestyles."

The prosecutor reviewed the psychiatric testimony and emphasized, "I didn't tell Dr. _____ [the second psychiatrist] what to think. I even gave him Dr. _____'s [first psychiatrist] report. If he had agreed with it, we wouldn't be here today. But *he relied on the facts*. He says Brad is delusional, but that such people can still make decisions and have rights. Brad made criminal decisions. If you make criminal decisions, you can be held responsible even if you are mentally ill."

He concluded: "You have enough exhibits [e.g., photographs, police records, mental-health assessments, the Sneaky Kid article, letters produced by Brad's mother, everything entered into evidence] to last two more weeks. At least 10 of the 12 of you must agree. Keep your bias out of any verdict. That way, when you give your verdict, we won't have another tragedy."

And the defense attorney, whom I came to despise with a passion, nevertheless seemed to sum it up best. It was his theory (hunch, interpretation, premise) that I became incorporated in Brad's delusions by continuing to attempt contact with him while he was undergoing psychiatric treatment. "Wolcott is sticking himself into that boy's life if he can, but what he's really doing is sticking himself into that boy's delusional system," he concluded. That "boy" was the 24-year-old waiting for a jury to vote his future.

If at 3 p.m. on a Friday afternoon the jurors were tired, they were also tired of the long, drawn-out trial. They were determined to put the case to rest before adjourning for the weekend. By 9 p.m., with time out for a dinner paid for by the court, they returned a unanimous verdict: guilty on all three counts.

"Would You Like to Make a Statement?"

It was another two and a half months before Brad appeared for sentencing. In the interim, more reports were prepared anticipating that final hearing and the ruling the judge would make. There was no audience in the courtroom this time except Brad, the prosecutor and defense, others awaiting sentencing, and our faithful observer Sam. Norman and I were out of state and would not take up permanent residence again for another year.

The proceedings went so quickly that Sam had to reconstruct most of the dialogue after the event was finished, so for this text I quote the trial transcript. There was time for only the briefest exchange between lawyer and client, during which Brad was asked the usual question ("Have you been taking your medicine?") and had learned the proper response.

The prosecutor reviewed the charges and announced that for sentencing purposes the three counts had been merged into the most serious one, arson, which called for a 20-year sentence "with a minimum of 10 years served." It was not clear at the time (and has never been clear) what that meant, since Brad served less than five years total, including an extra year for parole violation. But his fate was sealed as prison-bound, in spite of last-ditch efforts by his defense counsel and himself (see below) to be sent to a mental hospital. The defense emphasized how Brad's safety would be at risk in prison "because of the facts of the case, his serious illness, and the kind of overtures that will go on in a jail setting." (The defense's personal opinion, expressed earlier to a courtroom spectator, was that, if sent to prison, Brad was likely to be killed—that prison for him was a death sentence.)

The court asked Brad whether there was anything he wished to say. I provide his complete statement because these are the final words that he gets to utter in this retelling, except for the proclamation he made at his first parole hearing: "I don't even think about Harry Wolcott any more." By now, you, the reader, should feel sufficiently familiar with the case to understand the references.

Your Honor, there is not a doubt in my mind Professor Wolcott hated me for ruining his property and he broke me so I couldn't become famous. What that man did to me was a crime and I could not let him get away with it.

Your Honor, if I do five years I will be a virgin until I am 29 years old, and then how am I supposed to meet a girl when I don't know anybody? I am not going to go to a prostitute, or any girl, I don't want any girl. I want Lucy. I am not that bad. She wouldn't meet me in the county jail between the glass, but when I get to a prison or in the county hospital, she might meet me there and I can show the Parole Board I have the prettiest girl in the world, that can be the most prettiest girl in the world and have a big house and a swimming pool and a Corvette with my name on the license plate and they will know I will leave the school teachers [i.e., Harry and Norman] alone.

Your Honor, in being famous it is good looks or good luck, and I have good looks. I know I could be a movie star or model or dancer. When I was 19, I cut down Professor Wolcott's precious trees. I didn't know I did anything wrong. I could have cleaned up the place. I could have said I was sorry, but he didn't want me to become famous.

Your Honor, that was a low-down, dirty, disgusting perverted thing to do and that is what I have to live with for the rest of my entire life.

Your Honor, Professor Wolcott screwed with my head, my ass and my life too much. He knew there was something wrong with me and he thought it was funny.

Your Honor, I think I should have been found guilty except for insanity. I couldn't control myself. I couldn't control myself. I was obsessed with hate for that man.

Your Honor, I had been dead my whole life and my life won't begin until I make love to Lucy, so I would hope you and Lucy have some sympathy in deciding when my life is to begin, and, your Honor, I couldn't live the rest of my life thinking that that house, where my potential career was ruined, was still standing. Thank you.

The judge then read his decision:

It is the judgment of the Court that the Defendant be imprisoned for a term not to exceed 20 years. The Defendant is committed to the legal and physical custody and control of the Corrections Division of the State of Oregon for service of that sentence and is remanded forthwith to the custody of the Sheriff to be transported to the Oregon State Penitentiary for service of the sentence. It is the recommendation of the Court that the Defendant be considered for and receive a mental health evaluation and treatment as it may be deemed appropriate and necessary during the period of confinement. [Instructions on rights and procedures for appeal omitted here.]

The Court is bound by the verdict rendered in this case. The Defense has been fully presented to the jury and they have considered it and rejected it and the Court is bound by that. Nevertheless, the Court shares the view expressed here this morning that the Defendant is in dire need of assistance and rehabilitation in that particular and it is my hope that he receive it. In addition, having that recommendation in the sentence order, the Court must send an order to the institution to the same effect so they will be advised of that situation upon receipt of the Defendant.

The Court derives no pleasure in imposing a heavy sentence on a young man, but the crime was enormous and I share the view of the State at the present time and certainly in the circumstances that are described in the evidence before the jury that the Defendant was and continues to be dangerous, even more so on his own statement. He is unable to control that. That will be all.

Model? Movie star or rock star? Dancer? . . . Dancer! Strange to contemplate how well Brad might have been suited for that: agile, muscular, light of foot, fearless, good sense of balance . . . How differently it all might have turned out!

The Article on Trial

Where do our studies go, and what do they do there? It shouldn't take too much to convince you that one place an anthropologically oriented researcher would never want a life story document to go is to court, to be used against the person who gives it. But it was hopeless to try to keep the Sneaky Kid article under wraps. It had already been published and in circulation for almost two years when Brad returned. It was one of the first things mentioned to investigators to establish how well I knew him.

At the time of the fire I had also drafted what eventually became the second piece of the trilogy, "Life's Not Working." I was looking for a home for the newer article while continuing to revise it. My comments were based mostly on the literature I was looking at, rather than on any further information about Brad himself. As was my custom, I had put a copy of the current working draft on reserve in the university library for students who might be interested in what I was writing at the moment.

Given Brad's unexpected return and the events that followed, I was not anxious to add fuel to the fire, figuratively or literally. From my hospital bed I sent word immediately to withdraw the new draft from circulation, since it dealt, however conjecturally, with Brad's seeming choice to take the "crazy" route. As sides quickly became drawn, I was advised not to give the defense ("the opposition") any ammunition. However, I did think that the prosecutor might find the paper of interest, since Brad's sanity was now looming large as a critical issue. Yet another source (there's lots of advice floating around under such circumstances) warned that anything turned over to the district attorney's office had to be passed along to the defense as well. So I gave the paper to my lawyer, who could then tell the prosecutor he had something of possible interest, if he cared to drop by.

But the original Sneaky Kid article enjoyed no such restricted readership. I could only imagine how it would be used as evidence to indict Brad and to show him already well on his way to a life of crime ("in the chute," as I had expressed it), although my intention had been to show how Brad seemed to be succeeding at getting his life together. A social scientist's worst nightmare: Brad's freely given account of his misdeeds now turned back to haunt us both.

Well, not quite. With his confession already in hand the morning after the fire, there was no real need to strengthen the case against Brad. From the prosecutor's perspective, the article was, at most, incidental. But in terms of impugning me as a credible witness and person of integrity—ah, plenty of potential there. If a strong offense is the best defense, that would be a way to deflect the damage Brad had caused, explaining, or at least rationalizing, his actions as a consequence of abuses he had suffered at my hands. Discrediting the article, and the person who wrote it, became another element in the defense, a diversionary tactic that ran a nice parallel to "concerns" about my sexual orientation. Combining the two was even better. The defense fired such questions at me point blank.

"Didn't you have a duty to add about the homosexuality in the article? Isn't the article about deviant behavior?" I was asked. My response was that the article was about social, not psychological, behavior, and about society's direction with schooling. It was not an exposé. The point I had raised was to ask what can be done to help people like Brad. "And anyway," I added, "I don't consider homosexual behavior 'deviant'!"

The defense pounced on this as an opportunity to raise the kind of tricky question about which I had been warned: "As an anthropologist, don't you think that people in this society think homosexuality is wrong?" Had he asked whether I thought that both the prosecuting attorney and the defense thought homosexuality wrong, I could have answered, emphatically, "Yes." But the phrase "as an anthropologist" gave the defense an opportunity to denigrate a whole academic discipline, just the opposite of what he would have done had I been called on for expert testimony. He had already primed the jury for my appearance:

Harry Wolcott is not Mr. Average Fellow; he's a genius. I think you'll see it when he's on the stand. You will see when he answers the questions. Tough person to deal with as a witness. Ph.D. Has got some other degrees . . .

But he's an anthropologist, who first studies foreign cultures, but our culture now. . . . And the way he does that is he integrates himself, insinuates himself, perhaps, into human situations, makes himself accepted as just sort of part of the fabric. . . .

And part of his business, and a necessary part of that, is that he knows people. He is not some abstract ivory tower that backed into a situation here. As part of his job he manipulates people. He manipulates them in a higher cause to find out the truth, to reform our schools, to make our society, quote, a better place, by showing us the truth. . . .

He is the kind of guy who is prepared, for example, to follow around for a whole year, two years, a school principal, and integrate himself in, invade himself into the fellow's life, and then basically write a full book. Maybe it says some good things, but also showing what a failure, in many respects, this person is, with the idea that he is going to reform education.

This guy has expressed all sorts of humanitarian ideas throughout his life, caring for people. But in doing that, in getting close to those people, he is a person who has studied "How do I appear when I want someone to talk? What do I say so people won't shut down when I'm around? How do I direct the situation so that I learn the information I want?" And he's done that as part of his profession, and you'll see that.

And he does that with Brad. . . . He manipulates the situation so that he initiates this relationship, and that is what the evidence is going to show. . . . As part of that process, he writes this article about Brad, something of a sneaky boy, "Anatomy of a Sneaky . . . ," I don't know. We will hear about it in detail. It's a long article. He pays Brad to talk to him. You can decide whether that was part of the seduction process or not, bringing this boy in, to contact this boy, that is really living on subsistence level, with no father figure, that is looking for some company, and led it into that . . .

In that article which Wolcott publishes he is basically saying things [like] "This boy, since he's left school, is not getting any skills or education, dropped from the system. What can we do to help this poor boy?" And that is published for basically an audience of teachers, university professors, people that will use it. Perhaps he's got some suggestions as to how do we make our schools better.

He never tells those people that he's established a homosexual relationship with this boy. He doesn't tell them that. He doesn't tell them that he's got any relationship with this boy that he is using as the basis for telling the rest of us how to structure our schools. Doesn't tell them anything like that.

He also doesn't say that he sees any signs of mental problems in the boy, which would be pretty obviously significant if you're going to be using this boy as a paragon, an example, a study for which we can just change all of our schools and our books with kids like this, with normal kids, because that is the approach it takes.

Has this relationship. He writes this article. I think that article, when you look at it and you hear it, is fundamentally dishonest. And think, all those are things that you have to take into account in weighing Harry Wolcott's credibility as he testifies about this. He is not an honest person.

[Court recorder transcription.]

Similar comments by the defense helped to show me in a bad light, as someone constantly taking professional advantage of the situation:

• Harry writes Brad that Lucy doesn't exist. Harry will say that he was trying to help Brad. And he encourages him to take his medicine. Now the average person might not know or pick up on Brad's mental problems, but Harry is closer to being able to describe people and how they act and think.

• Harry gets Brad's mom and dad to come to the cabin to further his article [?]. He pumps them for information for his article. In the article he says that Brad is headed for trouble, but he doesn't tell the mother or father.

• Because of the letters, Brad thinks Harry wants to maintain contact, sending photos of the cabin. The assumption that can be made here: Harry is saying, "Come back to me." Harry is not letting go. Yes, there's affection, but it's exploitative love. Harry tells Brad in a letter, "My article is coming out. Sign the enclosed release so I can get more psychological records."

• Harry was the most intelligent person in the courtroom and he knew it. Smarter than me and smarter than Brad. He's a professional. As a professional, he manipulates people. He uses masks.[2] It's part of his daily work.

The prosecutor was equally relentless in pursuing the matter of ethics, asking whether I felt it was intellectually dishonest to write an article about someone with whom I was involved, or failing to mention the emotional involvement. My answer during testimony:

No. This is an article about schools and educational effectiveness, not about a relationship. The relationship was irrelevant for purposes of the article. It's simply not thinkable to me to put anything like that in this article and embarrass either one of us. The article stressed cross-cultural dimensions, not psychological or individual ones. The article was about the shortcomings of the American educational system and how it might be improved.

That was much too fancy an explanation for one of the testifying psychiatrists, who summarized the thrust of the article thus: "It was my impression that Harry was picking a bone with the school system." When asked whether he used the article in making his assessment, the psychiatrist answered, "No, it was pretty much secondhand, so I didn't base too much on that [i.e., the article is Harry's interpretation]. I used psychological reports and what Brad himself said." Question: "And what did he tell you?" "That throughout a lot of his youth Brad thought he wanted to be a criminal."

When convenient, however, the Sneaky Kid article was also cited in support of points being made. It offered ideas about where to ask, what to look for. For example, Brad's father, mother, and stepfather were all asked about stolen bicycles. Brad's father, who seemed to have a difficult time recalling any negative evidence, did in fact recall that there had been bicycles that mysteriously appeared when Brad was living with him.

Drawing upon the Sneaky Kid article for support, the prosecutor reiterated the (academic) purpose of the article and asked jurors to look at the facts within the article, which meant to examine it as testimony to Brad's antisocial nature. Thus the article itself earned his seal of approval, although its author did not: "You might say, 'I don't like that man [Harry], I don't trust that man,'" he told the jury. "But you see how it fits together" [i.e., how the observations in the article are corroborated by the reports of others]. "Brad told Harry these things at a time when the relationship was good between them. Harry wrote the truth, and Brad OK'd the article."

The most astounding dismissal to me was the implication that the Sneaky Kid article—or at least the majority of it—was fabricated by Brad, this the one time when I felt I had really gotten the story straight and gotten the straight story. Brad's mother stated as much by testifying under oath that she thought Brad had made up *the whole thing,* although I seriously doubt she ever read it. That idea was supported by the testimony of one of the psychiatrists, who explained:

> I had the impression Brad was creating an image—a fantasy—to please Harry, a fantasy of a man who had hard breaks but was succeeding. Harry wanted to prove this intellectually. It was a mutual game they were playing.
>
> I think Brad thinks that Harry finally got the advantage and abused him. But Brad could still manipulate. Initially Brad was the aggressor, in moving onto the land. Brad wanted to present an image of an individual abused by his parents and by school who was now making it on his own. But Brad didn't do most of the conning; it was mutual.

Q: Are you as confident about Brad conning Harry regarding the article as you are confident of your diagnosis of an anti-social personality?

Yes. I think Harry saw the whole thing through rose-colored glasses.

Q: Was there a disregard for the truth?

Yes, that's how Brad was living, by "conning" Harry to some extent. He was living off Harry.

The idea that Brad and I were conning each other appealed to the prosecutor as a satisfactory explanation of the relationship between us. In private, he offered another interpretation as well, that he wondered if the underlying problem had nothing to do with me, but was about working out the unsatisfactory relationship between Brad and his father. Was I perhaps just an innocent bystander? Ah, but he would not have wanted to portray me as "innocent" in the courtroom. Making me out to be a "father figure" was much more sinister.

Notes

1. For those familiar with my other writing, this is the person referred to as "Alfred" (Wolcott 1990, 2001). Small world!

2. This oblique reference to "masks" is from a chapter in *The Man in the Principal's Office* (Wolcott 1973). Presumably, the defense intended to develop the idea that anthropologists use masks [i.e., yet another form of deceit] in gathering data, but it was too convoluted an argument to pursue.

Chapter Five

More Truth, More Consequences

IT was good fortune that Norman and I already had plans to take sabbatical leaves even before the fire. Subsequent events dramatized our need to get away, underscored by the fact that we had no home (or belongings) to tie us down. Repeated delays for beginning the trial began to worry us as we wondered whether the trial might hold us captive.

A major decision I had to make was whether to rebuild. At the time of the fire, I had lived at that house for 20 years. From the moment I set foot on the property, I felt that I had truly found my place. With the trial behind and Brad locked away (for a while, at least), I decided to rebuild. A new house would be built on the same property but at a different site, slightly higher and set farther back from what was fast becoming a busy thoroughfare.

I had already given some thought to the kind of home I wanted, and I took great delight in designing it. The builder offered structural advice, his wife drew up the plans, Norman made important artistic decisions, and the three of them kibitzed on everything. Plans drawn, Norman and I left the country for a year, leaving construction of the house the responsibility of our reliable contractor and friends willing to oversee the work. We returned in June 1986 to the newly built home, where we continue to reside today.

The trial—which had once seemed to shatter whatever was left of our lives after the trauma of the fire—seemed largely forgotten. People congratulated us for getting on with our lives, as though we had some choice in the matter. (Even on the night of the fire, one of our friends consoled Norman, a devoted cook, with the comment, "At least you'll get a new kitchen out of it.")

There were two major changes in our lives: one a consequence of the fire, the other a consequence of the trial. We are more observant about security measures, especially when returning to the house. In spite of development in the area, the house still sits alone on a country road, and we do not cherish the idea of walking into another ambush. And the trial that so effectively publicized our sexual orientation served ample evidence that America's tolerance for diversity is not so widely shared that people feel free to be open about their sexual preferences. It is critical to have people who are not afraid or ashamed, and who are publicly "out," proclaim, "This is our life; this is who we are." A gay lawyer counseled at the time of the trial, "Once you are out of the closet, never let them put you back in." Perhaps this is not in-your-face gay identity as much as it is don't-tread-on-me gay identity.

One could hardly argue from my telling of these events that academics live entirely in their own little world. Indeed, for most of this adventure, the world was too much with us. But academic writing and publishing go their own way, taking their own meander. There is no way academic writing tries to keep up or be timely in the sense of being newsworthy. During the year of the trial, the second article I had drafted about Brad found a home in a volume being prepared by two colleagues. By then, however, what had been presented conjecturally, and from a social perspective, had proved a reality from a psychological standpoint. The article stood as written, but I wanted to inform readers that the story was not at an end. I appended an important footnote prior to the article's publication in Noblit and Pink's *Schooling in Social Context* (1987):

> In the interim between completion of the manuscript and publication of the book, Brad did return, just as several readers of early drafts predicted. Within hours of his arrival he produced sufficient evidence of "craziness" to be incarcerated. Long beyond the moment for timely help, the state's resources for dealing with him punitively seemed limitless.
>
> I do not yet understand those events or their meaning in terms of Brad's life or my own well enough to relate them; I am not sure I ever will. Bizarre as they are, the ensuing events do not change what I have written. In retrospect, my comments seem almost prophetic. But Brad had been equally prophetic years earlier when he reflected on what had been and what was yet to be: "I always seem to screw things up at the end." [Wolcott 1987:317n]

The rather obtuse reference to Brad's having given "sufficient evidence of 'craziness' to be incarcerated" was as much as I wanted to add at the time. Those events far overshadowed the point of the paper, and I did not want the point to get lost: Brad perceived a far different set of options in contemplating his future than I would have identified in facing mine. If, at some future date, I was going to take the account further, it would have to be done separately, and I was not sure what else needed to be said or how best to approach it.

The issue of Brad's and my personal relationship, and some consequent finger-pointing, had been introduced at the trial, suggesting that I could/

might/should have disclosed something of that relationship as well, even in the original article. But whose business was that? Maybe I had taken the story far enough.

Putting "Sneaky Kid" Before a Larger Audience

In spite of the trial, or maybe because of it, I felt that the original article made a valuable contribution to understanding a social problem, especially through using interview data to get an insider's perspective. But who was reading it? I doubted that anyone ever saw the original report submitted to the Office of Education. And the readership of the *Anthropology and Education Quarterly* was not very large. I wondered if there was a way to bring the article before a larger professional audience, encouraged by the words of John Singleton and others who felt that it deserved a wider readership.

That opportunity arose in connection with a project I had been engaged with for years, with the American Educational Research Association (AERA). AERA is headquartered in Washington, D.C., and boasts a huge national and impressive international membership of educational researchers. A move was afoot at the time to temper the educator obsession for measurement with accommodation for a growing minority of educational researchers pursuing other strategies, broadly labeled as "qualitative," or, in those days, "alternative," methods. AERA decided it needed not only to acknowledge but to serve its growing minority of qualitative researchers, or risk losing them. That effort was directed toward making available a series of taped lectures dealing with several of the better-known qualitative strategies. The tapes would, of course, be available to all, but they were especially designed to be used in institutions too small to have faculty prepared to offer instruction in qualitative approaches. Holding fast to the idea that collectively these approaches constituted "alternative" strategies (i.e., alternative to the real thing: research conducted with control groups and quantifiable data), the tapes were titled "Alternative Methodologies in Educational Research." As you probably have guessed, I was invited to prepare the lecture on ethnography.

The idea of the tapes, and the tapes themselves, proved highly successful, so successful that AERA eventually decided to invite the original contributors to turn their spoken lectures into printed chapters bound together as a research manual, under the gentler title *Complementary Methods for Research in Education*.

Volumes prepared under the auspices of organizations or the direction of a committee can be long in the making. A dialogue about this book began as early as 1981, the year I conducted my formal interviews with Brad. By the time the book was beginning to take shape, the Sneaky Kid piece had been published. The book did not become a reality until 1988. With space now available for supplementary material (bibliographies, study questions), authors were also asked to select an exemplary case study to illustrate what they had discussed in their lecture notes–turned–printed chapter.

I inquired ever so modestly if we might choose something we had written ourselves. I had decided that I would like to use the Sneaky Kid article as my illustrative example. Not only did it provide an excellent model for presenting information obtained through observation and interviewing, it also underscored a major element in the anthropological perspective on education, the distinction to be made between education, writ large, and schooling.

Once it became available, the AERA publication gave a huge boost to the readership of the Sneaky Kid article. When I originally prepared the article, I did not think of it or intend it as a model of research. But for the purposes of illustrating and extending my discussion of the ethnographic approach, it seemed to provide an illustration of both the process and the product of an anthropological life history. It demonstrated ethnography in action. The bias in educational research has always favored what is referred to as large Ns— big samples that usually produce enough cases in each cell to warrant high-powered statistical treatments. I intended my example of an extended dialogue with one individual to be an antidote.

Another Invitation to Write

The year was now 1987, the caller a longtime colleague in qualitative research, the late Alan Peshkin. Alan had called about an invitational seminar he and Elliott Eisner were planning to hold at Stanford University. Several key topics (e.g., objectivity, validity, generalizability, ethics) were each to be addressed by two authors, followed by a critique from a third scholar. The total seminar output was to be revised for subsequent publication as a book, tentatively titled *Qualitative Inquiry in Education,* to be coedited by Eisner and Peshkin.

I rather doubted that he was telephoning just to tell me how excited he was about the idea. I waited patiently to hear which topic they had pegged for me. I just *knew* it was going to be ethics. The time had come to bare my soul about my personal relationship with Brad, rumblings that had begun even before the ashes had cooled.

My reputation seemed to be getting tarnished regardless of how anyone had heard pieces of the story. Sneaky Kid was implicated in one set of rumors, that I had been involved with my informant. And if my informant was not involved, had I simply "picked up a trick" who subsequently beat me up and set fire to my house? The arson did seem a bit extreme, but it is not unheard of for older homosexual men to be preyed upon by their prey. Whatever they heard, most colleagues were too polite to ask for details, and the details seemed overwhelmingly complex to explain. "Now here it comes," I thought, awaiting my instructions.

I was so surprised when ethics hadn't been selected as my assigned topic that I instantly let my guard down, at least long enough to hear the topic that had been proposed for me. It was the issue of *validity*. But my relief was short-lived. "Of all people, why me?" I queried. "I'll have to look up the term just to make sure I don't have it confused with reliability." Unfortunately, Alan assumed I was joking, and he quickly went on to explain, "No, don't do that. We don't want a literature review. We are inviting you as someone who has done research and who deals with the issue implicitly in your work. How do you deal with validity if you are not self-conscious about it?"

Put that way—that I was a researcher who demonstrated validity implicitly, even if I didn't know it—I accepted the assignment. The wheels quickly began to turn: Even if I hadn't been assigned the topic of ethics, maybe this was the opportunity I needed to take the Brad story a step further.

When I tried out an early draft of the new paper on my graduate students, Tom Schram asked, pointedly, "Is this the paper you would have written, regardless of which topic they had assigned?" I had to admit that it was—that once I began writing, I had found a time and place to tell more of the Brad story, which by now had become the "Brad and Harry" story.

But along the way, I did address the topic of validity. I began with a review of how the term had found its way into favor among its early proponents. I followed this by discussing what I do that contributes to the validity of my own work, or at least what I try to do to keep from having the charge leveled against me that my accounts lack validity. By the time I finished, I thought I had pretty well laid validity to rest.

My chosen title, "On Seeking—and Rejecting—Validity in Qualitative Research" (Wolcott 1990a), serves notice to how my argument proceeds. Roughly halfway through the article, turning from accounts completed to an account in progress (it was 1987 when I started the writing, 1988 the year the seminar was convened, years during which Brad remained incarcerated) I shifted direction with a new subtitle: "When It Really Matters, Does Validity Really Matter?"

The major point I wanted to make was that *understanding* seemed to provide a more useful criterion than validity. Understanding, for which I found the simple definition "the power to make experience intelligible by applying concepts and categories," proves no less abstract than validity, but it points more clearly to what we try to achieve. I think there is a prevailing assumption that validity is a rigorous measure. But unlike reliability, which can be quantified by the application of a standard formula, there is no equation for determining validity. As anthropologist H. Russell Bernard so clearly stated at the time, "Valid measurement makes valid data, but validity itself depends on the collective opinion of researchers" (1988:54).

I sought to explain why *understanding* seemed so much more worthy a goal than *validity* by introducing the Brad story. With Brad at that very time being regularly evaluated for parole eligibility, psychological assessments loomed again as important measures related to both his and my own well-being, and the standardized measures employed were touted as valid ones. On the basis of his performance on some paper-and-pencil tests and a few brief conversations, Brad was now eligible for release. I could observe philosophically that my sense of freedom would be greatly diminished the moment he regained his.

To be able to make that point, it was necessary once again to review the events that began when I first encountered Brad on my property and allowed him to stay. A quick review of the events described in the Sneaky Kid article now carried forward to include his abrupt departure two years later and his return some two and a half years after that. I condensed my review to about four pages of printed text, hoping that interested readers would consult the original Sneaky Kid article and/or the newly published second installment, "Cultural Alternatives to Career Alternatives." But it was also time to make public the nature of our relationship, something that had figured prominently in the trial and continued to hang as a specter over the whole case. If I have ever written a single electric sentence, it was the following, sandwiched between two complementary sentences intended to soften the impact:

> In the course of a year of casual contact, then working together on an ambitious project, he [Brad] became more talkative and revealing about himself. We found ourselves becoming more intimately involved, psychologically at first, and, in time, physically. After that there seemed no topic that we could not discuss, no aspects of his (or my) life about which we did not talk freely. [Wolcott 1990a:137]

But Who Would Have Known?

When, in April 2001, we first discussed the idea of the book you are now reading, my publisher and longtime associate Mitch Allen asked, point-blank,

"Why did you even have to mention the homosexual issue? If you hadn't written about it, no one would ever have known."

Mitch had first attended to the validity chapter when we were planning to pull together articles that had appeared all over the place and to publish them under one cover as *Transforming Qualitative Data*. It was in that volume that the Brad Trilogy was born; the three pieces had never appeared together before. They represented a story and written account that had evolved over a decade. Why, indeed, did I even need to mention it? No one would ever have known.

From the publicity of the fire—the announcement that my house had burned down and that I had been seriously hurt—and public scrutiny at the trial, it seemed to me that *everyone in the world* knew. Or at least everyone in *my* world knew that something had happened, something terrible, even if only a few knew more than that.

Brad's trial was over. But even at a trial ostensibly about assault and arson and insanity, there were other considerations, ethical ones about intimacy in fieldwork and becoming involved with an informant. Candor: Why hadn't Harry been forthcoming with this information from the outset? Responsibility to informants: Had the research actually hurt Brad by being turned against him? Abuse of power: Wasn't this a relationship in which one individual was powerful, the other relatively powerless?

Reading an early draft of my paper to my students seemed to bring no condemnation from them. Perhaps that was the power thing again, but for at least some of them I became a profile in courage. Many had been around at the time of the fire and during the trial that followed. While the trial was still in progress, I announced that I would devote a class session to giving a candid report about it, and anyone was welcome to attend. Locally, the fact and facts of the trial were discussed openly. It was my need to reach beyond my own campus, to make information available to others whose careers were invested in qualitative research, that prompted my going public.

The fact that my students took it all in stride may have given me a false sense of confidence. I submitted an advance draft of the paper to the conveners of the Stanford seminar. I wondered if they might suddenly discover that the book was going to be "too long" and some material (i.e., my chapter) was going to have to be cut. But neither Eisner nor Peshkin expressed any hesitation. My appointed critic, Philip W. Jackson, commended the "courage it must have taken" to tell the story of my relationship with Brad.

Authors had not been given any length limits for the written chapters they were preparing, but our oral presentations at the invitational seminar had time constraints to allow for discussion and comments from the assigned critics. I could only give a portion of the full paper. I cut right to the chase, glossing over how I endeavored to achieve validity in my earlier studies and turning immediately to the Brad story, the trial, and where things stood at the present.

My candor introduced a moment of high drama. In the silence that followed my presentation to an august group of about 25 colleagues and graduate students, the chair announced an unscheduled break. These colleagues were not familiar with the details, and what I could tell them in an abridged version of the chapter hit different chords of response. The power relationship seemed to be most disconcerting to the new feminists among them, but the atmosphere was charged and I did not get a sense of a common reaction, only a stunned sense that they had all been profoundly moved, but not all profoundly impressed. Today one sometimes hears the words, "Get real!" My impression was that I had gotten too real for some hearers, while appearing unusually brave and forthright in the eyes of others. Almost 15 years later, that is my assessment of where we are today.

The chapter served, and continues to serve, two audiences. It is usually included as a reference in any discussion of the validity issue in qualitative research, though I am less certain that those citing it today have read it—they just know it ought to be cited. More importantly, the chapter serves as a lively opening for instructors who want to talk about, or preach about, ethics in field research. By exhibiting candor about my own work, I hoped that I would serve as a model to other fieldworkers for being more candid in reporting theirs. I did not realize I would become the whipping boy for ethical issues more generally. But for students being introduced to fieldwork through its literature, my case was one of few available, unless instructors cared to admit to some more innocuous indiscretions of their own.

Part Two

Where Do Our Studies Go?

Chapter Six

The Rebound

PRIOR to this book, I have written only one other piece about the Brad story. It deals with how the material can be used and some questions it raises for research, not with further details of Brad's life. And that is the direction this book now takes, looking at lessons from the case, not from the story of Brad.

As a matter of fact, I do not know more details of Brad's life beyond what I have said here. I did not even know whether he was still living, until it occurred to me during this writing that the Social Security office might be willing to help me with that fact. They did confirm that he is alive, or at least he was in summer 2001, the time of my inquiry. They are allowed to do that, but no more. Brad would now be in his 40s. He lives in Southern California.

The Brad story separated itself from Brad years ago as it became involved in a host of issues dealing with ethics, intimacy, and the politics of research. And I can bring the story of the Brad *story* right up to the present.

Ethics is, or quickly becomes, one such focal issue. For instructors willing to bite the bullet, a class discussion can turn on the question of researchers' responsibility to their informants (although the term *responsibility* serves notice that the issue is to be treated as a self-evident moral obligation) or, couched in what strikes me as a more neutral approach, on the broader issue of intimacy in fieldwork. Given one popular definition of fieldwork as "long-term, intimate acquaintance," the Validity chapter prompts a delicate question: Just how intimate is intimate?

For the writing in question, I was invited to prepare a response to an article that Reba Page submitted in 1996 to the editors of *QSE*, the *International Journal of Qualitative Studies in Education*. In the article, Reba described a one-term course she had been teaching for several years. She had her students read and discuss the Sneaky Kid article, among many topics probed. Then, for a later class session, she had them read and discuss the Validity chapter. Students were asked to reflect on implications of the chapter for a fuller understanding of the earlier piece.

Reba organized and conducted her class sessions entirely through reading and critiquing existing work, rather than through the more familiar hands-on technique, in which students conduct field exercises or do a mini–qualitative study. She selected topics and readings with care, and her class discussed them in great depth.

The editors of *QSE* were pleased to accept Reba's article, but they were anxious to offer me an opportunity to respond, given the critical reading to which my two articles had been subjected in her class discussions. The editors opted to invite several responses and published the pieces together. By the time the discussion appeared in print in 1997, the Sneaky Kid article had been around for 14 years. It was apparent that the Validity chapter, and the issues it raised, were keeping the account at the forefront, especially in classes and seminars like Reba's, where instructors were intent on introducing dilemmas of fieldwork beyond the "gaining entrée and maintaining rapport" stages.

In the article, Reba described the general sequence and tenor of class discussions, with particular focus on the pair of Brad-related articles she had used to raise the issue of validity. One can marvel at the analytical acumen her students achieved under what I assume was some gentle but persistent prodding. Her account is a masterful critique and an example of masterful teaching. Students are first led down a primrose path: empathy for Brad, coupled with admiration for Harry's skills at interviewing and reporting. Then they are sparked with caution and doubt once the previously unreported relationship is revealed. Questions arise as to how much Harry's account—and Harry himself—are to be trusted. Finally comes the kind of healthy skepticism that I think Reba intends to instill in her students—not only toward research reports but toward the whole research enterprise.

Where do our studies go and what do they do there? When I wrote the Sneaky Kid article, I intended it to raise issues about out-of-school youth and what might be added in some educational way to shape the course of their lives. When I wrote the Validity article, I intended to call into question the notion of validity itself, and to join with others who were calling for terms better suited for assessing the worth of qualitative studies. Reba's article was evidence and illustration of how my Validity article was more generally received, raising broad issues about relationships in fieldwork and candor in reporting.

Those issues were indeed issues I wanted to see raised. I had not realized that whatever I had done in confronting them would become the fodder for such a debate, but by then I had been living with questions raised at the trial some dozen years earlier. I responded in a manner intended to keep the discussion focused on issues relevant to fieldwork—which was what Reba was doing—rather than allow the dialogue to degenerate into a character assassination, as had happened at the trial. I faced that issue head-on by noting in my rejoinder to her piece:

> I never anticipated that the "Validity" article would be turned back on the original Sneaky Kid one to prove me a rogue and rascal for becoming so involved with a younger guy whose life ever so gradually became inextricably wound up with my own. [Wolcott 1997:158]

I didn't really feel like a rogue and rascal (well, rascal, perhaps, just a bit). Given the widespread and varied response the Validity chapter—or the combination of chapters—seemed to provoke, I felt vindicated in having presented students and colleagues with a real live set of dilemmas to discuss. I say "set of dilemmas" because there did not seem to be a single issue universally defined.

Too often, the issue of homosexuality became central; but in those instances I really felt vindicated, because it was certainly time for my fellow researchers to realize that they, too, were wearing rose-colored glasses. Questions of intimacy in fieldwork needed to be addressed, as did issues of what needs to be disclosed, and when. If I had not anticipated all the avenues that needed exploring, I could at least rejoice in having presented a case that would introduce more candor into discussions about fieldwork and the reporting of fieldwork.

All this might well have come along at the wrong time, or at least at the wrong time in my own career. (For an unfortunate example, see Werth 2001.) In that respect, I simply was lucky: a modest bit of courage coupled with a careful reading of the times and, frankly, not much alternative. I was 60 when the Validity chapter was presented. My career was well established; my work was respected among the people I respected, in spite of my having been run over roughshod by the court. Although I am not a great believer in the idea that it is better to be spoken of badly than not to be spoken of at all, I was bolstered by a feeling that, in some eyes, at least, I had become a crusader for candor. I was willing to take the heat for other researchers not so far along in their careers or so secure in their personal lives that they were willing to divulge highly personal aspects of fieldwork.

Shortly after publication of the Validity chapter I was invited to address a conference held on a major eastern campus. A few moments before I was to speak, a distraught conference organizer had to deliver the unsavory news that a faculty member was planning to embarrass me publicly at the conclusion of my talk, with questions about my sexual orientation and my ethics. That threat, although not carried out, had the effect of reassuring me that I had done the right thing in bringing such issues before the public.

Today, the three Brad articles are most easily accessed in my own volume of collected essays published in 1994, the volume that "created" the trilogy. If the Validity chapter is responsible for keeping the other two alive, the original issues posed by the Sneaky Kid article have not been entirely overshadowed. Through the years, usually with the blessing and encouragement of their instructors, students who have come across, or, more typically, been assigned either the Sneaky Kid chapter, that chapter coupled with the one on validity, or the entire trio, have contacted me through telephone, letter, and now, increasingly, by e-mail. They want to know if I have anything to add by way of insight or recent developments.

For instance, while writing the first draft of this chapter in July 2001, I was startled to see the name Brad pop up as a subject when I checked for e-mail messages one afternoon. The writer, a graduate student taking a summer session course in qualitative methods, wanted to know whether I had written more about the case (strange that I had been doing just that all day, and the previous weeks) or had anything else to say about it. As usual, the ethics question, prompted by the disclosure of the Validity chapter, loomed large, but it was refreshing to have the ethics issue itself posed as a question: "Is there an ethics issue here?" It was even more refreshing to know that the issue that had prompted the original account had not been lost sight of:

> As a group we came up with many issues related to your research—education v. schooling, how do we deal with these fringe kids who seem to slip through the cracks and have no real advocates for themselves.

Alas! When it came time for their class presentation, the group assigned to discuss my work took the road more traveled by. They followed the usual Sneaky-Kid-then-hit-'em-with-the-Validity-chapter sequence. A lively discussion followed; it is virtually guaranteed. What happens from that point determines the depth and direction of the lesson. If the ethical question is couched as one demanding judgment, then I don't think much ever comes of the dialogue besides moralistic venting. When the questions are cast in a broader way to examine the role of intimacy in fieldwork, then each researcher must resolve for him- or herself how to go about a particular inquiry. I made that decision for the Sneaky Kid study more than 20 years ago. I have no regrets, only a slight sense of disappointment.

Brad himself should have been my biggest disappointment in all this, but I suppose I am still in denial and like to think that the Brad who came back determined to do harm was a different Brad from the person who had lived on my property for two years, determined to survive. My biggest shock was how I was treated in court. Personally, I will hold the counsel for the defense in contempt . . . forever.

A Member Protests

Along professional lines, my treatment at the hands of one of my professional organizations, the American Educational Research Association, proved a huge surprise and disappointment, making Phil Jackson's words about candor as "risky business" ring true. This particular sidelight reminds us that our studies can be turned back against not only our earlier works but also ourselves. Reba Page's article, in contrast, did no such thing—most certainly she highlighted lessons to be learned, but the treatment I received from her was coolly analytical, constructive, and aboveboard.

I have reviewed how the Validity chapter has been used to raise issues and spark much soul-searching as to what we expect in behavior and in reporting qualitative work. But I was hardly prepared for it to be held up as a reason for withdrawing support for the original Sneaky Kid piece and for condemning its author as well. If nothing else, this part of the story is a reminder that institutional support can disappear quickly in the face of controversy.

In the previous chapter I reviewed how my essay on ethnographic research, prepared for the first edition of *Complementary Methods for Research in Education*, came to be augmented by appending the Sneaky Kid article as an illustrative example. That chapter and the supplementary reading were well received, as was the volume itself. Had preparations for the revised edition proceeded as quickly as originally planned, I might have escaped the hullabaloo that surrounded the inclusion of my Sneaky Kid chapter in the revision. But there were the usual delays, new chapters to be added for more inclusive coverage, recalcitrant authors to be coaxed into completing their revisions. And during those years, the Validity chapter, published in 1990, was being read and talked about. Its original appearance in the Eisner and Peshkin book had been augmented with publication of the complete trilogy in my own *Transforming Qualitative Data* (1994), which enjoyed sales of well over 5,000 copies in its first three years.

From those two readily available sources, the Validity chapter was widely circulated among students and instructors in classes on qualitative research. Some instructors surely were dismayed by the complexities revealed about my relationship with Brad, but they talked out of my hearing. Others more audibly expressed appreciation for the opportunity to raise and examine sensitive fieldwork issues that were also addressed in such landmark books as Kulick and Willson's *Taboo: Sex, Identity and Erotic Subjectivity in Anthropological Fieldwork* (1995) and Lewin and Leap's *Out in the Field: Reflections of Lesbian and Gay Anthropologists* (1996).[1]

But in my response to Reba Page's article, I felt it necessary to report on a disturbing set of events taking place at that very time, from January to November 1996, in connection with revising *Complementary Methods*. If things continued as they seemed then to be going, I would lack a forum for chronicling what had happened. So I made special mention of the problem I was currently facing. I wrote:

> Although the Validity chapter has been in print for 6 years, newcomers continue to "discover" it. . . . Even as I write, the American Educational Research Association is seriously considering dropping the Sneaky Kid article in a revised edition of its highly successful *Complementary Methods in Educational Research* because *one member* (out of a reported 22,000!) has called my integrity into question for failing to reveal the nature of our [i.e., Brad's and my] relationship. We will know the eventual outcome of their deliberations if my contribution to that collection is missing from a second edition already long overdue.
>
> Given such knee-jerk reaction in the educational research community, I feel I did the right thing in extending the original account and adding to its complexity by writing the Validity chapter, but it is disheartening that some readers are unable to recognize its far different purpose from the initial invitation to offer an anthropological perspective on educational adequacy. [Wolcott 1997:158–59]

That "one member" had taken it upon himself not only to set his students on a course of Right Thinking but to raise formal objection about including the Sneaky Kid piece in the revision of *Complementary Methods*. His objection started off innocently enough with a casual e-mail inquiry to editor Richard Jaeger as to whether he was "aware of the fuller story of the Sneaky Kid case" (i.e., did he know about the Validity chapter published six years prior)? And did he intend to include the Sneaky Kid chapter in the revised edition?

Editor Jaeger offered a succinct reply:

> I really don't see the ethical issue here. He [Wolcott] might refer readers to
> the later article if they're interested in the tragedy of the finale, but the
> "kid" was beyond the age of consent, Wolcott's sexual preferences are irrel-
> evant, and . . . it isn't clear that what he reports about the "kid's" views on
> education and schooling would be invalidated by the relationship, even if it
> were going on during the research study. Am I just being dense about this?
> What's the ethical issue here?

What's the ethical issue here? My detractor now addressed himself directly
to me. "You clearly failed to live up to your own standards for conducting and
reporting on ethnographic research," he wrote in a long letter. "You advise the
researcher, for example, to 'let the reader "see" for themselves,' 'report fully,'
and 'be candid.' In your account of the Sneaky Kid story," he continued, "you
failed to practice what you preached and implicitly claimed you practiced. You
omitted the significant fact of your intimate involvement with Brad. In short
you have deceived me and other readers." And what to do about it? He urged
not only that I withdraw my chapter from the revision of *Complementary Methods* but also that I prepare an erratum notice for publication in the *Anthropology and Education Quarterly* for my "misleading account of the sneaky kid story"
published in that journal some 13 years earlier!

He looked no further than to his students and an office mate for wholehearted support of his position that decried not only the Sneaky Kid chapter
but everything I had to say about ethnography, and, by extension, everything
I had ever written. In seconding his reservation, his office mate wrote:
"Because Wolcott was not straightforward to begin with, my class is sure he
still is not being straightforward. They also doubt that he was straightforward
in any of the rest of his work. . . . They do not trust a word he says. . . . I, in
good conscience, cannot continue to use *Complementary Methods* as long as it
contains the Wolcott material." Their letters were accompanied by two student papers in support of these views. One of them concluded, "I'm tired of
Wolcott justifying the importance of his tainted research as he conveniently
overlooks his responsibility for creating his own victimization."

The heat was on, turned up a few notches in the letter—which was written to me but also generously distributed. I assumed that my answer might be
my only opportunity to state my case, and I took great care in its preparation.
Fortunately, I was teaching a class in ethnography at the time. My students
were already familiar with the Brad Trilogy. Now they got an inside view of the
ethics and politics of research and publishing. Here I had the advantage of an

audience on whom I could try different versions of a written response. Initially, my class worried that my anger and frustration were getting in the way of the more reasoned response they expected and felt I needed to write. It took six drafts before we collectively felt I had expressed myself adequately.

The Letter

I thought it especially important to defend my choice of the Sneaky Kid article as an exemplary model. My detractor was reported to be a specialist in survey research and measurement, so I pointed to some critical differences between his approach and qualitative ones. But if his righteous indignation was rooted in ethics, I pondered some issues he might want to consider for himself. Here is the letter I sent, dated May 5, 1996, quoted in its entirety. To this day, the questions I posed remain unanswered.

> I have received and pondered your letter and suggestions for how to go about ordering my professional and personal life. Be assured that the purpose of this letter is not to solicit another one from you, although I would never deny your right to write to me in any capacity. Indeed, I am sorry it never occurred to you to set up a conference call while your "class" was in session, if they were as intent as you seem to have been in making ethical issues the core of a class purportedly instructing them in research design. Ethical issues have their place, but I hate to see them substituted for content in the limited exposure students have for being introduced to research.
>
> But what students? What class? What syllabus, with what readings and exercises? How strange for you to fault me for failing to tell all of a story, yet confront me with two papers supposedly written by students from an unspecified class with an unspecified enrollment? How many students, at what level, were deeply concerned with questions you raise that look so suspiciously like your own? Where are the papers from the other students? Surely not all your students write so well or share the single view represented here. What were their opinions? It is hard to imagine that in a class of any size, someone would not have been grateful for being presented with genuine issues in research and feel some compassion for a researcher/author who is still trying to "get it right," to understand and relate in an instructive way a series of events that really, deeply matter, including how much to tell, for what purposes, at what time. It is hard for me to believe that not a single student would defend the value and integrity of the model or recognize the once-in-a-lifetime opportunity of having an informant whom one *believed* would be able to talk freely about *any* aspect of his life. I hope no one in your

class has ever reported on a comment of a spouse or lover, for clearly intimate personal knowledge has no business in your conception of research.

You are entitled to your opinions and to express them, but I am astounded at your arrogance in presuming to speak for the entire 18,000 members of AERA [the figure was nearer 22,000, I learned later]. For all your concern with power relationships, what gives you the right to act as censor for what those members and their students can read? Your logic escapes me: you are interested in teaching about ethics; my work, with *or without subsequent developments*, raises ethical concerns; therefore my chapter should be hidden away. You seem to have lost sight of the fact that when the [first edition of the] AERA book came out, my chapter on validity hadn't even been written. The bold decision to write it took the case in a different direction from where I started. Only then did the more personal dimensions become important as I realized how little we ever understand others or even ourselves. If you were well read in qualitative research you would have had all this before you half a dozen years ago. (I trust that you were ethical in your class use of the Validity chapter as well and had students buy the book, not just xerox a single chapter.)

You have given me, as I trust you have given editor Jaeger, the best possible evidence for the power of qualitative research to bring real issues into the dialogue of educational researchers, in support of his original decision asking contributors to include illustrative cases to demonstrate methods in action. But one can't accomplish everything in a single chapter. The purpose of my chapter was to discuss ethnographic research and to demonstrate the ethnographic concern for context. Educational adequacy was the issue at hand, pursued through a brief anthropological life history. That was enough for one article. Don't confuse deception with focus.

You state as personal opinion, "It seems to me to have been highly dubious ethically for you to have undertaken a 'life history' study with a youth with whom you had been 'intimately involved.'" Did you miss the point that it was the intimacy that prompted the idea of pursuing a formal study? At the time, I was trying to figure out how to offer an anthropological perspective on learning outside school, and here was a learner in my own backyard with whom I could talk about virtually anything. Must I underscore that I don't do survey research, run "experiments" on "subjects," or conduct evaluations on programs? In the case with Brad, after he had hung around for a year and a half, I realized I was in touch with a real live dropout who would probably give me a straight story about himself and his perceptions on life. He seemed willing and interested in the idea—and a few easy bucks—so we gave it a try with a few taped interviews. His comment about anonymity is included in the case. He was sufficiently comfortable with the idea of "informed consent" that he tore up a form I prepared and wrote out his own consent in longhand instead.

"Assaying ethical matters in particular cases of research often remains a matter of personal judgment," you observe, but apparently only your own judgment matters, for you state, "In short, you have deceived me and other readers." Have I really? There's more to every story, of course, but that brings me around to trying to figure out yours. What are you really up to here? For instructional purposes, the importance of the Sneaky Kid article is to show how qualitative research is designed in the making and how much we can learn even from an N of 1. From my perspective, it would have been "highly dubious ethically" to have presented a case study of this sort without having a sense of intimate personal knowledge of my informant. What has been changing recently is that researchers—in the social sciences, at least—are becoming more up front about the nexus between their professional roles and personal lives. You provide good evidence of the uphill battle this will be in educational research.

"This doesn't help me one jot in learning how to conduct educational ethnography," writes one of your "students." In spite of his angry jottings in three tightly written pages, I'll hazard that he has learned plenty! Without the typical educator preoccupation with method, the Sneaky Kid chapter is an excellent model for getting and organizing information presented primarily through interviewing. Some kind of relationship has to develop to get such information. You survey research types with your hit and run tactics never really get at the heart of matters, but to pass that off for ethics is to divert attention from the fact that you substitute breadth for depth. In this case, a personal relationship that evolved over a year and a half paved the way for exploring still another relationship in which even Brad thought his story might help someone. That in itself was a pretty big breakthrough for him.

I had no idea of the magnitude the problem of homeless youth would present for us in the decade ahead, but that was the problem focus in the initial writing. The account remains an excellent illustration of and model for taking the in-depth alternative to the psychometric approaches dominant in educational research. The model exemplifies Karl Popper's caution: Observation is always selective. It needs a chosen object, a definite task, an interest, a point of view, a problem. Instead of beating my article and me to death, did it occur to you and your students to ask, What can we learn from this? Did you really try to assess risks and benefits, the power of the Sneaky Kid article as it stands, to provide some insight into all those we do *not* reach through our ceaseless efforts to school them? And thinking for a moment about the researcher himself, did you seriously take into account that the case was written in 1981, only six years after American psychiatrists reluctantly relinquished a huge source of income by declaring that homosexuality was not a mental illness? How about tempering your classroom discussions of ethics with a bit of compassion?

Now some advice for you, if you take it as well as give it. I urge you to communicate once more with editor Jaeger. By all means, reaffirm your position—I'm sure I have not changed it—but do allow that you speak for yourself, without insisting that what looks suspiciously like personal indignation should determine the organizational or editorial policy for 17,999 others. And tell him enough about the mystery class to assure him that the two letters were freely volunteered (rather than, say, a class assignment in which you displayed some power of your own), and [confirm] the extent to which they represent class consensus. I think it would also be a courtesy for you to let him off the hook by not holding him personally responsible for the works of his contributors, as apparently you do. With others, both of us have been working at this project for years with not so much as a thank you. If you don't like the book, use another. If righteous indignation about researchers who behave like people is a source of energy for your teaching, you and your students ought to have a field day with Kulick and Willson's new *Taboo* (1995) from Routledge.

As long as I remain an invited contributor to the volume, the Sneaky Kid piece will remain and I will point to it as a model. To date most readers have been able to make a distinction between research and researcher that apparently you cannot make: "Your 'sneaky kid' account is, in my view, simply not worthy of being held out as a model of such research." So be it; that's why they make chocolate and vanilla ice cream.

And how did AERA reward my forthrightness? The editor buckled. He wrote that he remained in "personal support" but was unwilling to claim he could act on behalf of the entire organization, in spite of the fact that he had been shepherding this project from taped lectures to a printed edition to an almost second edition for the previous 20 years. No sooner had I received a copy of the correspondence detailing the complaint than I received a phone call asking if I had a different piece I could substitute in place of Sneaky Kid. The second edition was ready to go to press. Did I have something less controversial that I could use as my illustrative piece?

Those were fighting words. My answer was a decisive "No." To expedite publication, I offered to withdraw my entire submission; just leave ethnography out of the second edition entirely. But I noted that my contribution would remain available if there were a subsequent decision to accept the material as originally submitted—essentially an updated version of what, by that time, had been in circulation for nearly a decade.

The editor wrote personally: "I'm as fed up with this flap as you are! I hope it soon is resolved, but I have no choice but to follow through as the Professional Development and Training Committee has directed. It is a very unfortunate delay in what is already an unconscionably long publication process."

After much hemming and hawing, it was decided that the case would be submitted to a panel of judges selected from within the organization. Three AERA "ethicists," as they were referred to, would advise on the acceptability of what I had submitted. Before that internal review got under way, all parties gave permission to circulate what they had written. For my part, that included my proposed submission for the second edition, complete with the Sneaky Kid article, plus the Validity chapter and my letter quoted above, which was my formal response to the critique. For his part, my detractor included permissions to circulate what he had written, the echo by his office mate, and statements written by two students. I was fascinated by the correspondence from one of the students. She gave permission but noted that what had been submitted was part of a midterm exam that she never imagined would be so widely read. She underscored her concerns and objections about using the Sneaky Kid piece as an exemplar of ethnographic research, but emphasized that her essay was written to address an exam question and thus represented a more "bookish" writing style than she normally used.

Except for correspondence I had already seen, none of this matter was made public. I was never told who the judges were. To my surprise, I learned that I squeaked by with a two-out-of-three endorsement, when I expected (well, hoped, in any case) every one of the other 21,999 members to be in wholehearted support. The delay used up another year. The second edition of *Complementary Methods* was in production as long as the first, a half dozen years in all.

The editor still felt he was walking a fine line by including the Sneaky Kid piece. He wrote that he had received further inquiry from my detractor: "From his response, it seems likely that I've not heard the end of it. I let him know that I considered the decision firm and hoped he would not pursue it further. We'll see."

For the moment, at least, the matter was dropped. But, in my opinion, so was the ball. As long as there are vigilantes ready to pounce on researchers to stifle efforts at candor, or to censor the kinds of studies and problems brought before students, then the safest route, especially for neophyte researchers, will be to follow a maxim that keeps such matters off the table entirely. Don't ask, don't tell.

Or else, remain fully cognizant of the risks, and never assume that candor comes without cost. Joan Didion is reported to have warned, "I am so small, so neurotic, and so inoffensive that people invariably forget an important point: the writer will *do you in*" (attributed in Miles and Huberman 1994:287). As a researcher, you also need to watch out for your colleagues. If you don't do or present research as our self-appointed standard-bearers feel it should be done or presented, they may try to do *you* in. It is always safer to fault research reported by others than to present your own.

Notes

1. Kulick and Willson's collection deals with sexual issues surrounding fieldworkers. Lewin and Leap deal specifically with lesbian and gay issues during fieldwork and writing. Since publication of those two works, there have been several books and collections on related topics. See, for example, Grinker 2000; Markowitz and Ashkenazi 1999.

Chapter Seven

A Play on Words:
The Brad Trilogy as Ethnodrama

ALMOST from the moment Brad left my place, I felt there was another story to be told: not an academic study like the Sneaky Kid piece but a play or novel that might capture his romantic Robinson Crusoe life and the relationship that developed between us. I didn't know just how far to go with that part of the story, but I wanted to get at least to the point of revealing my affection for him.

I kept the idea in mind, usually visualizing the story as it might be staged, but tempered with the reality that I would have better luck writing a novel. Flashbacks seemed the most obvious vehicle for relating the story in play form, perhaps with me sitting at a desk on one side of the stage drafting letters, Brad sitting at a table on the other side of the stage reading them aloud, until correspondences blended into a series of vignettes with the two characters in action and spoken dialogue.

During the year after Brad departed, I drafted the second article, as described previously. The Sneaky Kid piece had been published that spring. I shared the new draft with a friend in theatre, Lou Salerni, both to get his reaction to the article itself (he had served as a critical reviewer of things I had written and once helped with a major editing project) and to see if he agreed that an expanded account would have the makings of a novel or play. He was encouraging about the story possibilities. He voiced only one caution: Yes, there's stuff for a novel or play here, he reflected, only *you* can't be the one to write it!

Those were not the words I wanted to hear. Still, I suspected that Lou was right, and on two counts, not just one. In addition to my lack of skill or experience at any kind of writing other than academic, I was much too close to this story. I still found (and find) myself brooding over Brad's unexplained behavior at his departure, his unsettled mental state, the discouraging news about the "bizarre" behavior his mother reported after he returned to Southern California, and the fact that he had not kept in touch as promised. There was little doubt in Lou's mind that I could ever get the distance from the story that I now had from Brad himself. Nor was it clear exactly what the focus of the story was, or whether anything could be resolved other than the fact that Brad had been here, he was now gone, and I missed him.

Brad's unexpected return would soon enough provide plenty of tension, even suspense, should the time come to develop the account further. For the present, however, I channeled my writing energies to polishing the second part of the trilogy, with its seeming resolution in mental illness. Eventually I turned to drafting the third piece. I still held the thought of someday trying my hand at a novel or play, the dramatic elements now clearly apparent. But I could not escape the counsel Lou had offered, that although there was good material here, someone else would have to work it up.

If nothing else, creating the trilogy—pulling the three articles together under one cover—provided an opportunity for me to discuss the *idea* of developing the account into some literary form. Even as the possibility of ever achieving that objective seemed to be fading away, I had come up with what seemed a great title, *Finding My Place.*

My projected title offered entrée into the story by giving different twists to the meaning of "my place." I tend to organize and present material in sets of threes, so it seemed natural to envision *Finding My Place* as a story told in three parts. The first part would find Brad on my property and would review some of his prior life experiences that led him to build his cabin and, in his words, begin to get his life together. The second part would focus on the evolution of our personal relationship, from uninvited squatter and wary landowner to a caring relationship between a younger man and an older one, an unintended consequence of proximity and personal inclinations. I must admit that, to be as forthright as I intended, I recognized the advantages of writing a novel rather than a play for this portion of the story. I imagined that some recounting of sexual intrigue would be expected. Even if I did not target the writing to prurient interests, whatever gratifying detail I offered would underscore that this writing was not just more of that stuff professors write. (I also wondered if writing would help get Brad out of my sexual fantasies.)

The tragedy of Brad's return would mark the shift in emphasis from the personal dimensions of the first two parts of my proposed script to the societal dimensions of the third. In the final section, *Finding My Place* would refer not simply to the trial but to society's efforts, through the courts, to make sure I was put in *my place* for my indiscretions: I had gotten what I deserved and could serve as object lesson for all.

If I was never going to write such a script—and it was beginning to look that way—at least I might pique the imagination of readers who could envision what I had in mind. I did not intend such thoughts as a challenge, to see if anyone would recognize the potential of the material for being rewritten in another form. If anything, I was putting the idea to rest. But I liked my proposed title and the sequence that seemed to follow from it for developing the material in more dramatic fashion.

Enter the Playwright

Small world again: In the autumn of 1980, only four months after Brad appeared, I took a leave for one term to accept an appointment as a visiting professor at Arizona State University. My assignment was to help establish qualitative research in the graduate program in education. Qualitative methods did eventually become established in the curriculum. Both instructors who taught qualitative courses had also attended the Stanford seminar when the Validity chapter was originally presented. It was included in their course readings.

With their encouragement, a colleague from across campus in that university's theatre department, Professor Johnny Saldaña, had become interested in qualitative research and had begun wide reading in the field. During a term of sabbatical study leave, he joined qualitative research seminars to immerse himself in those methods. That was when *Transforming Qualitative Data* first became available: the three Brad pieces now under one cover, accompanied by a brief commentary describing a play or short novel—the script I probably was never going to write.

Johnny Saldaña was captivated by the Brad Trilogy when he discovered it in *Transforming Qualitative Data*. He wrote me to express not only his enthusiasm but his surprise at the level of candor:

> I was transfixed by your Brad stories, especially when you "came out" in the final selection. . . . I am openly gay, and I was utterly surprised at your revelation in the final chapter of the book (what a climax!). When I find out that men I admire turn out to be gay, it boosts my pride and gives me an emotional high. I admire the courage you displayed in revealing such a personal side of yourself in your work.

Johnny concluded his note with the observation: "I doubt that our professional travels will ever bring us face-to-face. But . . . thanks again for your inspiration."

Where do our studies go and what do they do there? Johnny did not mention how or why he happened to be reading *Transforming Qualitative Data,* except for noting that he was "fairly new to qualitative research" and had also read some of my earlier work. I, too, doubted that our professional travels would bring us face-to-face, but I found it flattering to receive accolades from someone outside the customary circle of qualitative researchers.

Five and a half years went by before I received another correspondence from Professor Saldaña. Having learned from a preliminary announcement that I had been invited to give a keynote address at the second Advances in Qualitative Methods conference, to be held in Edmonton in 2001, he sent an e-mail with a specific question in mind: Would I be willing to let him adapt and direct an ethnographic performance text of the Brad Trilogy, the play to be presented at that conference?

I could not imagine committing myself in so short a time to producing a play that had not even been written. But in the period since we had first corresponded, Johnny not only had pursued his inquiry into qualitative methods but had made ethnodrama something of a specialty (see Saldaña 1998a, 1999). He had also written and produced an ethnotheatre piece of his own, *"Maybe Someday, If I'm Famous . . .,"* a play about an adolescent actor (Saldaña 1998b).

I was delighted with the idea. I replied immediately by e-mail that I was happy to grant permission and to offer my enthusiastic endorsement, although I was in considerable doubt as to exactly what he might need from me other than formal permission.

By the next morning, Johnny had outlined the things he needed to do and a time frame for mounting a production 10 months hence. He sent an e-mail that described in detail how he intended to get the new project started. First, he would reread the trilogy, this time "with a playwright/director's lens." Then he would read or reread whatever related materials of mine he had at hand, including the exchange with Reba Page and the commentary I had added to introduce each of the trilogy chapters in *Transforming Qualitative Data.* Then he planned to generate a set of questions for me. To that last item, he gave as examples: "What did Brad look like? What did/do YOU look like? Remember, we've never met!" And he posed the issue of how, whether, or how extensively, we might work together: "What kind of final review/approval process do you want to negotiate as the script develops?"

What role did I wish to play in developing the adaptation? I felt that Johnny should be free to adapt and develop the play as he wanted. My approach should be strictly hands-off. I was intensely curious as to which story, or stories, he would choose to tell. All I knew about him was that he was in theatre, was interested in ethnodrama, and was gay. I imagined the latter point was an important reason for his expressing admiration at my candor. I assumed that he would play up the relationship between Brad and myself. Would that be the play's preoccupation? And, if so, could I live with it?

I tried to think of all the possible stories or combinations of themes that might be developed from the account, aspects that would lend a dramatic element. I realized I needed to assess carefully whether I would be comfortable with allowing free interpretive reign. As it turned out, I need not have worried, but I was putting both Brad's story and my own in the hands of a stranger. There was little doubt, for instance, that there would be sexual intrigue, but would it be played as a love story, a seduction, or, as was suggested at the trial, little more than two people intent on conning each other?

And how far to take the story? Happy ending or sad? One ending might depart from the text at the moment of Brad's original departure, romanticizing a fictional and happier return. We could take up where we had left off (as both Brad's mother and I had anticipated might happen) or celebrate some new, improved life circumstances or direction (e.g., entering the military; finding a suitable partner nearer his own age; even returning to life at the cabin, resolved to make it work).

Alternatively, and remaining true to the account, Brad's return could chronicle his efforts to bring down everything around him, the two of us included. How much of the mental illness would need to be introduced, a latecomer to life at the cabin but, as I now realized, a major preoccupation, to some extent even an occupation, after he left? An upbeat story of triumph against odds, or a story of loneliness and despair? And how about a villain? Was it essential that there be one? Might the villain be some external force, such as mental illness, or a society that abandons its youth once they escape its schools? Or did the role of bad guy have to go to one of the two of us . . . or even to us both?

A question I might have wondered about at first, but did not recognize until later, was: How close to the "real" story does an account based on a real story have to be? What did terms like *ethnodrama* or *performance text* imply, and were there subtle distinctions to be made between them? (Johnny uses *ethnographic performance text*, *ethnotheatre*, and *ethnodrama* interchangeably [Saldaña 1999:60]; for more discussion, see Denzin 1997.) I found myself comforted by the prefix *ethno-*, which suggested that ethnographic integrity would be preserved, the performance staged in front of an audience of colleagues interested in research. Johnny gave me pause when he emphasized that he was interested in producing "good theatre," which made me wonder whether he would subordinate ethnographic integrity to achieve high drama. But that was not what he meant. He simply didn't want a second-rate production passed off with the excuse that ethnotheatre is somehow less than, or an inferior form of, "real" theatre.

It quickly became apparent that, if the play was to be faithful to real events, there was a vital role that I could—and should—play as a sort of technical assistant to the playwright: the dramaturg. There was no way I could avoid being involved if Johnny intended to supplement what he already had by way of published material with details that had not been described in print.

Our relationship quickly became a collaborative one. My role was to expand on the information he had at hand or to correct impressions. At times I am sure I told him more than he wanted to know, but I felt that he could pick and choose from whatever I could offer of details or my perceptions of what had happened. The script itself remained in Johnny's hands; he has always held the master copy, and his decisions are the final ones. At the same time, he always deferred to me: "Nothing goes into the script without your approval."

Once early drafts of the script could be shared between us, I realized that Brad's character had, in the main, already been written. It existed in relatively natural speech because all Brad's lines originally had been spoken. My words, to whatever extent Johnny intended to draw on them in the original, existed only as written text, written in academic style for academic audiences. Would the playwright make up dialogue for me, or would my utterances all be professorial ones? As Johnny noted, he had never heard me speak. What he had for my character were long and often convoluted sentences that, with some wordsmithing, had been made to read OK. But they were virtually impossible to speak. Consider being handed a line like this one, quoted earlier, to read at an audition:

> I never anticipated that the Validity article would be turned back on the original Sneaky Kid one to prove me a rogue and rascal for becoming so involved with a younger guy whose life ever so gradually became inextricably wound up with my own.

At first I didn't recognize the problem, or realize that I *was* the problem. It was an ego trip to imagine myself enacted, my written words now to be spoken on stage. As the person who had written them, if anyone could read them I certainly could, and it was exciting to find them treated as dialogue (well, monologue, usually, but exciting, nonetheless) and to recognize them not only as my own but presented exactly as written. I also experienced a sense of awe not only at how faithful Johnny had been to preserve and present my words as originally written but how carefully he had sifted through so much of what I had written elsewhere, combing my studies for pithy phrases or relevant insights into fieldwork. Heady stuff indeed.

Johnny set himself a seemingly impossible task. In his determination to remain faithful to my words, he seemed to have restricted his selection almost solely to phrases already in print. In my own self-interest I had to encourage him to take liberties lest I appear a stodgy professor unlikely ever to have become intimately involved with Brad in the first place. Eventually we realized that this dilemma was part of a bigger issue—how close to the details, or at what level of detail, should ethnodrama be to the actual events being portrayed? If your immediate response favors high fidelity, keep in mind that the play covers a period of roughly five years in a real-time period of about 90 minutes, including intermission.

Script in hand, I had a better sense of what more to describe in places where all Johnny had was an idea of what might possibly have happened. My suggestions always seemed welcome and largely acceptable. I must admit to some surprise at the extent to which I worried over and worked to create a favorable impression of myself. As interested and objective as I intended to be during this process of adaptation, my suggestions usually dealt with ways to soften my research role, to make me appear wise rather than smart, caring rather than opportunistic, more the humanist than the detached observer. Of course, until I could actually see the production, I had no idea how it would be directed. But I'll admit to lots of ego involvement with the presentation of this particular self. I point that out as reminder to fellow researchers: No matter how sensitive we think we are or try to be in portraying others in our studies, when we are the subjects, we become acutely aware of what delicate business this is.

I tend to include too much detail in my reporting. That practice was appropriate in my role as dramaturg—I was the key source of data. Johnny selected what he felt was needed from the rich fare I had to offer, basing his decisions on how much an audience needed to know without being subjected to information overload.

An instance of this was the decision about whether to introduce Brad's imaginary girlfriend, Lucy, into the script. Lucy entered Brad's delusional system only a few weeks before he left the cabin. He mentioned her occasionally but was not having much success convincing Norman or me that she existed, and we did not encourage talk about her except as a sort of reality check. She resurfaced in Brad's monologues in Southern California and again during his statement at his sentencing. In the latter, he described her as "the prettiest girl in the world" and anticipated that she might visit him in prison or a mental-health facility. For completeness, she might have been mentioned in the script. But simply to add another name into the story seemed to accomplish little. Brad's "craziness" was established through other actions and words spoken by the actor. Lucy was important to Brad's case history, but not to the purposes of the play. I note this to show how ethnodrama might be described as "minimalist" ethnography, employing the least detail necessary to make a point or convey a context. It contrasts markedly with the accolade "thick description" that we prefer in reference to our written studies.

Yet that issue, always in process of being resolved rather than ever being totally resolvable, reveals how workable our collaborative arrangement was. I can jump ahead here to the post-production editing, for we have continued to work together that way: me supplying new information or insight, Johnny weighing potential additions but remaining final arbiter as to what gets included. It is not that the facts keep changing, but that new information is uncovered (such as the trial transcription, which I had not known about before) or new insights present themselves. With my penchant for editing and editing again, there will always be new material that can be reviewed, new interpretations to consider. But at some point, as in final preparation for including a version of the script in this collection, we have to declare, "That's it—at least for now."

The story as Johnny seemed to be developing it was constructed essentially around two sources. For Brad's part, the interview material contained in the Sneaky Kid article was virtually the sole source. Since I collected it through interviews, it was natural to have Harry interview Brad in the play, or to find ways for Brad to share his thoughts and reflect on his experiences. Harry's reflections and advice on fieldwork are presented through musings throughout the play, sandwiched between an opening monologue about the setting and context and a closing monologue pondering lessons and meanings of the experience. The discussion of fieldwork, particularly fieldwork conducted primarily through interviewing, is also the vehicle that invites the audience into the play. The script retains a didactic quality, informing audience members as to how one goes about doing this type of research, reflecting Johnny's abiding interest in qualitative approaches to research and his careful perusal of much of my written work.

I was not clever enough to recognize that allowing myself first and foremost to be portrayed as a researcher—indeed, as a model researcher—might be as counterproductive in this instance as identifying the Sneaky Kid article as a model of research had proven to be a decade earlier. From the beginning, I should have been on the lookout for any confusion created between collecting a brief life history and being involved in an intimate personal relationship that overshadowed the research project.

Thus, reality was not inevitably a blessing, not always on my side. There were occasions when I wished I had written something differently, but since

Johnny took my sentences right from the printed page, the record was already there. Most often the problem resided in my professorial language, long utterances difficult to shorten and almost impossible to memorize or to say, as we discovered once the two actors were chosen and began to speak—or try to speak—the written lines. If anything, Johnny was probably too respectful of lines as I had written them. The character of Harry was trapped in Harry's own verbiage. And the longer some of those long lines remained in the script, the more Johnny began to regard them as my natural way of speaking, and the harder I had to argue on behalf of modifying them. From the first, however, Johnny displayed great skill in crafting the play and great care in fine-tuning it. Unlike what usually happens when I am doing the editing, the running time of the play did not seem to get longer. I think Johnny felt that the play was just the right length. If a line or two was added one place, an equivalent cut would be made somewhere else.

Johnny took the title I had proposed, *Finding My Place,* as his title. He coupled it with the subtitle *The Brad Trilogy,* which he felt was essential to communicate to an audience of qualitative researchers. And, perhaps intuitively, he followed the plot outline I had in mind for the trilogy as I had once thought of writing it. To my surprise, however, the parts into which he divided the story were built around a different threesome, the "description, analysis, and interpretation" framework into which I had set my studies in *Transforming Qualitative Data.*

Johnny premiered the play on his own campus in performances given on three consecutive nights (February 15, 16, and 17, 2001). He later learned that there had been some initial confusion that anyone who attended only one of those evenings was not going to see the entire performance, only one of its three parts. But he was comfortable working with a story told in three sections—he made them "scenes" in the production—with a prologue and an epilogue to provide necessary context.

We never felt we were working at cross-purposes, but there were differences in our orientation. Johnny's concern was about actors delivering lines and an audience needing to be informed about the play and its purposes. We were in agreement on that, for I have always advised that it doesn't hurt to make the statement of purpose sentence one of paragraph one of chapter one in any study. From the very first draft, Johnny had the actor playing the part of Harry state the purpose of the play:

> The purpose of this play is to render from research-oriented personal experience an account that offers to a discerning audience a level of insight and understanding into human social life. [Draft July 17, 2000]

Those, of course, were not exactly my words. I had not written the play, so I had never thought about an introduction for it. But one gets a sense of Johnny's awareness of an audience, of the performance, and of drawing the two together—with just a hint of well-placed flattery. I would be loath to flatter readers that way, inclined instead to worry whether they would find the idea of an unspecified "level of insight and understanding" adequate as a criterion for judging the worthiness of my reporting.

Before embarking on the project, Johnny and I had not met. We did happen to meet at a professional gathering shortly after he proposed writing a script, but at that time he had not yet begun work on it. I gave a brief presentation during those meetings and later learned that Johnny sat in the audience taking notes on me—that is, on anything that might be useful in portraying me in the play. We did not meet again until the play had its international premiere in Edmonton. Our communication while the script was being developed and the performance was being staged was entirely by e-mail. We have a record of everything we ever wrote to each other, as well as the evolving script itself, which was in its eighth draft by the time of performance. Two months before the performance, Johnny also began sending videotapes of rehearsals, so that as well as reading what they had to say, I could see how the actors were being coached.

Johnny perceived the play as presenting a short treatise about ethnographic research, along with an illustrative example of that approach, embedded in an account of the relationship between an older man and a younger one. The arson and assault were somehow to be underplayed sufficiently to allow for reconciliation in the finale. That was a good reason for me to stay out of the way and let him take the story where he wanted (and where I would have much preferred it to go). I think Johnny held out hope that there could be a happy, or at least more satisfying, ending. He envisioned the play concluding with a final tableau, Harry and Brad staring intently at each other. In the first draft, Johnny had Brad caressing Harry's beard, leaving the audience with the impression that some tender feeling between them remained. Alas, if the script was going to remain true to the actual account, that was never going to be. Harry and Johnny both had to come to grips with that fact.

Two aspects of the rear projections planned for the play gave me pause, at least until I could see them in production. First was the use of slides to project scenery, so that the play required few props and was highly transportable. I feared that projected photographs would be too small to be seen, but the images were clear and of good size. I was able to contribute a few slides of my own, such as photos of the charred remains of the house, or of Brad's cabin, taken several years after he'd left. (The cabin still stands today, though it is now yielding to the effects of weather and a tree that is relentlessly crushing the roof.)

Along with the projection of images, there were also projections of phrases—title words taken from the script, key phrases spoken by the actors, or words that helped introduce or underscore ideas. I worried that the play was already excessively wordy, and that more words would distract. Instead, I found that the phrases and titles helped audiences focus on key terms, something akin to supertitles for opera performances. This is, after all, a play of words, a so-called performance text. Making key words accessible via more than one sense seemed to reinforce rather than diminish their impact.

Finding My Place in Performance

The play's four performances—three on the Arizona State campus, one at the Advances in Qualitative Research conference held in conjunction with the University of Alberta—received favorable audience response. With Johnny Saldaña's permission, the most recent version of the play is reproduced here in full in the appendix. This will give you another way to view these events. Should you someday consider doing an ethno-performance yourself, you can see what was done here. Our problems will become your problems as you breathe life into your characters and decide how to tell your story.

I note that the performances received favorable response. However, the play's message received varied interpretations and mixed reviews. At issue for me was the order in which things happened. It was never clear, or clear enough, that my intimate relationship with Brad did not develop until his second year, that it was a consenting relationship, and that the nature of our relationship was, in part, impetus for doing a life history project.

The play provided opportunity to clarify the order of things, and I paid particular attention to how the sequence was handled. The script seemed satisfactory. But the message did not get across, or did not get across as emphatically as I had hoped. On Johnny's campus, this did not particularly matter, for his audiences included theatre people intrigued with aspects of production, and research students already familiar with the Brad Trilogy. In Canada, however, the voices of the incensed rose above those of the impressed.

Not at first: In invited commentaries that immediately followed the production, the talk was about how powerful the play had been. In my own remarks, I expressed deep admiration and appreciation to Johnny and to the production team for a job superbly done. But in a follow-up panel the next morning, a session ominously titled "Deconstructing Harry," our sense of celebration was quickly dampened. A vocal minority held the discussion to the topic of my ethics, focusing on issues of consent and a researcher "taking advantage" of an informant. This view ignored the fact that Brad was a willing subject of a life history, and that our formal research relationship occupied only a few hours of taped interviews.

Detractors argued that, by offering the story as ethnodrama, the relationship was being condoned. The researcher was presented as a model—a most unsavory one—of fieldwork in action. With the playwright and his dramaturg collaborator sitting there as resource for a panel discussion, plus the two actors and the person who ran the slides, the discussion never achieved its potential to examine the effectiveness of the production, the nature and power of the messages conveyed (other than disgraceful ethics), the actors' perceptions of their roles, or how one goes about creating a play from written text. Ethics became the trump card, effectively cutting off dialogue by subverting it.

Later that same day, I was accosted by still others who demanded to know why the play was presented at all, since it "had nothing to do with research."[1] And traveling overseas later that year, I was astounded to learn that someone who had been in the audience now anticipated my arrival with an e-mail warning my overseas hosts that they had invited "one of America's most controversial researchers in qualitative methods." The e-mail recounted the highlights of the Brad story and play (Brad conveniently viewed as a teenager), and how my unethical behavior had been presented as a model of research. My lack of contrition was offered as further evidence of what a bad model I really am. I would rest more easily if such observations were presented as questions, rather than as statements of fact. In question form, they might do some good.

Johnny has continued fine-tuning the play. We hope to see it produced someday by people not so close to it emotionally. The version you have here may make clear the distinction that is so important to me about the sequence of events. That is not necessarily the part that is important to others; there are many issues for reflection. In the final chapter I will address some questions about research—qualitative work in particular—the Brad Trilogy raises for me. You can take it from there.

Notes

1. Two critical letters to the editor followed in November 2001, in *Qualitative Health Research* (11:6), the journal most closely associated with the conference. A more thoughtful and constructive review of the play by Thomas Barone appears in the *Anthropology and Education Quarterly* (33:2) and brings the account full circle back to the journal in which it originally appeared two decades ago.

Chapter Eight

Drawing Lessons

Only connect.
—E. M. Forster *(Howard's End)*

IN each generation, it becomes fashionable in the social sciences to include certain names among one's citations and to somehow try to weave one's interpretive framework around a cogent quotation from at least one of them. In recent years, such names as Pierre Bourdieu, Jacques Derrida, Wilhelm Dilthey, Martin Heidegger, Hans-Georg Gadamer, Jacques Lacan, and Herbert Marcuse spring to mind. At the mere mention of them, the reader is presumed to recognize that an author travels (or travails) in good company.

Cynics have observed how curious it is that we go far afield literally and figuratively to find our philosophers and theorists. I take some comfort in that observation because it supports my bias that the study of human social behavior is not well served by taking how theory works in the natural sciences as our model. We catch ourselves trying to validate our interpretations by looking for pithy observations selected from an approved list of intellectuals. The roster keeps changing, so while it is hard to keep up with everything that is going on, one can give an appearance of doing so. But flat-footed ethnographers like myself tend to be so firmly rooted in the idiosyncratic nature of everyday occurrence that we are loath to make any generalizations at all, and are especially reluctant to nest our modest observations in lofty theories.

Yet I must concede that the language of our appointed theorists of the day is rich with insight and fresh perspective, especially when we bring our cases to them for examination in their light, rather than setting out with their ideas and endeavoring to prove them right. And so I go the next step, to borrow an idea that lends a fresh perspective to the account I have been developing and, especially, to the coherency I have imposed on it.

The late Pierre Bourdieu is the source for the insight and caution to which I point here, an observation he has termed the "biographical illusion"

(Bourdieu 1986). Bourdieu's notion—paraphrased for you just as it was for me when I came across it (in Järvinen 2000:372)—stems from his critique of traditional life history research that "forces the lived life's chaos into a straightforward, one-dimensional logic."

Bourdieu argues that the life history is a social construction, an artifact that is a consequence of our insistence on, and pursuit of, order. The life history organizes and reports the events of someone's life as internally consistent, reciprocally meaningful units. They are presented as functional parts of a larger whole because it is in the interest of both the narrator and the listener, or author and reader, that the story assumes a logical and clear-cut pattern. This sense of logic and order is accomplished "by linking together life episodes into long, causal sequences and singling out certain events as especially significant." Human life itself, Bourdieu argues, is incoherent, consisting of "elements standing alongside each other or following each other, without necessarily being related. It consists of confusion, contradictions, and ironies, and of indecisiveness, repetition, and reversion" (Järvinen 2000:372).

I have been guilty of creating this very kind of biographical illusion. I have created order out of chaos to make this account, just as I created order out of chaos to present Brad's original story. Even without the mental-health aspect, there had been plenty of chaos in Brad's life, and he most certainly added chaos to mine. I read Bourdieu's concern as a caution, but only that. It is something to be aware of, but something I am not able to do much about.

I created this biographical illusion for both personal and professional reasons. As the report it was intended to be, the original piece—even without the appended snappy subtitle "The Life History of a Sneaky Kid"—seemed intrinsically interesting because it opened the door on a life to which academics like myself are not ordinarily privy. That project, I remind you, was completed before there was any hint of what lay ahead. The journey into schizophrenia opened another door. Whether or not Brad is "over it" (the prognosis is not very good, and there is no way I intend to disturb him to find out), I opened that door in recognition of the fact that the mentally ill are around us, and we must take responsibility for them. The court case was another eye-opener, as you may someday experience if you ever find yourself in court with neither side on your side and nothing to win, no matter what the outcome. Still, the lasting power of the Brad story is a phenomenon to behold, for now both printed and performance versions are with us today, some 20 years after the fact.

Considering Consequences

What lessons can we draw from examining this case? What general advice can I pass on to others wondering about the fate of their studies? What safeguards should they observe? I hope it is clear that there is no way one can ever anticipate every possible place a study might turn up, or what its effect might be. I was tempted to write, "how it might be used or misused," but that would add a moral dimension, suggesting that there are right and wrong messages to be derived. On that, I think we have to take our chances. We may have our hopes and preferences, but the uses to which our studies may be put are totally beyond our control once we make them available. Note only that they are created without malice; perhaps that is the quality that was missed in the courtroom.

We can make some effort to control circulation, but such efforts may draw attention as well as divert it. We can change names or locations in an effort to restrict the number of people in the know, but that tactic can backfire if those in the know take delight in letting outsiders know just who is who. There are other ways we try to protect our informants. I think it incumbent on every researcher to review how important it may be to honor tenets of confidentiality and anonymity, as well as to inform those among whom we conduct research that there are no absolute safeguards. Nor can we assume that confidentiality itself is necessarily desirable. In Brad's case, it was my concern for confidentiality, not his, that resulted in his pseudonym. As he aptly observed— aptly at the time, at least—"No one knows who I am anyhow."

Thinking now of the original Sneaky Kid piece as having started it all, the case illustrates the need to be accurate and compassionate in reporting, and modest in claims of what we have accomplished and what we understand. I was tempted to fall back on the old saw "First do no harm," but that would be a cop-out, for I do not believe one can do this kind of research at all without there being risk, if only by having attended to some things and ignored others. Even studies intended to paint a glowing picture can inadvertently produce stress among other groups equally deserving but not chosen.

I think the realistic approach is a risk/benefit analysis, a weighing of possible risks and negative consequences against whatever is to be gained. In this, I would give the edge to satisfying our basic curiosity about how other people identify the problems they must solve and how they go about solving them. A clear sense of purpose is the best overall guide, with details assessed on a case-by-case basis.

As much as I agonized over the fact that the Sneaky Kid piece was introduced in court, I do not think it harmed Brad, any more than it enhanced my esteem in the eyes of jurors. The psychiatrists discounted it as secondhand and claimed to have based their assessment of Brad as anti-social on the basis of earlier reports and Brad's own statements during interviews. I had wondered whether Brad would find his own misdeeds a bit brazen when he first read about them in my report, but they seemed to give him no pause. Although his peers, too, were essentially illusory, he had them in mind as he looked for anything that might create a poor impression. I have noted my tendency to keep the same thing from happening to me, particularly in the play.

There is little we can do to keep our studies from falling into the wrong hands or being used in ways we never could have predicted. But I think we can be more proactive in trying to reach audiences we *do* want to reach. I stand by the Sneaky Kid story as a good model. If my position is not yet clear, I personally regard the account as remarkably insightful from Brad's perspective and superbly crafted from my own. I felt it was much too good to be buried and forgotten in an obscure government publication.

Therefore I took, or, more accurately, made, an opportunity to publish it in the *Anthropology and Education Quarterly* when I assumed editorship of that journal, thereby ensuring that it would reach my closest professional associates. When I was asked to select an illustrative case to accompany my article on ethnographic research in a publication of the American Educational Research Association, I immodestly chose it once again, this time placing it in the hands of hundreds and hundreds of graduate students learning about qualitative research. Certainly not every author has such access at just the right time, but I helped to create those opportunities. It wasn't just luck! When I was able to convince publisher Mitch Allen to let me put together a book of readings of a number of my shorter pieces, there was the Sneaky Kid article again, this time joined by two subsequent articles, together forming the Brad Trilogy.

I did something else to promote the case, something I have consciously tried to do since first setting out on an academic career: I mentioned and cited these articles in my subsequent writing. I kept circling back to incorporate them in my thinking and writing, writing about research and about culture and about cultural acquisition. I never left my studies to flounder for themselves. I drew lessons from them, used them as examples, and reflected on their insights for new situations I faced.

I cannot say I have confronted and contained the idea of a biographical illusion; rather, I have endeavored to create that illusion. Looking back with a post hoc analysis, I can make sense of my career and what I know of Brad's career as well, placing odd bits and pieces into a mosaic that gives the appearance of order and logic. You expect to find such order in the careers of others, even though you know it isn't happening exactly that way in your own!

I turn now to some specific points I want to underscore. I begin with a discussion about ethics.

On Ethics

Blow all the blue smoke you wish about research ethics, but please, leave my work out of the discussions. Ethics as an abstract phenomenon seems a wholly desirable quality, a goal toward which—supposedly, at least—we all strive. In practice, ethics seems not to be something we attain but something we do not want others to find absent from our work. It is a quality noted in the breach.

I do not want my work challenged—and thus faulted—on ethical grounds. As far as I am concerned, one can be ethical or one can conduct social research, but one cannot be both ethical and a researcher in such settings.[1] I'll opt for the label of researcher. I'm prepared to take my lumps.

Matter of fact, I have been taking my lumps on ethical issues for years. I have grown weary of being confused for being ethical, or attacked for being unethical, when it is not a claim I wish to make or a standard against which I wish to be judged. I am more in tune with the declaration made some 20 years ago by Matthew Miles and Michael Huberman, that "fundamentally, field research is an act of betrayal, no matter how well intentioned or well integrated the researcher" (1984:233). Bless their hearts, they didn't back off from that stance when they revised their popular *Qualitative Data Analysis* a decade later:

> Field research can, at bottom, be considered as an act of betrayal, no matter how well intentioned or well integrated the researcher. You make the private public and leave the locals to take the consequences. [1994:265]

In my heart and soul, I like to think that I am as ethical as I can be and still do the research I have done. But I am finding it difficult to defend the claim and wearisome to argue it. It seems to get in the way, rather than open the way, to helping others understand what I do and how (and why) I go about it. What I hope to accomplish here is to invite—or dare—you to join me in rejecting ethics, to refuse to allow yourself to be boxed in by pretending to be something you cannot possibly be if you are active in field research.

Alternatively, if my position is anathema to you, I would like to back *you* into a corner where you can be not only ethical but *superethical*. The only condition I impose on you is that you never ever claim, or pretend, to conduct qualitatively oriented research into human social behavior. Management guru Peter Drucker once observed that people can either meet or work, but they cannot do both at the same time. I suggest a parallel in social inquiry: You can be ethical or you can conduct social research. You cannot do both. The reaction of that small but vocal minority voicing their objections to the production of *Finding My Place: The Brad Trilogy* at the Edmonton conference finally drove me to the position I take here. Forced to make a choice, I will side with the researchers.

I have been writing, and writing about, qualitative research for years. Since publication of my first book in 1967, there have always been at least a few ready to step forward and take issue with what I have written. Most often this has been collegial, constructive, and well intended. Taking a long view, I can even situate myself in what has been called the "age of ethics" in the kind of field research in which I engage. This was an age in which the ways and motives of the fieldworkers who were my models for research came under close scrutiny as we sought to reposition ourselves vis-à-vis those among whom we studied.

But since the publication of my Validity article in 1990, my detractors have included a different type of critic: one who sits in moral judgment of *me*. If you regard sexual behavior between same-sex, consenting adults, or the attraction of an older person for a younger one, as perforce unethical, unnatural, perverse, and so on—in other words, if your personal moral standards dominate your ethical ones, and they are so universal that you feel privileged to impose them on the world around you—then I doubt you can hear me even if you pretend to be listening.

But the problem for at least some readers was that I did not make clear enough, or forcefully enough, the order in which things happened. To misconstrue that order put me in a less-than-flattering light as a social scientist who abused his role by seducing his (somehow the term *powerless* always seems to creep in here) powerless young informant.

Or was it just that readers and listeners hear what they want to hear? For those who held me responsible for a seduction, rather than recognizing that I had made an informant of someone with whom I was having sex, judgments crept in before there was any opportunity, even any need, to hear the full story. The same is true for those who failed to recognize the relationship as a consenting one.

Books and articles go on to have lives of their own. There was no way I could add an explanatory footnote to the third piece in the Brad Trilogy once it was in print. From the moment I first presented the material, during the invitational symposium at Stanford, there were voices of criticism. There were voices of encouragement as well. I embraced them all, rather than feeling I ought to be, or needed to be, on the defensive.

The trilogy itself did not exist until the three pieces that comprise it were published under one cover in *Transforming Qualitative Data*. In that writing, I introduced each of the three pieces with a brief new discussion. Unfortunately, I paid too little heed to the fact that among a growing number of readers there were also a growing number of vocal critics offended by the relationship between Brad and me. They wanted to know why I failed to mention the nature of our personal relationship in the *original* life history, written almost a decade earlier.

In 1981, Brad's sexual behavior could be dismissed socially as "hustling," a behavior among younger men in dire straits that allowed such acts to be viewed as an economic necessity, and therefore forgivable. Brad certainly wasn't hustling me, but he had a ready alibi and he allowed it to be played heavily in the eventual trial. Although by then I had lived with my partner Norman for almost 15 years (and still live with him today, after almost 35), we were both teachers, and we had no desire to see how far we could push the boundaries at the time. Honoring diversity is easier said than done. We live in a seemingly enlightened era, but under the specter of fundamental (and the reality of fundamentalist) disapproval.

Controversy doesn't hurt book sales. Boldly stated fieldwork issues offer real cases that are valuable for seminar discussions, and the tenets of fieldwork as intimate, long-term acquaintance are indeed an invitation to moral disaster. I have encouraged and appreciated instructors who used the articles in *Transforming Qualitative Data,* especially the trilogy included in it, to raise such issues.

If anything, my effort to encourage more candor in reporting may have taught just the opposite, that efforts to be candid are likely to be costly. There was no consideration of whether these things can and do happen in fieldwork. For me, the lesson is that ethics and research are ill suited to each other. It appears safer to take the moral high ground than to allow oneself to become a truly human instrument.

There is safety in numbers. My counsel for those who want to take the ethical high road is to stick with numbers. Make your samples so large that no one runs any risk in gathering or examining the data. Of course, one can put entire populations at risk that way, but as long as the numbers are large enough, you are more likely to be applauded for what you uncover than for any discomfort you cause.

Protection of Human Subjects Versus Institutionalization of the Protection of Human Subjects

I am not opposed to keeping confidences and respecting the rights and privacy of those whose lives we invade, but I do not think such declarations can be made in absolute terms. Casting this process in words suggesting that those among whom we study need to be protected from us also gets us off to a poor start. These days, it is often researchers who need to be protected: from their human subjects, from those who assume responsibility for protecting those subjects, and from those who use their authority to silence unwelcome findings or to purchase the results they desire.

I am dead set against the end result of the collective concern for human subjects that has resulted in the procedures formally designed to confer that protection through Institutional Review Boards (IRBs). Most certainly there have been circumstances where harm—psychological, and sometimes even physical—has come to people being researched. But the machinery that has evolved to protect them is a boondoggle that has turned human research into a bureaucratic nightmare, a series of steps and procedures designed ultimately to protect only the institutions themselves. They also provide busywork for a largely self-selected coterie of research monitors.

I came of age in research before such policies were institutionalized. By remaining calculatedly uninformed, I have generally managed to escape them. The best advice I can offer to researchers confronting formal review procedures—and these days this includes virtually all researchers—is to treat the bureaucratic process with about as much reverence as you would in renewing your driver's license. Do what you have to do, tell them what you need to tell them (i.e., what they need to hear), and get on with it. Ethics are not housed in such procedures.

Some awfully petty personnel find comfort in enforcing some awfully petty rules, which takes up the valuable time of others trying to keep them from completely closing down the discovery-oriented approaches qualitative researchers follow. An example is the notion of obtaining written consent, so easily insisted on by an IRB, so impossible in some situations and impractical in others. Today, one is expected at least to speak to the issue of informed consent in most research. If nothing more, it is another box to be checked in the inventory of deeds and possible misdeeds.

I once had a person in authority tell a doctoral student planning to do research in a village that she would need a signed permission slip from everyone in the village before she could even begin her study. Another student returning to her native country to conduct research was told that she would have to get a signed consent form from every villager she intended to interview that explained that their names would not be used! And, in the spirit of retroactive protection, the editor of a scholarly journal inquired whether I had on file a permission slip from everyone who attended a potlatch event about which I wrote, an audience numbering in the hundreds.

The only time I ever requested formal consent in any study I have ever done was from Brad himself. I did it as much to inform him how research was conducted as to ratify his permission to use what he had volunteered. I prepared a brief form on letterhead stationery for his signature. He read it. Then, in his customary impatient style, he tore it up, informing me that he would write his own release. He did it with a simple sentence or two. Far more important to him, as he came to realize but could not anticipate, was my assurance that I would turn off the tape recorder any time he wanted to go off the record, and that he could read and critique what I had drafted. He was willing to give my completed draft one reading. He was not even particularly interested in doing that until I told him I would pay him for his reading time as well as his interview time.

Ethics in the Brad Story

Please be aware of my intent. Although confession may be good for the soul, I have not undertaken this examination of the Brad saga to unburden myself. My purpose is to serve reminder that qualitative research is laden with such problems. If you are going to pursue qualitative work, your agony will not so much be about the violations themselves as whether or not, or to what extent, you will choose to disclose them. The yet-to-be-discovered secret is why the topic has not been addressed more candidly and more often, for these are realities in fieldwork.[2]

Ethically, I do not find as much to fault with the Brad study as have my critics. Brad himself was satisfied with the initial account as drafted. Certain of his exploits that I thought he might wish deleted or at least muted (breaking into houses, stealing bicycles, a failed attempt at robbery) gave him no pause. His concern seemed to be for an imagined audience of peers who might fault some of his word choices. He even expressed the wish that his story might help people to "understand," although exactly what he meant was never clear.

I doubt that either of Brad's parents held me in high esteem, but ethics do not reside in the esteem people have for one another. In their view, I assume that I am seen as the one responsible for his landing in prison. I don't hold them in high esteem, either, in a general sense for throwing him out so early and so often (though, admittedly, he was a handful), and in a particular sense for failing to warn me that he had returned to Oregon with the stated intent to do harm. With fair warning, they easily might have prevented all this; they chose to look the other way. I will always wonder whether they intentionally chose the option that allowed Brad both to wreak his revenge *and* to be locked away.

During the trial, Brad's mother was overheard remarking, "I suppose Harry will get another book out of this." True, but the book has been a long time coming, and the story has not produced a fortune. Did the Brad story bring fame and notoriety? Perhaps the answer is yes, especially if the terms are taken literally. Did the story make my career as a researcher? The order in which I conducted my research studies should dispel that notion: The Brad sequence was the last of my fieldwork ventures, not the first. My more recent writing has focused on issues of method. I wondered at the time of the trial whether the account might bring my entire professional career to a halt, which it did not. But, most certainly, neither did it launch it.

What dismayed me at the time of the trial was that my case study— Brad's account of his life as volunteered in his own words—was introduced as evidence *against him* in the trial proceedings. Not much was actually made of the article, but the jury had it as an exhibit, and under the circumstances it hardly offered testimony to his stalwart nature. I cannot imagine a worse professional nightmare than having a life story collected for research purposes being introduced as evidence against the person who gave it.

In a deep and personal way, Brad's own ethics disappointed me. He turned the nature of our relationship around to make me out to be the bad guy in what I would wager were the best years of his life. But I understood where he was coming from. Once he had committed the assault and arson, the only thing he could do was make me appear culpable. He managed to do that with both a literal and figurative vengeance. Know this: Were similar circumstances to occur today, knowing what I now know of the risks involved, I would probably let another Brad take refuge on my place. I have never been sorry for letting him stay or for becoming involved with him. I have been deeply grieved at how it all turned out, and deeply sorry if there was something I might have done that would have helped. My sorrow does not reach the depths of remorse, just a wish that it all might have turned out differently.

Over the course of the past 40 years, I have made some good ethical decisions and some not-so-good ones. I have made no decisions that I deeply regret. Sometimes I have been ethical where I did not need to be, in the sense that what I regarded as ethical did not matter to someone else, and what they regarded as ethical did not look that way to me. But my ethics in the Brad case are intact. You can find more serious breaches in my other studies, if you really need to. But if you do, you are heading away from doing your own research and into looking at the research of those about you. That is the only way you can be superethical.

Finding "Typical" Cases

Watching helplessly as Brad seemed to drift away from reality in his last weeks at the cabin, I could not believe that under my very eyes I was seeing someone slip into mental illness (or mental illness slip into him). At the time, I felt one could read the signs either way, that it was a passing phase of depression that Brad might have been playing up, or a sign of something deeper, to which he was unwittingly surrendering. For Brad, those days were both the best of times and the worst of times. His sometime job as a landscape-gardener's helper resulted in the unusual event of an occasional payday. He purchased (purchased!) a few things that made life at the cabin pleasanter, including a fancy two-burner campstove.

But by the final week preceding his departure (several weeks after that purchase), nothing seemed to be going right. Brad had explored the possibility of joining the armed services, and, at my gentle but persistent urging, he had been to the county mental-health clinic. Now he delivered the final ulti-matum: He was leaving. Yet he seemed to have no idea where he would go, or what he was hoping to find there.

It seemed unlikely that introducing a world of uncertainties would stabi-lize him, and once he departed, there was no way I could learn of his fate unless he contacted me. Telephoning his mother was not a consideration; he had been adamant about not returning there. I felt that a call to her would only introduce needless worry if she felt any concern for him at all, and at that point I doubted she did. Brad had made it quite clear that he would not be welcome in his stepfather's house. To my surprise, it was Brad's mother's call to me, weeks after Brad left the cabin, that brought word of his travels and troubled state of mind, which by then had become acute.

I began thinking and writing about the different set of options that Brad had considered in his final weeks at the cabin, but it was clear that the one that had become a reality was the mental-health issue. If his mother had overstated the case by describing him as "insane," it was nevertheless apparent that his behavior was anything but normal. What I had observed just prior to his depar-ture were the early signs of a full-blown psychosis. Helplessly watching that hap-pen to a young and otherwise healthy person who desperately needed to keep his wits about him was to experience tragedy in the making. I had watched from the first undetected moments as the tragedy began to unfold, and Brad went from OK to not OK, from normal to not normal. To this day, I find the memory of those circumstances sad and depressing: a physically capable and healthy young body deprived of its complement in a mentally capable and healthy mind. Rose-colored glasses? Perhaps. But I never embraced the idea of Brad as hopelessly anti-social, only as someone who had taken a long way to come around.

Initially, I was sorry to see the mental-health issue elevated to the posi-tion of a major player in the continuing Brad saga. But never for a minute have I felt any remorse about having sex with him, and/or subsequently doing a life story with him. Had he not returned as he did, the personal aspect of our relationship need never have been made public. It was strictly a private matter until he chose to make it otherwise.

In that, the mental illness played a major role. Once I learned that he had not miraculously snapped out of it, that his mental condition had worsened into something serious, I wondered what effect his present mental condition had on the veracity of the Sneaky Kid account. In the original interviews, as well as in all but the last few months of his two years at the cabin, Brad had expressed and demonstrated an idea of who he was and what he was up to. That was what made his story compelling. Looking back on the account now as the ramblings of a madman, might everything be reinterpreted as signs of impending mental illness waiting patiently in the wings? After all, don't crazy people do crazy things?

I realized that what I wanted was to normalize Brad, to make him appear as typical as possible, in order to lend credibility to the case study. I wanted the case to be generalizable. Every qualitative researcher faces dilemmas like this, anxious to be acknowledged for recognizing what is unique to an individual case, but equally anxious to have the case recognized for its broader implications. Here is one place where research ethics really reside, cautioning against making more or less of certain aspects of an investigation, so as to present the case in its best light.

I decided early on to bite the bullet, to raise the question (or specter) of the mental-health issue, without letting it overwhelm the case. In the "Cultural Alternatives to Career Alternatives" piece drafted soon after I heard from his mother, I wrote:

> If the case [i.e., the previously published Sneaky Kid account] is diminished because its young protagonist crossed a psychological threshold and lost some touch with reality, there is still something to be learned.
>
> As noted, being a paid and full-time crazy person is becoming an "occupation" for a discernible portion of our population, a social group whose distinguishing economic characteristic is that they are remunerated on the basis of their incompetence rather than their competence. Further, no one is crazy all the time. Even during the moments when they do act crazily, the cultural repertoire from which so-called crazy people draw remains essentially the same as for those around them. Even inappropriateness must be exercised in culturally appropriate ways. In his paranoia, Brad did not bury his fingernail clippings, cast a magic spell over his cabin and belongings, stick pins in voodoo dolls, or run amok. Rather, he hitchhiked a thousand miles, cast about for several weeks, and then suddenly began making collect telephone calls to his mother from freeway points conveniently accessible from her home, insisting that he was broke, hungry, and lost. [Wolcott 1987:323–24]

I was tempted to make Brad seem as normal as possible so that I could counter the inevitable challenge, "But is this case really typical?" We are bedeviled by the idea, and ideal, of randomness, as though it is somehow sinful to select the cases we study. Students being introduced to research are enjoined to employ the model of our quantitatively oriented associates and let some external system choose our subjects for us. When that seemingly desirable procedure is impossible or impractical (as is usually the case in qualitative study), then we strive to identify cases that are "typical," and thus at least somewhat representative of the phenomenon under study.

That is an unfortunate misreading of research. First, a caution about the merits of random sampling. I take my maxim from something I learned from sociologist Robert Dubin, that we only randomize when we don't know what we are doing—that is, when we don't have any idea of the population from which our cases are drawn. If you want to study shopping behavior at a Saturday market, you don't randomize the days of the week, you observe on days when you expect something to happen. You make the most informed selection you can according to the purposes of your study.

True, in the selection of informants or cases or villages, we may have little or no choice. Pure randomization is usually out of the question. You hope that you can find one of a kind where there is any possibility of doing research at all. Margaret Mead wrote to this issue years ago in what she described as the problem of "anthropological sampling" (Mead 1953:654). I find her answer instructive and reassuring. I pass her advice along even though she is no longer in the quoting circle of the current generation of fieldworkers. You may wish to take her answer for your own in responding to the objection that our cases are not, and can never be, selected at random:

> *It is simply a different kind of sampling*, in which the validity of the sample depends not so much upon the number of cases as upon the proper specification of the informant, so that he or she can be accurately placed, in terms of a very large number of variables. . . . Each informant is studied as a perfect example, an organic representation of his complete cultural experience. [Mead 1953:654–55]

Seasoned fieldworkers are all too aware that the individuals most willing to talk to us are often marginal to their own group, or at least are not typical of other insiders. But that observation can be turned around to ask just who is ever typical or representative. Instead of trying to inventory the features that would make an individual average, and then hoping to identify and enlist such an individual, Mead points a way that allows us to work with whoever is willing to work with us. Or, as in Brad's case, whoever happens along.

With no exact idea of how to proceed, I had been looking for a learner. But for months after Brad happened along, it still had not occurred to me that here was a perfect example of a learner, and right in my backyard. From an anthropological perspective, I knew only that I did not want to focus on school learning. I wanted to look at education in its broadest sense.

Brad was a learner. That's all I needed. He could be accurately placed within a wider community of learners. Qualitative sampling cannot answer questions of frequency or distribution—those questions must be researched in other ways. There are other Brads out there—that was enough to satisfy my purposes. And if Brad headed into mental problems, that, too, could be specified. If one were to count him among the homeless—living in a crude shelter without amenities or address—then the fact of mental illness actually served to make him more, rather than less, typical. I did not seek Brad out, nor did he seek me. When our paths crossed and I eventually invited him to be my informant for a brief life story, I did not concern myself with his typicality.

I can attest to the fact that there never was and never will be anyone quite like Brad. But according to syndicated columnist Bob Herbert, who is published in my daily newspaper, there are now "nearly 5 million people aged 16 to 24 who are both out of school and out of work." The article continues:

> These youngsters live their troubled lives beneath the radar of most public-policy planners. They are jobless, but most of them are not even counted as unemployed. To be officially "unemployed" you have to be actively looking for work.[3]

For purposes of a case study, I did not need a random sample drawn from a population of 5 million. I had only to identify the characteristics that help to specify where Brad fit into a larger picture. In this case, the picture was of a white middle-class homeless suburban youth. Mead categorized her subjects with a number of such characteristics ("variables," as she referred to them): "age, sex, order of birth, family background, life-experience, temperamental tendencies (such as optimism, habit of exaggeration, etc.), political and religious position, exact situational relationship to the investigator, configurational relationship to every other informant, and so forth" (1953:655). Such a list of properties could be expanded indefinitely. Mead wanted only to suggest some ways that an individual can be placed in a broader context and still be a perfect example.

The purposes of the research help determine the relevant characteristics to be identified. As to the "exact situational relationship to the investigator," I think she would have been satisfied with what I reported, not condemned me for what I did not disclose. Writing in the 1950s as she was, anthropologists were still having to be encouraged to put themselves into the settings they were describing! Give me credit for doing that!

I could have done without the mental-health issue. I could have done nicely without the violence, and without the agonizing trial and subsequent prison sentence. I would just as soon have continued to look through rose-colored glasses, if that is what I was doing. But these elements became part of the case. My initial reaction to each untoward event was a lament that it made the case less typical. On reflection, they all may have contributed to making it more timely, more in tune with the reality of everyday life. Anthropologist Arthur Kleinman has written:

> I would hazard the suggestion . . . that the search for social theories of the human misery of violence, poverty, and oppression will preoccupy the next generation of ethnographers. [1995:241]

Voilà! Brad has dragged me (battered and bruised rather than kicking and screaming, I'm afraid) into the concerns of the next generation of ethnographers. I would rather not be here. But here I am.

On Serendipity

Which brings us to a consideration of serendipity in research. Pursuing the case study led in directions I would never have anticipated. The beauty of a discovery approach is that one is free to follow leads suggested by the case itself. From the very first, Brad's life and explanations led to circumstances I might never have faced or understood.

Without the strictures of hypotheses carefully formulated in advance, fieldwork reaches its apex as an act of discovery, not through earth-shaking revelations but in discerning patterns of behavior and our human capacity for both creating and coping with problems. There are always choices to be made in pursuing a course of research—one cannot venture down every path and make any headway toward a destination. But if one can maintain an openness to inquiry without losing focus, our studies can be as unpredictable for us as are the uses that others may make of them.

The Brad story serves as case in point, looking back over its impact on my thinking and subsequent experience. I'd read a lot about alienated youth, I'd just never met any. Nor was I particularly conscious of the fact that the term itself is no longer in fashion. The labels keep changing; the problems seem to remain. In classes and seminars, I often included books and articles dealing with the topic of alienation. My experience as a teacher in an Indian village on the west coast of Canada put me somewhat at the forefront in discussing problems of cultural diversity in the schools. An early and frequently reprinted article from that experience, "The Teacher as an Enemy" (Wolcott 1974), helped establish that my experience with such students was firsthand and insightful. It was also quite limited.

My experience of dropouts, delinquents, the homeless, and the unemployed was of the same order: I was familiar with the literature, read reports and statistics, and served on doctoral committees dealing with the topic. I'd just never met any. My firsthand experience with these social categories remains about the same today. Living in a medium-size community in the Pacific Northwest, on the outskirts of a city where it is still possible to have a 20-acre plot and live within five miles of a large university, I remain buffered from the realities of urban blight and people who live unusually hard lives. Realistically speaking, if I was ever to have informal contact with these problems—that is, contact outside of my role as professor or researcher—they would have to come to me.

In the form of Brad, they did: alienated youth, dropout, delinquent, homeless, unemployed, all rolled up into one 19-year-old. Who stayed. I try to avoid categorizing people, but, in any case, the negative categories are not the ones that would have come to mind except that I had never known anyone on food stamps. It had not occurred to me that a physically able youth would be a recipient of, and dependent on, them. But I also saw a more admirable set of characteristics: rugged individualism, resourcefulness, bravado, daring, and craftiness (in both a good and less-good sense). He was a keep-to-yourself kind of person, not a type you necessarily would associate with in social circles, but a person you would be glad to have as an ally in the face of adversity. I could not help but be curious as to how he survived, which, in his own terms, was what he was doing. How did he go about it, what were his days like, his thoughts for the future, his worries?

I gained some insight into most aspects of his life, but it was slow work. We did not see much of each other for the first several months he was on the place, although there were occasional jobs on which I needed help, and I recognized his need for cash. I realized that his attitude toward other people's property probably included our property as well, but living at the edge of town, and being away weekdays, we had always been careful about locking things up, house and tools especially.

I found his arguments convincing for living the way he was living. I recognized that his choice of a spot on which to build his cabin did put him at a disadvantage for taking a job in town, even if he had been able to find one. The cabin site was about 700 feet above the floor of the valley. Getting back to it after a trip to town meant a steep climb, the final portion on an often-muddy trail. My delinquent, dropout, homeless, unemployed homesteader became instead a woodsman-survivalist, his choice of options nicely rationalized.

I found myself wondering how society could help him do what he had set out to do. I was surprised to discover how little it helped, how much it threatened. In society's terms, he was still a delinquent, dropout, homeless, unemployed youth.

Trial by Trial

Second only to the shock of finding Brad inside my house, intent on doing harm, was the shock of the trial as case and case study of the American justice system. Serendipity found me there, and an anthropological perspective helped me get through it, but I am saddened by the experience. As with my vague notion of what psychologists and psychiatrists do and how they go about making their judgments, my expectations for the courts were based on idealized notions of how things should work, not how they actually do. I wonder if that has not been my lifelong engagement with anthropology: studying how social systems really work, as contrasted with how I have been led to believe they should work.

I have described what I perceive as a paradox in how this trial proceeded, that under the guise of gathering as much evidence as possible, the mechanisms for introducing evidence worked instead to restrict information and to bundle as much information as possible into either/or issues often irrelevant to the case. Two attorneys conducted the trial; theirs were the only questions to be answered. Objections raised to questions or answers served constantly to interrupt the train of thought. The defense attorney grasped at straws to delve into irrelevant aspects of a case of assault and arson.

The question before the jury was whether Brad could "conform" his behavior and pursue his anti-social acts, or whether he was driven by mental forces that overrode his ability to control himself. As it was fairly clear that he remained essentially in control, having waited two and a half years before returning, one would have been hard-pressed to insist that he could exert no control, although I will forever wonder how, or even whether, he was able to control himself at the height of the skirmish. He did, after all, douse me with gasoline. He did not know whether or not I was in the house when he set it afire. It was interesting that the judge hearing the case harbored reservations about Brad's sanity. Although he followed the jury's instructions, he took care to see that Brad received psychological counseling and that he be placed in a special program in prison.

But I found the proceedings themselves, although giving an appearance of exceptional civility, to be exceedingly rude. The lines of questioning were allowed to go far astray. The time spent on everything except the disagreement among the two psychiatrists was irrelevant. The whole trial was a waste of money: six months after Brad confessed to the crimes, the jury discovered that, yes, he did it. Summoning people to testify and then working to discredit everything they said, and asking questions in such a way that they could not be answered, were both counterproductive and demeaning.

Sensing how often the defense counsel was asking convoluted, nonsensical questions, at one point I made an effort to let him swing in the breeze, at least for a while. I insisted he repeat one of his badly phrased questions. He stumbled in doing so, and I asked the court recorder to read the question back because I still could not discern a question in his rambling. The court recorder read back from the stenographer's tape as well as she could, until she had to confess, "I didn't get it." I got my two cents in by adding, "Welcome to the club" (which she did get). But I had long grown impatient with the way I was being treated—bullied, really—and my regard for the court is a consequence of the regard I felt the court had for me.

To be there because of Brad was the last thing I wanted, and to be his adversary was unthinkable. It was not a trial in which justice eventually triumphed, but in which everyone lost everything, dignity included. Somehow I anticipated that when it was all over, everyone would feel OK about it, that at least there had been a fair hearing of relevant issues. When the trial did finally end and the verdict was announced, Brad reportedly snapped his fingers and shrugged his shoulders, in a manner suggesting, "That's the way it goes." An unannounced verdict was that Brad's court-appointed defense attorney was the worst thing that could have happened to him.

Several weeks went by before Brad's sentencing, so the suspense was not over for him. Norman and I were glad to be leaving town and heading out of the country for a year, where we would no longer wonder what the local paper had to say about us or the trial.

Where do our studies go, and what do they do there? The Sneaky Kid, both as article and as the real thing, went to trial, and that part of the story would seem to have ended there. I did not know that the verdict had been appealed about a month after sentencing. As might have been expected, the point of appeal was as irrelevant as most of the trial to the issue of Brad's sanity. It dealt with whether the judge's ruling about the nature of any other of the *victim's* (i.e., my) prior homosexual relationships was germane to the case. Might the existence of any such relationships have been of consequence in the determination of this one? Based upon another ponderous 15-page legal document, the (public) attorneys for Brad, now referred to as "the defendant-appellant," respectfully requested that the conviction be reversed.

You may make what you want of the appeal court's reply affirming the judgment of the circuit court in disallowing such testimony. I see it as a reprimand, and a severe one, of the defense counsel. Not really worth my waiting 15 years for, but I had no idea that an appeal had been filed or acted upon. Here is the summary statement:

> The fatal flaw in defendant's argument, which was never addressed below or
> on appeal, is the complete lack of relevancy of the victim's prior homosexual

activity to defendant's alleged mental disease or defect. Defendant's motive for introducing this evidence is clear; he sought to prejudice the jury about the victim's lifestyle rather than establish any evidence of his alleged mental disease. However, the victim's character was not at issue. Defendant's conduct and his responsibility for this conduct was the issue. The trial court did not err in excluding this totally irrelevant and unduly prejudicial testimony.

That statement, though unlikely to see the light of day or ever come to my knowledge, was signed by the then–attorney general of the state, who later became president at my university. Why none of this was ever made known to me, the victim, tends further to diminish whatever feelings I might have had that ultimately justice will prevail. They are compounded by my bitterness that the man who so ineptly presented Brad's case and so thoroughly disparaged me was subsequently appointed to a judgeship. Judge not.

The fact of the appeal has one further consequence for the Brad saga. Whether or not an appeal is successful, a judicial review elevates a circuit court trial to the status of law. Future cases can be argued on the basis of the findings of this one. So in the annals of Oregon state law, there will exist forever a case to which I here give a pseudonym: *State of Oregon v. Brad*. With court costs, prosecutor and public defender costs, psychiatric examinations, and years of institutionalization, that was one expensive addition to the law library!

On Intimacy

I could not possibly identify all the places where our studies might turn up. But surely this inquiry into where one study went suggests how far afield they can go. At that, I seriously doubt that I have identified all the places where the Brad Trilogy made an appearance, or all the uses to which it may have been put. Even estimating readership is impossible, for the original Sneaky Kid account first appeared in a journal that is sent to many academic libraries. It may have been read, or copied, in uncounted numbers. Not even publishers can be relied on for accurate records of book sales, especially when the current owner is not the original publisher.

At the same time, I hope I have not made a bigger issue out of the case than is warranted, or given it a more prominent role in the annals of qualitative research than it deserves. What I have intended to underscore is that we never know how our studies will be used or where they will go. Nor is there any way to guarantee that they will go anywhere at all.

If you would like to help your studies attain wider attention than they might otherwise enjoy, you will have to stump on their behalf, as I did with the original Sneaky Kid article, and as I have done now with the entire trilogy. Most certainly I suggest that you draw on your earlier studies in analyzing and interpreting subsequent ones, constantly circling back for deeper insights and a broader perspective. In that way you not only make fuller use of your own work but provide a model for less experienced scholars who may think it in vogue to deny their earlier research so as to appear more mature and sophisticated.

From the experience reported here, it is probably safe to say that another way to gain notoriety—a surefire way, it would seem—is to include an element of scandal or sex in the account. "Only recently," writes anthropologist Sally Cole, "have some anthropologists begun to be frank about having acted as sexual selves in the field—and not always to the critical acclaim of colleagues" (Cole 1995:178). That "safe sex" warning cautions you to restrict your observations to reporting on the activities of others—what they do or are reported doing with each other—rather than on your own involvement. Even reporting on the intimate relationships of others, especially if you have not made it clear to your subjects that you intended to make that an aspect of the research, can lead to a sense of betrayal that puts future fieldwork, particularly your own, in jeopardy.

I should not pass up the opportunity to underscore that in this case it was Brad's betrayal of our relationship that precipitated the problems that developed. I attribute that betrayal to a mind beset by illusion that I simply got mixed up in. It was not that we did not have sex. We did. We enjoyed it at the time. There should have been no regrets afterward. When Brad started enjoying it less and became distracted with other thoughts, we stopped.

Perish the thought of another confrontation, but if Brad has regained or ever will regain his wits, I doubt that he would be able to offer what I could accept as a satisfactory explanation for what happened, or why I became the fall guy for his troubles and troubled mind. I think we would argue endlessly over who started it. I can live with his observation that I was "more consenting" than he was. I took the lead; he followed. I would remind him that he knew Norman and I were in a longtime relationship. An attractive young man like him does not take down his pants to ask if his penis "looks all right" with no thought as to what may follow. Rather than bear the wrath of his mother for his hustling activities after he left the cabin, it was easier for him to put the blame, now encased in guilt, on me. He had convinced me of his amoral nature; now he needed to rediscover his moral one to get back into his mother's good graces as he once again became dependent on her. That's what I think happened. It just happened to be with someone who cared about him—perhaps, like poor Othello, not wisely but too well.

But there is opportunity lost if the case is not probed further for a critical issue it raises about the role of intimacy in fieldwork. Most of my detractors' energies have gone into examining issues of *my* behavior, or condemnation of *my* actions as a researcher, rather than looking at the broader question of intimacy itself. Intimacy is an issue of degree. How intimate is intimate, and how much intimacy is allowed, condoned, even essential in fieldwork? What does it mean to describe fieldwork, at least the ethnographically oriented approach that many of us pursue, as "intimate, long-term acquaintance"?

I did not invite Brad to do the life story project on the basis of our sexual intimacy. I did assume our intimacy to be a clear advantage, because I believed that it would allow us to discuss virtually any aspect of his life. That he remained guarded in his revelations surprised me; nonetheless, I felt I knew him better than anyone I had ever worked with in a formal research capacity, and at least as well as those with whom I interact informally. Age and circumstances separated us—formidable barriers, but not impossible ones.

I daresay this is not the first time a researcher has become sexually involved with someone in the group under study—nor will it be the last. Unfortunately, what has happened as a consequence of such cases means that it is probably less likely that we will see an outpouring of such revelations in the near future. Granted, there have always been a few brave souls willing to tell more than expected. But what can we offer by way of guidelines or advice to future fieldworkers?

An easy cop-out is to suggest the same guideline that helps with the issue of level of detail: Delve as deeply as necessary to answer the research question. That ought to keep instructors in safe territory when discussing a dicey topic in class. But intimacy is also a matter of the heart, of emotions, of physiological response as well as intellectual response. And it has a negative side as well. How do we cope with individuals whom we despise, those who stir no feelings or stir strong antipathy in us? Do we pretend to hide such emotions from ourselves, to claim an objectivity we know we do not have?

Viewed in terms of risks and benefits, the issue of intimacy is an aspect of fieldwork that warrants deliberation. What we need, however, is not resolution but a heightened sensitivity toward the problem. It is up to the individual fieldworker to map the course for each situation. Platitudes are an easy starting place, but it is important for each fieldworker to recognize the distinction between real and ideal behavior. It is crucial to be honest in such matters. The degree of candor appropriate for one's various audiences will always vary with the circumstances and, especially, with the times.

Our attention should be directed to one's comportment *during* fieldwork, rather than how revealing one intends to be about it afterward. A number-one rule should be to not be dishonest about anything one says, which is not to say that one is therefore advised to reveal everything. Whoever said that discretion is the better part of valor coined a good aphorism for fieldworkers. I think fieldworkers are better prepared when sent into the field alert to the *issue* of intimacy than armed with a set of rules to follow. Neophytes caught between Human Subject Review Boards on the one hand and their moralizing mentors on the other—faculty teaching about research but not doing it—may more often need encouragement about how to achieve sufficient intimacy than warned against its obvious excesses. I find it easier to look for what constitutes too little intimacy for authentic fieldwork than to come up with platitudes for guarding against excess.

A good starting place is to be more revealing about ourselves. In our sometimes grim determination to learn all we can about the individuals with whom we conduct research, we forget that others can be quite curious about us, including why we are curious about them. One can marvel at how much fieldworkers have been able to learn and report about the lives of others. On reflection, I think one can also marvel at how incomplete is our knowledge, even of those close to us.

Muddy Waters

The problem of intimacy, as it unfolded in the Brad Trilogy and was discussed in *The Art of Fieldwork* (Wolcott 1995), became the basis for an ongoing discussion among a group of six researchers at the University of Vermont. They labeled their group "Muddy Waters," aptly describing the difficult issues they were tackling. The group jointly authored one of the rejoinders to Reba Page's article "Teaching About Validity" that appeared in *Qualitative Studies in Education* and was discussed in chapter 6 here. As they reported in their response:

> Our dialogue gradually evolved . . . into a deep, reflective conversation about the complexity and power of intimate human relationships generally, and in research, specifically. We began to consider and acknowledge intimacy as a unique medium for learning. In juxtaposing our perspectives on learning-through-intimacy to the Brad Trilogy, our central question surfaced: If intimacy is a route to understanding, what should we, as researchers, consider as we engage intimately in relationships as part of our research? [Busier, Clark, Esch, Glesne, Pigeon, and Tarule 1997:165]

The Brad Trilogy did, indeed, muddy the waters. It presented their group with a complex case in which their professional sympathies lay with the researcher role, but their concerns were for the researched, interpreted through a feminist perspective as an imbalance of power. And power, they cautioned, cannot be ignored in intimate relationships: "A certain discomfort remains around using data obtained through intimate relationships or, at least, from relationships that breach celibacy, that are viewed as too intimate" (1997:165–66).

Yet they also recognized, following feminist researcher Patricia Maguire, that "without close, empathetic, interpersonal interchange and relationships, researchers will find it impossible to gain meaningful insights into human interaction or to understand the meaning people give to their own behavior" (Maguire 1987:20–21). They were left with questions that I relay to you: How can we achieve "a comfortable balance between revealing too much or not enough about our intimate relationships in our attempts to enable readers to understand our work and to share in our discovery"(Busier, et al. 1997:167)? And, can one ever retell *all* the understanding that emerges from an intimate relationship (p. 168)? For, as they note, the only thing as challenging as getting tangled in the "underbrush of relationships" is trying to write about them.

As the Muddy Waters group speculated about what they called the "Brad/Harry connection," they found themselves disclosing more and more personal information about and among themselves. They began struggling with how to connect their personal lives with their professional ones. The Brad saga was a catalyst for introspection into their own roles—both as researchers and as women.

Where do our studies go? Sometimes they seem to get to just the right place, and to do something worthwhile there. My own foibles, although duly inventoried in the group's brief response, appeared to be forgiven as they realized that fieldworker relationships with those they study are the critical issue. They concluded:

> We are grateful for the way that Wolcott's willingness to take risks in the research community has provoked such conversations as the Muddy Waters one. We may have gotten here without the Brad Trilogy, but we doubt we would have done so as quickly or as passionately. [p. 169]

In their response, the Muddy Waters group commented, "In recent years, a few researchers have been forthcoming about intimate relationships which resulted from fieldwork experiences" (p. 166). From the citations they included, I would say the number of researchers has been few indeed. They identified only two (Cesara 1982; Cole 1995), and, of course, added the Brad Trilogy to the list for readers unfamiliar with it. However, as the group noted, an intimate relationship may or may not involve a sexual one, and a physical relationship does not automatically make a relationship intimate (p. 165).

Perhaps I have been presumptuous in implying that Brad's and my relationship was intimate. What I said in the Validity chapter was that our relationship became physical, which leaves the question open to speculation, my own included. I am not sure that Brad had an intimate side. Turning again to the psychological problems to which he eventually succumbed, intimacy may have been one of the experiences denied him. The physical sex may only have been practice for one of the roles he was prepared to assume. The hugs may have been far more important. The sex was satisfying at the time and became invaluable as a rationalization for his later behavior. He never voiced any objection to the hugs. Ever!

The important thing for fieldworkers is the nature of intimacy in an activity defined as "intimate, long-term acquaintance." What we have in the literature are mostly platitudes and cautions. The experiences I have reported with Brad and the Brad Trilogy are not likely to encourage fieldworkers to be more forthcoming. But if you can't take "heady candor" as a personal mantra, you can at least come to grips with the question—and your own resolution—of how intimate you want, intend, and need to be in order to achieve the level of understanding you seek. This will necessitate a careful delineation of exactly what you mean by intimacy. The questions may best be served by using other, less ambiguous terms than intimacy itself.

Among the different disciplines that pursue qualitative approaches, intimacy has a wide range of interpretations. And I am sure that male and female notions can be far, far apart, even among close colleagues. If the Brad story offers a way to raise questions of fieldwork practice to a new level, I would say it has performed a good service. I hope I have not inadvertently raised such concern to a new level of caution. To assuage doubt, let me leave you with a question that the account raises for me: Can one ever be intimate enough in learning about the life of another?

Only Connect

It all began with a rather straightforward idea: to write a brief life story of an out-of-school youth and to examine the influences on his life. This has been the story of what happened as a result. More than 20 years later, the story is still unfolding. It amply demonstrates how we can keep some stories alive at least partially through our own efforts. But it certainly is true that not all the things that happen are what one hopes or intends. I counsel you to make your stories as accurate and as complete as you intend when you release them. While you may exercise some control over some of the places they go, you cannot possibly imagine all the places they may go or what they might do there.

Brad is not the only person in my life or the only thought in my head. In these same 20 years, I have taught a lot, learned a lot more, and generally done a heap of living. But I admit to having made Brad something of a preoccupation. That is because he kept recurring in my own life story. I have chosen to link these themes rather than treat them as isolated events. Brad's physical presence is limited to the two years when he lived here, a period ending shortly after his 21st birthday, now 20-plus years ago. Since then, I have been the one to weave activities into the sequence you have here. Were Norman writing this, Brad's entry into our lives would have been brief and unremarked. As for Brad himself—were he inclined toward such endeavors—anything to do with me might disappear altogether.

I have tried to show how the Brad story touched many facets of research, finally settling most resolutely in discussions of ethics and intimacy. That is not because those are key facets of his being here, but because they are key facets that interest us today in research. I would like to think that I have had some influence on your thinking about the role of the mentally ill as well. I am convinced that we already see more of such folk around and increasingly will be expected to cope with them on a daily basis rather than simply wish them away.

I have never been sorry for allowing Brad to stay, for taking the trouble to get to know him, or, for a while, for knowing him in the biblical sense as well.

Years ago, Norman Cousins offered some advice along these lines in the now-defunct *Saturday Review of Literature*. I must have followed his advice without ever realizing that my "man" would come in such conventional clothing, be as young as Brad, or actually live on my property for two years. Still, the words haunt me, and I have never regretted recognizing Brad as the stranger in my life:

> Compassion is not quantitative. Certainly it is true that behind every man whose entire being cries out for help there may be a million or more equally entitled to attention. But this is the poorest of all reasons for not helping a single man. Where, then, does one begin or stop?
>
> You begin with the first man who puts his life in your hands and you continue so long as you are able to continue, so long as you are capable of personal mobilization.
>
> How to choose? How to determine which one of a million men surrounding you is more deserving than the rest? Do not concern yourself in such speculations. You will never know; you will never need to know. Reach out and take hold of the one who happens to be nearest. If you are never able to help or save another, at least you will have saved one. Many people stroll through an entire lifetime without doing even this. To help put meaning into

a single life may not produce universal regeneration, but it happens to represent the basic form of energy in a society. It also is the best of individual responsibility.[4] [Cousins 1961]

What for me seemed at the time the best of individual responsibility has become, for at least a few others, the worst form of the abuse of power. Certainly I did not "save" Brad. I did help him, as even those who insist that I was only helping myself must admit. So be it—we focus on different parts of the act, we derive our satisfactions and self-worth accordingly.

I wish we had Brad's views: Brad's views now, after the same 20 years; Brad's views without his mother, or the courts, or two disagreeing psychiatrists, all whispering in his ear. I am not so sure this was all that important to him except as a means to what he wanted. And what he wanted to do was to survive. Which, I guess, is exactly what he is doing.

Notes

1.   Hear Jason Ditton on this topic: "Participant observation is inevitably unethical by virtue of being interactionally deceitful. It does not become ethical merely because this deceit is openly practiced. It only becomes inefficient" (Ditton 1970:10, quoted in Hobbs 2001:212). Or Ken Plummer: "All life story collection involves ethical troubles and no life story-telling in social science is ethically neutral" (Plummer 2001:403).

2.   Nor has it been totally ignored. For recent examples, see de Laine (2000), or entries in the *Handbook of Ethnography* (Atkinson et al. 2001).

3 Bob Herbert, "Out of work, out of school, out of mind." [Eugene, Oregon] *Register-Guard*, September 5, 2001. Used by permission of Bob Herbert.

4 Used by permission of *The Saturday Review*.

Finding My Place: The Brad Trilogy

A play adapted by Johnny Saldaña from the works of, and in collaboration with, Harry F. Wolcott

CHARACTERS

HARRY WOLCOTT, early 50s, bearded, glasses; professor of educational anthropology; gay; passionate about his work; warm, empathetic, insightful; though his language is formal, his tone is both informal and emotion-laden.

BRAD, 19 at the beginning of the play; wiry but muscular; a bit shifty in manner, streetwise, a self-proclaimed survivalist; searching for his sexual identity; progresses into paranoid schizophrenia as the action of the play continues.

SETTING:

Eugene, Oregon; the 1980s.

PRODUCTION HISTORY

Finding My Place: The Brad Trilogy premiered at Arizona State University (ASU), Tempe, February 15–17, 2001; then at the Advances in Qualitative Methods conference, Edmonton, Alberta, Canada, February 23, 2001. Both performances featured the following production company:

Harry: David Vining

Brad: Charles Banaszewski

Directed and staged by Johnny Saldaña

Lighting by Aaron Severtson (U.S.) and Joe E. Norris (Canada)

Projections by Lori Hager

Dramaturg: Harry F. Wolcott

Production support was provided by the ASU Department of Theatre, the ASU Katherine K. Herberger College of Fine Arts, and the University of Alberta's International Institute for Qualitative Methodology.

Producers interested in staging *Finding My Place: The Brad Trilogy* can contact the author for permission and terms at: Arizona State University, Department of Theatre, P.O. Box 872002, Tempe, Arizona 85287-2002; phone (480) 965-5337; e-mail Johnny.Saldana@asu.edu.

Finding My Place:
The Brad Trilogy

PRESHOW

A rear-projection screen upstage left shows a SLIDE of a densely wooded area in Oregon. Downstage right is a small desk with books, notepads, a phone, a cassette tape-recorder and tapes, a box of Triscuits, and a drafting stool behind the desk. Downstage left is a backpack. A bow saw lies on the ground up center next to a large portable radio. As the audience enters for seating, rock music from the late 1970s and early 1980s plays: "Sunglasses at Night" (Corey Hart), "Harden My Heart" (Quarterflash), "What's Love Got to Do With It?" (Tina Turner), and "Call Me" (Blondie).

During the next song, "Slow Hand" (Pointer Sisters), HARRY, wearing casual gray slacks and a dark purple shirt, enters reading a letter and drinking from his coffee mug, sits on the stool, and clears away some of the clutter from his desk. As he snacks on Triscuits, he flips through a book and makes notes from it on a notepad with a Bic pen. He then sorts a large number of 3-by-5-inch cards with notes on them into three piles, reading them carefully before making a decision, sometimes labeling or writing additional brief notes on them. Now and then he lays a card in one pile, thinks better of it, and puts it in a different pile. At times he thinks carefully of a card's placement; at others, he writes a question mark on it and places it in a "to be sorted" pile for later examination. He does not acknowledge the music playing.

Also during "Slow Hand," BRAD, dressed in faded blue jeans and an unbuttoned faded red flannel shirt, enters carrying items from one offstage side to the other, such as freshly cut logs and a kerosene lantern, pieces of lumber, a frying pan and water jug (which he drinks from and leaves on stage), a toolbox (which he sets by his backpack), and lawn chair (which he unfolds and sets center stage). BRAD sometimes lip-syncs, sings with, or dances to the music as he passes by. At some point he removes his shirt, revealing his muscled torso in a tank top. He then brings on a broken bicycle and attempts to repair it with various tools that he's laid out on the ground. Neither character is conscious of the other's presence.

At the beginning of "Ride Like the Wind" (Christopher Cross), HARRY exits to refill his coffee mug and takes the box of Triscuits with him. BRAD continues fixing his bike, but turns the radio off in reaction to a distant voice he thinks he hears; after realizing there's no one around, he turns the radio back on. He goes to his backpack, pulls out a dictionary, a spiral notebook, and a pen, and practices writing words. After writing awhile, he rips the sheet from the notebook, folds the paper, and stuffs it in his back pocket. Towards the end of the song he picks up the bow saw and imitates playing it as a guitar along with the music.

When "Sweet Dreams" (Eurhythmics) begins, BRAD turns the volume up and moves to the music; this is his favorite song. HARRY enters with fresh coffee and reads a second letter; he sits at his desk and continues sorting index cards. BRAD moves his head and body energetically to the music. Occasionally there are serendipitously similar movements between the two men, such as turning their heads or stretching at the exact same time. After a while and out of frustration with his unsuccessful repair of the bike, BRAD gives up and storms offstage, putting his shirt back on. HARRY rubber-bands the three piles of cards, but seems puzzled by one single index card remaining; he rises, paces, and thinks. BRAD reenters with a Playgirl *magazine and looks at the pictures. Toward the end of the song, the two men cross each others' paths but are too absorbed in their tasks to notice. HARRY gets an inspiration and sits at his desk; BRAD stares intensely at one of the magazine photos, rubs his chest, thigh, and crotch, then unbuckles his belt and unbuttons his jeans to reach inside and masturbate.*

(SLIDE: Eugene, Oregon)

(SLIDE: The 1980s)

(SLIDE: Prologue)

BRAD exits as HARRY continues working on the single index card. House lights fade and stage lights rise on him. "Sweet Dreams" fades out.

PROLOGUE

(SLIDE: "The purpose of this play . . .")

HARRY

(methodically working/pondering out loud to himself the key phrases of what he wants to say, perhaps even writing or crossing out and changing something already written on the card)

The purpose of this play . . . to render from personal experience . . . to a discerning audience . . .

(scans the audience with a quick glance to check if they're ready)

a level of insight and . . .

(pause as he reaches for just the right word, then writes it down)

understanding . . . human social life.

(to himself, looking at what he has written)

Yeah, that seems to say it.

(to audience; rises with card in hand, crosses to projection screen)

You gotta get the statement of purpose worded just right.

(SLIDE: {purpose statement in quotes, as worded below})

The purpose of this play is to render from personal experience a research account that offers, to a discerning audience, a level of insight and understanding into human social life.

(SLIDE: Finding My Place: The Brad Trilogy)

(indicating title slide)

How about my title? Did it reach out and grab you?

(acknowledges it may have not, for some)

I've written with a particular audience in mind: people who engage in fieldwork—

(SLIDE: book cover for Harry F. Wolcott's Ethnography: A Way of Seeing*)*

ethnography, the rendering of the ongoing social activities of some individual or group from a *cultural* perspective. In fieldwork, you immerse yourself personally—with passion, without apology—for the purposes of research. Fieldwork beckons, even dares you, to become part of what you study.

(SLIDE: book cover for Wolcott's The Art of Fieldwork*)*

I'd never deny unabashed efforts to approach my work artistically. In its own ways, art is every bit as rigorous and systematic as science. Artists portray. That's also what ethnography is about: to present material in a sufficiently engaging manner to hold the interest of an audience who may not expect to be entertained, but hopes not to be bored.

(SLIDE: "No two individuals ever get exactly the same message.")

(to an audience member)

If you fall asleep, I need never know. To hurry through is to miss the point of what both fieldwork and life itself are all about. These are my words, my sentences, my ideas; I stand by them. So, attend to a discussion of *my* problems and solutions and don't remain too preoccupied with your own. I need an audience of others, multiple and complex. No two individuals ever get exactly the same message.

(SLIDE: Ethnography by the Numbers)

(returning to desk, holding up cards)

From interview tapes or handwritten notes, I transcribe statements in sentences or brief paragraphs, writing them by hand. I put them directly on 3-by-5 cards for easy labeling and sorting into broad categories suggested by the account itself. You'll find a mechanical cast to much of the advice I offer. Instead of wheedling you to attempt great leaps of intuitive insight, you're more likely to find me arguing in favor of careful coding and sorting to construct a solid study one brick at a time.

(*SLIDE: book cover for Wolcott's* Writing Up Qualitative Research, *second edition*)

I appreciate being told that I'm a good writer—by academic standards, not literary ones. Good writing doesn't call attention to itself, it enhances what is being written about.

(*SLIDE: The Darker Arts*)

But the cold, hard fact is that a few rare moments of ecstasy over something well written or favorably reviewed are meager compensation for all the agony endured to achieve them. The extent of the author's suffering and sacrifice isn't factored into judgments about the worth of the fieldwork—anything from an intellectually rich to a . . . psychologically devastating personal experience.

(*SLIDE: Heady Candor*)

This account addresses personal issues in a manner I describe as "heady candor": being open and up front about both the research process and the researcher, and to be as frank about what I don't understand as what I do.

(*HARRY moves to center stage*)

Today's fieldworkers are encouraged to put themselves into their scripts. Put yourself squarely in the scene, but don't take center stage.

(*HARRY realizes where he is and moves off center; BRAD enters from behind and looks at HARRY, sits on the lawn chair*)

(*SLIDE: book cover for Wolcott's* Transforming Qualitative Data: Description, Analysis, and Interpretation)

Qualitative study consists of a trilogy of dimensions: description, analysis, and interpretation. When you emphasize description, you want your audience to see what you saw. When you emphasize analysis, you want your audience to know what you know. When you emphasize interpretation, you want your audience to understand what you think you yourself have understood.

BRAD

(*to HARRY; HARRY does not look at him*)

Anything you've ever heard, you just remember and put it all together the best you can, that's good enough for me. Help people—understand.

(*he rises and exits; HARRY looks at him as he leaves*)

(*SLIDE: In Anticipation*)

HARRY

Brace yourself. I still don't understand all that led up to these events, nor am I ever likely to understand all that they mean. That's a reminder that we never get the whole story, and we aren't likely to fully understand whatever part of the story we get.

(SLIDE: A Personal Account)

Little's to be gained in becoming defensive or apologetic about the past. Since issues have arisen about this particular study, I've taken the occasion to unveil them.

SCENE ONE: DESCRIPTION

(SLIDE: Scene One: Description)

HARRY

(holding up one pile of index cards)

Description is the starting point, square one. The strategy of this approach is to treat descriptive data as fact to answer the question, "What is going on here?"

(SLIDE: Serendipity)

I first came to know Brad through what ethnographers sometimes refer to as serendipity.

(music up: "Heart of Glass" by Blondie)

(HARRY finds a bow saw on the ground, picks it up, looks at it curiously)

Literally as well as figuratively, I discovered Brad in my own backyard, unannounced and uninvited.

HARRY: I discovered Brad in my own backyard, unannounced and uninvited.

(SLIDE: {BRAD's cabin})

(BRAD enters, carrying a sapling, stops when he and HARRY see each other; BRAD sets the sapling down, shuts radio music off; they look at each other warily)

A 19-year-old had managed to construct a crude but sturdy 10-by-12-foot cabin at a remote corner of my densely wooded, 20-acre homesite, which my partner Norman has shared with me since 1968. He didn't know on whose property he had built his cabin, perhaps hoping he had chosen public land next to mine.

(hands BRAD the saw, which he grabs)

BRAD

(defensively, to HARRY)

Can I stay?

(SLIDE: Early Encounters)

HARRY

(beat, as HARRY looks BRAD over; to audience)

I attach great importance to first impressions.

(HARRY stares at BRAD; BRAD starts packing up his tools)

At the moment of our first and unexpected meeting, I felt hesitant about allowing him to remain on my land; yet I felt an even greater reluctance in insisting that he leave.

BRAD

(to HARRY)

I needed some place to get out of the wind and keep dry. The rent ran out. I knew the rains would continue and I'd have to do something.

HARRY

(to audience)

He had no money, no job, and no place to go. I couldn't see how I could claim to be any kind of humanitarian and throw him off my property.

(SLIDE: Courtesy and Common Sense)

(HARRY picks up the sapling and examines it; to BRAD)

I guess if you're going to be here, I need to know something about you: Where you're from? What kind of trouble you're in?

Courtesy and Common Sense

HARRY: I guess if you're going to be here, I need to know something about you....

BRAD

(takes sapling, saws into it)

I'm not in any trouble. I'm not that stupid. I used to live at this end of town; my father still lives here but I never see him. And I've lived in a lot of different places, like California, Portland, out in the country; different places in town, like the Mission—you had to sing for Jesus before they'd feed you there—a halfway house,

(slightly mumbling)

reform school.

HARRY

Reform school?

BRAD

(defensively)

Yeah, but it wasn't really my fault.

(SLIDE: Survival)

I picked up my sleeping bag and the stuff I had and headed for the hills. I didn't know exactly what to do. I saw this piece of level ground and I set up a tarp for shelter. There were plenty of trees around. I decided to build a place for myself, because I wasn't doing anything anyway.

(SLIDE: {BRAD's cabin})

(HARRY looks at the cabin as BRAD describes it)

I put up four posts and started dragging logs around till the walls were built. As I went along I just figured out what I would need. I got the stuff I needed—tools and nails—from new houses being built nearby. The roof's made of paneling that I carried up from some kid's tree fort. I knew about plaster because I had worked with it before, so I smeared some on the walls. So now, I've got this cabin. This is better than any apartment I've ever had, that's for sure. It really works good for me. Here I am.

(beat; BRAD shrugs his shoulders)

That's it.

(SLIDE: Getting a Start and Building on Later)

HARRY

It wasn't much of an introduction, but it marked the beginning of a dialogue that lasted almost two full years from that moment.

(returns to his desk; BRAD turns on his radio to a loud volume and returns to fixing his bike; HARRY glares at him, goes to the radio and lowers the volume; HARRY sits on the lawn chair and watches BRAD work)

(music: "Jump" by the Pointer Sisters)

I didn't expect him to stay. Norman has an aversion to people he identifies as "losers," and from the outset had as little to do with Brad as possible. But as time went on and Brad continued to make improvements, he gradually became as much a fixture about the place as was his cabin. We saw rather little of him at first, but I became *fascinated* with him and intrigued with his—

(BRAD removes his shirt; HARRY stares at his muscled torso)

chosen lifestyle.

(rises, crosses to desk, sits and shows audience a letter written on official stationery)

(SLIDE: Jumping Ahead with the Story)

I jump ahead in the story, almost a year and a half at this point, to an event that at first seemed totally unrelated to Brad's presence on my place. Congress happened to turn once again to the perennial issue of increased federal funding for schools, this time under a banner of "educational adequacy." A federal project officer was assigned to commission a set of position papers addressing the topic, and I was invited to prepare one from an anthropological perspective.

(the bike accidentally falls over)

BRAD

Fuck!

(he sets the bike upright and continues working on it)
(SLIDE: Place and Serendipity)

HARRY

There's a remarkable correspondence between what ethnographers choose to study and where they happen to find themselves. With Brad in mind, I inquired whether it would be OK to address the assignment through a case study of a school dropout, a more suitable anthropological contribution to such a project. If Brad was amenable to the idea, this would also give me a focus and rationale for inquiring more systematically into his life.

(SLIDE: Making a Case for the Single Case)

(HARRY gets a small tape recorder, yellow paper note pad, Bic pen)

My proposal: Instead of writing a conventional paper, I would present a life story of one out-of-school youth, underscoring a critical distinction that can be made, and needs to be made, between schooling and education.

(sets his materials on the stool, picks it up, crosses to center)

What can we learn from studying only one example of anything?

(as if the answer is obvious)

All we can.

(HARRY sets up his equipment, sits on stool as BRAD turns the radio off)

Everyone has a story to tell if the right person comes along to hear it. Like Blanche DuBois in *A Streetcar Named Desire*, fieldworkers must rely on the kindness of strangers to help get them where they want to go.

(BRAD sits on the lawn chair, takes the tape recorder and checks it out, inspects the cassette tape)

I discussed the idea of taping Brad's life story. He was willing to give the idea a try and seemed eager to discuss his experiences, his outlook, and his conscious effort to put his life together.

(SLIDE: Consent)

(HARRY takes back the tape recorder and gives BRAD a form to read)

I also explained the idea of informed consent, and I had typed up something for him to sign. He objected to my stilted language,

(BRAD tears up HARRY's consent form, takes HARRY's pad and pen and writes his own version)

and wrote out a simple release in his own words. And then we began.

(HARRY starts the tape recorder)

(SLIDE: Adequate Schools and Inadequate Education)

The earliest school experience he could recall was in a church-sponsored kindergarten.

BRAD

I went to Sunday school for a while. I heard all the big lessons: Jesus, Moses.

(BRAD returns HARRY's notepad and pen; HARRY takes occasional notes throughout; BRAD occupies himself with his hand tools)

HARRY

Hearing Brad use objectionable language, the teacher threatened to wash his mouth with soap. At the next occasion when the children were washing their hands,

BRAD

I showed the kids around me, "Hey, no big deal, having soap in your mouth."

(puts his cigarette pack in his mouth to illustrate; laughs)

HARRY

School personnel were forever testing him, though little seems to have resulted other than the performance of the ritual itself. In middle school he was eventually assigned to what he described as an educationally handicapped class.

BRAD

E.H.—with the other stonies! I don't know if I felt I was "special" or not.

HARRY

By his account he had often been slow or behind the rest of the class. He had trouble recalling number sequences and basic arithmetic facts.

BRAD

Lack of practice.

(pulls a folded sheet of paper from his back jeans pocket and stands close to HARRY to show him)

I can spell good enough. Handwriting, well, you just write the way you write. I don't worry much about that.

HARRY

His spelling and punctuation weren't very good. But he *was* remarkable in his phonetic spelling of a language that's not all that phonetic:

(SLIDE: {words as spelled below in BRAD's handwriting})

BRAD

(reading aloud the words as he points to them)

edgucate, beleve, egsagurate, angsiaty, conchens.

(BRAD goes to his dictionary and flips through it; whispers to himself the alphabet)

HARRY

He could read, but he faltered on "big words." Yet he was sufficiently intrigued with words he wanted to understand or to spell that he would try patiently to locate them in an old dictionary he procured for the cabin—no easy task for a phonetic speller who had to recite the alphabet as his first step.

(SLIDE: "It was boring, man.")

BRAD

Like, English class, I'd get there at nine in the morning and put my head down and I'd sleep through the whole class. It was boring, man. The people in college today are probably the ones who didn't sleep when I was in English.

HARRY

A school counselor remembered Brad as a somewhat troubled seventh-grader who had spent most of his time either in a counselor's office or "seeing the vice principal," the school disciplinarian.

BRAD

(SLIDE: "I've always liked learning, I just didn't like school.")

I've always liked learning, I just didn't like school. I was never that interested. If I knew I had to do something, I'd try a little bit. Maybe school could of did better. I could probably have tried harder. Everybody who knows me says,

(SLIDE: "'That guy had the world's record for ditching school.'")

"That guy had the world's record for ditching school." Like, when I was in ninth grade, Southern California, I didn't need P.E. I wasn't interested in sports. So I'd go get stoned. I'd take a walk during that class, go kick back in an orange grove, maybe eat an orange, get high, smoke a cigarette, and by the time I'd walk back, it was time for another class. I did that for a long time and never got caught.

HARRY

Sneaky kid.

(SLIDE: The Life History of a Sneaky Kid)

BRAD

(laughing, agreeing with HARRY)

My mom says that when I was a small kid I was always doing something sneaky. That's just the way I am, I can't say why. Maybe 'cause I was dropped on my head when I was little.

(sitting next to HARRY)

I remember busting into my second-grade classroom. I went to the school grounds on the weekend with another kid. We were just looking around outside and I said, "Hey, look at that fire escape door—you could pull it open with a knife." We pulled it open and I went in and I took some money and a couple of pens. That was the first time I broke in anywhere. We got in trouble for it; I don't know why I did it. Maybe I did it because I saw that I *could* do it.

(SLIDE: "I've stole lots of bikes.")

While I was growing up, I went pretty wild. We used to steal bikes all the time.

(goes to his bike)

We'd get cool frames and put all the hot parts on them. I've stole lots of bikes—maybe around 50. But I probably shouldn't have never stolen about half of them, they were such shit. I just needed them for transportation. I can't straighten out my old bike after that accident I had the other day, so I'll try to find one to steal—that's the easiest way to get one. Maybe a Peugeot or a Raleigh.

HARRY

What would your mother think about you stealing a bike?

(SLIDE: "dumb, smart?")

That it's dumb, smart?

BRAD

Neither. She'd just think that I must have needed it. She wouldn't say anything. She doesn't lecture me about things like that. When I was living with my dad— a total asshole—he didn't really notice.

(SLIDE: "I'd stay out all night.")

I'd stay out all night just looking in people's garages. I'd get lots of stuff; my room had all kinds of junk in it. You could walk into somebody's garage and take everything they have—maybe $5,000 worth of stuff.

(SLIDE: "I walk quietly.")

I walk quietly so no one will see me. They way I do it, I go out in nice neighborhoods, walk on streets that aren't main streets, and look for open garages, like maybe they just went to the store or to work and didn't close the door. Anybody that owns a house and three cars and a boat—they're not hurtin'. It's the law of the jungle:

(SLIDE: "If you snooze, you lose.")

"If you snooze, you lose." Someone might spot me looking around at all these bikes, but even if somebody says something, they can't do anything to you. The cops might come up and question me, but nothing could happen.

(SLIDE: "It's worth the risk.")

It's worth the risk, because I'm not going to get caught. I did it too many times; it's easy. I've gotten into churches and stores, apartment house recreation rooms, crawling through the windows. And I've broken into houses before. I went in one through the garage door, got inside, scrounged around, took some liquor, took some cameras.

(SLIDE: "I didn't have nothin' then.")

It's not my main hobby to go around looking to steal, but I didn't have nothin' then; I was looking for anything I could find. Just before I started living at the cabin, I kept having it on my mind that I needed some money and could rob a store. It seemed like a pretty easy way to get some cash, but I guess it wasn't a very good idea. I don't know what you'd call it.

(SLIDE: "Risky? Crazy?")

Risky? Crazy?

(he acts out the story)

I went into one of those little fast-food stores. I had a BB gun and this hood over my head with a little hole cut out for the mouth. I said to the clerk, "Open the register." And she said, "What, are you serious?" I knew she wasn't going to open it, and she knew I wasn't about to shoot her. So then I started pushing all the buttons on the cash register, but I didn't know which ones to push. And she came up and pulled the key. Then someone drove up in front of the store and the signal bell went "ding, ding," so I booked.

(SLIDE: "I could probably do it if I had to.")

If I was ever that hurting, I could probably do it if I had to. But you wouldn't get much from a little store anyway. I'd be more likely just to walk in and grab a six-pack of beer.

(SLIDE: "I'd steal before I'd ever beg.")

(walks to his backpack, picks it up)

Before I got food stamps, I'd go to the store with my backpack, fill it with steaks and expensive canned food, and just walk out. If anybody saw me, I'd just wave at them and keep walking. I'd steal before I'd ever beg. I guess food stamps are society's way of paying me to drop out.

HARRY

(to audience)

I never confront informants with contradictions, disbelief, or shock, but I don't mind presenting myself as a bit dense, someone who doesn't catch on too quickly and has to have things explained.

(to BRAD)

Why not get a job?

BRAD

I'd just be taking a job away from someone who needs it more.

(SLIDE: "I just get by.")

I'm not what you'd call a super thief. A super thief makes his living at it; I just get by. It sure makes life a hell of a lot easier. If I found anything that I needed, I'd pick it up and take it: sleeping bag, radio, stove, lanterns, tools, clothes, water containers, boots. If you took away everything here that's stolen, there wouldn't be much left.

(SLIDE: "my life")

I don't have to work my life away just to survive. And I don't think I'll have any big career. If I can't do super-good, I'll do good enough. I'm not in a big hurry with my life. Living this way is a good start for me; it's great.

(raising up his fists)

Jungle boy!

(BRAD turns his radio back on; music: end of "Hot Rod Hearts" {Robbie Dupree}, followed by "Eye in the Sky" {Alan Parsons Project}; he continues working on his bike)

(SLIDE: Cultural Alternatives)

HARRY

(to audience, looks at his index cards as if referring to notes)

Faced with jobs he didn't want to do and expenses he couldn't afford, Brad had chosen to change his lifestyle radically. He was basically a city boy making whatever accommodation was necessary to survive inexpensively. It wasn't an ideological search for an alternative lifestyle. Brad was too anti-social to become part of a socially inspired counterculture movement.

(SLIDE: A Free Spirit)

At first impression, his strategy for coping with life seemed as bold, resourceful, and even romantic as was his building of the cabin. He was free to decide how to spend the day. He arose when he wanted and retired when he wanted. He could eat when he chose and cook or not as mood—and a rather sparse cupboard—dictated.

(SLIDE: Cultural Know-How)

He had a keen sense of what for him constituted the essentials: Obtaining them provided his driving force. His attention was on what he needed, rather than what he might become. Survival was his challenge and his work, and he worked full time at it.

(SLIDE: All That Is Required)

The direction that process was taking seemed to reflect all too well what he felt society expected of him: nothing. He was left largely to his own resources to make sense of his world. Brad was trying to figure out for himself what he wanted in life and whether it was worth the effort.

(to BRAD)

Do you have anything to add?

BRAD

I've definitely had more experiences than some of the people I went to school with.

(SLIDE: "I've been more places and done more things . . .")

I've been more places and done more things. . . . In *some* ways, I'm wiser than other kids my age. I'm not really corrupt, but I'm not innocent anymore, that's for sure.

(sits close to HARRY)

I can be honest. I can be trusted, to some people. I don't like to *totally* screw somebody.

(SLIDE: "Can I trust you?")

HARRY

(smiling, almost flirtatious)

Can I trust you?

BRAD

(smiling back)

Yeah. Pretty much.

(walks to his bike)

I dunno.

(beat)

I always seem to screw things up at the end.

(he smirks; music fades up as lights dim; BRAD exits with bike, returns with a second one for next scene; HARRY exits)

SCENE TWO: ANALYSIS

(SLIDE: Scene Two: Analysis)

HARRY

(lights rise; a different bike has replaced BRAD's old one, but this, too, is broken, and he attempts to fix it; HARRY enters with letters, including a package addressed to BRAD, and hands it to him)

This came in today's mail for you.

(music fades out; BRAD unwraps the package; HARRY returns to the desk and picks up his pad and pen; to audience)

A second way of organizing and reporting data is to extend beyond a purely descriptive account with an *analysis* that proceeds in some careful, systematic way to identify key factors and relationships—to show how things work, how things fit together. But don't expect the parts to come together that easily.

(BRAD turns on his radio; music: "Private Eyes" by Hall & Oates; he opens the package and takes out a new blue flannel shirt and a letter; HARRY looks at BRAD and the package's contents)

(SLIDE: Getting Nosy)

There's a fundamental fascination with the way other people live. We may vigorously deny that we're voyeurs, but virtually everything that humans do is of potential interest to us.

(BRAD smiles as he reads the letter; HARRY picks up the tape recorder and strains to get a glimpse of the letter; though HARRY tries to be secretive, BRAD turns around and sees him)

BRAD

(grabs the tape recorder from HARRY and shouts into the microphone)

Sometimes my mom sends me clothes, or shampoo, or other stuff like that!

(he thrusts the tape recorder back to HARRY, turns the radio off, takes the package and exits, disgusted)

HARRY

(returning to his desk)

Humans aren't above making surreptitious observations, but we certainly hate to get caught making them.

(HARRY prepares cassette tapes for the next interview; lighting suggests dusk is approaching)

(SLIDE: The Ethnographer Helps People Tell Their Story)

When someone "gives" a life story, what should be offered in return? I tried to support Brad's modest but recurring need for cash by letting him work for me whenever he needed money, and I paid him well. Somewhat self-righteously, I suppose, I also felt I was helping him build character by insisting that he earn every penny he got. Brad usually avoided the lesson by working for me only as a last resort.

(BRAD enters for his next interview wearing his new flannel shirt, unbuttoned; he lays a blanket on the ground and sits on it; BRAD also has a large set of pulleys and rope for his next project; HARRY pulls a bill from his wallet)

He liked to goad me with the idea that it was easier to steal what little he needed than to put in the time and effort necessary to earn it. If he had more than a dollar or two in his pocket, he usually chose not to work at all.

(BRAD holds his hand out, HARRY gives BRAD $5)

He was also paid for his interview time, the dollars providing adequate motivation once initial enthusiasm waned.

(BRAD stuffs the money in his jeans pocket)

Altruism and research make strange bedfellows.

(BRAD works on looping and tying knots, with difficulty, for the pulleys)

(SLIDE: Fieldwork as Intimate, Long-Term Acquaintance)

During our year and a half of casual contact, occasional invitations to share a meal, and sometimes working together on outdoor projects, Brad had gradually become more revealing about himself. He seemed willing to talk about many aspects of his life, and I became intrigued with trying to piece together his own personal worldview.

(HARRY turns on the tape recorder, sits on the blanket)

BRAD

(SLIDE: "pretty wild")

After my parents got divorced, I was living with my dad. I had quite a bit of freedom. My dad was at work all day and there was no one to watch me. I was pretty wild. If I didn't want to go to school, I just didn't go. After my dad got remarried, I had no freedom any more. I had a new mother to watch me. I got mad at her a couple of times, so I moved in with her parents. Then I went to Southern California to visit my mother and I just stayed there with her and my stepdad.

(SLIDE: "hassle")

But I got into a hassle with my stepdad, and I ditched some classes. Anytime I did something, my mother and stepdad just said, "Back to Oregon." They didn't threaten, they just did it. My mom could have figured out something better than sending me back all the time. She could have taken away privileges, or made me work around the house. Suddenly I was on a bus back to Oregon. Then my father separated again and I moved into some little apartment with him. He wanted me to go to another school, but I said, "Forget it, man, I'm not going to another school. I'm tired of school." So I'd just lay around the house, stay up all night, sleep all day.

(SLIDE: "a good boy")

Finally I told my mom I'd be a good boy, and she let me move back to California. She used to cut out everything they printed in the paper about pot and put it on my walls and she'd talk about brain damage.

(BRAD turns on his radio; music: "Drive" {the Cars}, followed by "Millworker" {Bette Midler})

Then I got in another hassle with my stepdad. I ran out of the house and stayed with some friends for a few months, but then the police got in a hassle with me and they said I'd have to go back with my dad or they were going to send me to a correctional institution. The next thing you know, I was back on the bus.

(SLIDE: "another family")

(getting a bit angry and moody)

By then my dad had remarried again. My stepmom and my dad started telling me I wasn't going to smoke pot anymore, I would have to go to school, I was going to have to stop smoking cigarettes, and other shit like that. I wasn't ready for another family and I didn't like anything about that fucking house. I stayed about two days, then I split. I figured any place was better than living there, that's for sure. I just hung around town, sleeping anywhere I could find. I ripped off a quilt and slept out on a baseball field for a while. I stayed in different places for a couple of weeks.

(SLIDE: "no place to go")

Bad times for me were getting in a hassle with my parents. Then I wouldn't have no place to go, no money or nothin'. That happened with all of them at different

BRAD: *After my parents got divorced, I was living with my dad.*

times. They got pissed at me because I kept breaking into the house for food, so they called the cops on me. Running away from them, I broke my foot and had to go to the hospital. Then I got sent to reform school for eight months.

(beat)

I think the real reason was that I didn't have any place to go.

(throws the rope down and goes to his bike)

HARRY

(to audience)

By my count, he was reared in six households. Nothing ever lasted.

(SLIDE: "a big difference")

BRAD

I saw a guy a few weeks ago who's the same age as me. He lived in a house behind us when I was in fifth grade. He still lives with his parents in the same place. I think about what he's been doing the last nine years and what I've been doing the last nine years and it's a big difference. He went to high school. Now he works in a gas station, has a motorcycle, and works on his truck. I guess that's all right for him, so long as he's mellow with his parents.

(SLIDE: "I've never really held a job.")

(crosses to HARRY, sits on the lawn chair)

I've worked for my dad for a while—helped him wire houses and do light con-struction. I scraped paint for one company. I worked for a graveyard for about eight months, for a plumber awhile, planted trees for a while. Dishwashing. I've never really held a job. I wouldn't want to have to put up with a lot of people on a job that didn't make me much money. Like at a check-out counter—I don't want to be in front of that many people. I don't like a job where everyone sees you do it.

(SLIDE: "a loner")

I guess that I'm sorta a loner, maybe a hermit. I've had close friends, but I don't have any now.

(fighting back tears)

HARRY

(to BRAD)

Shall I turn the tape recorder off for a while?

BRAD

(shakes his head "no," tries to put up a brave front)

You've got what you've got. It doesn't make any difference what anybody else has. You can't wish you're somebody else, there's no point in it. Being by myself doesn't make all that much difference. No one knows who I am anyway.

(HARRY puts his hand comfortingly on BRAD's knee; BRAD remains still, looks as if he's about to reach for HARRY's hand, then pulls away, gets a wrench, and starts working on his bike)

(SLIDE: "a closer family")

If I had kids, I'd be a closer family. I would be with them more and show that you love them. You could talk to your kids more. And if they do something wrong, you don't go crazy and lose your temper or something. My dad's worked all his life so he can sit at a desk and not have to hold a screwdriver any more. But he just works! He never seems to have any fun. Who wants a second-class job so you can live in a second-class apartment and lead a second-class life? I don't have to work *my* life away just to survive.

(BRAD throws the wrench down in frustration)

But I've got to have a *bike* that works!

(BRAD pushes the bike over and storms offstage)

HARRY

(beat)

He had begun to figure out that *no one* really needed him.

(stops the tape recorder, turns off the radio, and sets the bike upright)

(SLIDE: Fieldwork as Personal Work)

When you inquire deeply into the life of nearly anyone, you can't help developing a sense of empathy. I was surprised to realize the myriad forces ready to pounce if Brad did anything wrong, the total lack of recognition for anything he did right. Many times I'm jolted by rage, even outrage, at the conditions under which so many people live. I can't imagine doing *any* study in which I had no personal feelings, felt no interest or compassion for the humans whose lives touched mine. Brad was no longer a subject of my research. He was someone who thrust himself into my life, and I was now trying desperately to understand him.

BRAD

(enters with a lit joint, and carrying an ashtray and two magazines)

(SLIDE: "When I was seven, . . .")

When I was seven, after my dad had beat up my mom, he picked me up and carried me down the lane on the farm where we were living, and said he was gonna drown me in the river. The only thing that stopped him was my mom screaming that he'd go to jail if he did.

(he takes a hit off his joint)

(SLIDE: "catch a buzz")

I don't know why I didn't get into drugs more. I've never really cared to take downers and uppers or shoot up. I've taken acid before and got pretty fried. I don't know if it was bad acid but it wasn't a very good experience. I like to smoke pot to catch a buzz. Sometimes when I want to be mellow, I don't say anything. I just shut up, smoke a joint, drink a beer—you just sort of melt.

(BRAD turns on his radio—music: George Michael, "Father Figure"; BRAD sits, reads through a Playboy *magazine)*

HARRY

(to audience)

Long before we began the life history project, I became aware that Brad had some personal hang-ups focused largely on his acceptance of his body, and a preoccupation with sexual fantasy. He recognized a new physical prowess in himself and remarked casually about the possibility of marketing his body.

(SLIDE: {a naked female})

His ideal sex-for-hire scenario was to have a

BRAD

beautiful woman

HARRY

offer him a ride and immediately take him home with her, where he would enjoy the good life as a handsome young stud.

(BRAD reads through a Playgirl magazine, removes his shirt to compare his muscles against the men in the pictures)

(SLIDE: {a naked male})

Brad also acknowledged that at his age and with his physique he could be attractive to males as well. The idea of easy money—pay to play, so to speak—had its appeal. Along well-known boulevards of certain metropolitan areas,

BRAD

San Francisco, Los Angeles,

HARRY

young males regularly hustle customers under the guise of hustling rides.

BRAD

(he rises)

I can drop my morals whenever I want.

(SLIDE: Hustling)

(BRAD stares at HARRY)

I've always been susceptible to older guys.

(beat; BRAD looks at his magazine)

HARRY

At first, the issue was a topic of occasional but guarded discussion. Eventually, I realized that certain provocative situations kept presenting themselves.

(BRAD turns up the radio volume, looks at the magazine, lip syncs and dances to "Father Figure," stares at HARRY now and then with a sly grin; HARRY crosses hesitantly behind BRAD, places his hand on BRAD's shoulder and embraces him from *behind; BRAD does not pull away; HARRY's hug becomes stronger and his hands move slowly all over BRAD's body; BRAD closes his eyes, smiles, and loses himself in the feeling. When HARRY's hands move below BRAD's waist, BRAD pulls away teasingly and walks backwards until he's underneath the "Hustling" slide; he dances towards his cabin and stops before exiting, giving HARRY a slight head gesture towards it, suggesting that he follow, and exits; HARRY moves slowly, contemplating a difficult decision; he then unbuttons his shirt as he follows BRAD offstage)*

(SLIDE: {BRAD's cabin})

(lights dim as music increases in volume)

INTERMISSION

(music continues through Intermission: "Do You Really Want to Hurt Me" {Culture Club}, "Just When I Needed You Most"{Randy Van Warmer}, "What a Fool Believes" {The Doobie Brothers})

(music fades as lights rise to suggest evening; HARRY enters, shirt unbuttoned, accidentally trips over BRAD's bike)

HARRY

It's been pointed out that with sexual liaisons, getting *out* of bed gracefully requires more art than getting in it.

(SLIDE: Be Candid)

(sets the bike upright, buttons his shirt)

How far to go with personal revelation? When in doubt, tell the truth. We initiated sex long *before* we began the life history project. The relationship itself was not accidental, not casual, not transitory, and it put us on another level of intimacy.

(SLIDE: "no secrets")

I felt that Brad was someone I *really* knew, *really* understood. There seemed to be no secrets, no taboo subjects, no topics off-limits. I turned off the tape recorder whenever Brad asked me to, though it was usually so he could toke up rather than talk about something that was too personal to record.

(SLIDE: Disclosure)

The reaction to my disclosure has, for the most part, been nonjudgmental. But in what sometimes seem these more enlightened times, I've been chastised by those anxious to impose their own moral standards on the world around them. Chastised by those who turn a deaf ear to the fact that the physical relationship preceded the life story project by several months.

(SLIDE: Self-Defense vs. Getting Defensive)

And chastised by those who see the relationship as an abuse of power, by somehow transforming a muscular and angry 20-year-old streetwise reform school graduate into a naïve and helplessly vulnerable victim of a lustful old professor. *(BRAD enters, shirtless; he and HARRY stare at each other; BRAD turns on radio; music: "Hold Me Now" {Thompson Twins}; BRAD sits on the blanket, HARRY sits behind him and massages his shoulders)*

You may think me a rogue and rascal for becoming involved with a younger guy whose life ever so gradually had become inextricably wound up with my own. But we each have our own lives to live, and I've sensed little loss of personal esteem, even from those whom I've disappointed.

(SLIDE: "consenting adults")

The ethical issues aren't about the private behavior of *consenting* adults. So, whatever shocks you about all this probably has nothing to do with what you've been hoping to understand. Some will hear only the story they want to hear. To borrow a line from *Torch Song Trilogy*, I'm embarrassed, but I'm *not* ashamed.

BRAD

(picks up the tape recorder and mocks HARRY's interviewing style)

"Can you tell me anything more about that?" "Are there topics we might explore that I haven't asked about?" "Ten years from now, what do you think things'll be like?"

HARRY

(laughs, takes the tape recorder from BRAD, turns it on)

Ten years from now, what *do* you think things'll be like?

BRAD

(SLIDE: "I don't want to be alone all my life.")

I don't want to be alone all my life. I might stay here a couple of years. I've got to get my life together before I can worry about just going out. If you get your life together, it means you don't have to worry so much. You have a little more security; that's what everybody wants. Money,

(as if dropping a hint)

a car. You can't have your life together without those two things. I'd like to go camping with somebody on the weekend. Have a cooler of beer and a raft or something. It's nice to have friends to do that with. If I had a car and stuff, I'm sure I could get a few people to go.

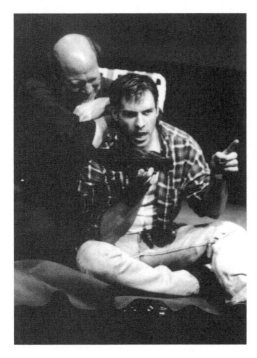

BRAD: Ten years from now, what do you think things'll be like?

(BRAD looks at HARRY)

Without a car, man—shit.

(BRAD pulls away from HARRY, rises, puts his shirt back on, goes to the desk)

After reform school, I got some work and the first thing I did was buy a motorcycle. I was riding without a license or insurance for a while. But even after I got a license, I kept getting tickets, so my license got suspended. My dad took the motorcycle and sold it to pay for the fines.

(SLIDE: "excelling only once")

(BRAD picks up the phone, dials a number he reads from his mother's letter)

HARRY

(to audience, as he turns radio music off and crosses to desk)

Brad expressed only resentment toward his father, but he often mentioned his mother's efforts to provide a positive influence. He recalled excelling only once in school: an art project in clay that was put on display and that his mother still kept.

(HARRY sits at his desk and shuffles through his index cards, as if looking for answers to new questions or to place them in a new order)

(SLIDE: "Mom")

BRAD

(on the phone to his mother; beat after each phrase)

Mom . . . yeah, I'm still living here in the woods. . . .

(SLIDE: "hiding out from life")

I guess I'm sorta hiding out from life. At least, hiding from the life I had before I came up here, that's for sure. . . . I'm not workin'. I don't need all that much. . . . I live on food stamps. . . . I sneak into some nearby apartments to wash my clothes. I pay for the machines. . . . I always wash up before going to town if I'm dirty. I don't want to look like I live in a cabin. . . .

(SLIDE: "a different way of life")

The life of a dumpy apartment and a cut-rate job? This is a different way of life. I do what I want. . . . What would I have been doing for the year and a half in town compared to a year and a half up here? . . . Like, all the work I've done here, none of it has gone for some landlord's pocketbook. . . . No, no girlfriend right now. . . .

(SLIDE: "a friend")

(he looks at HARRY and says cautiously)

A friend . . .

(turns away from HARRY)

HARRY

(to audience)

Good actors aren't the only performers who learn how to fake it.

BRAD

The last time I got kicked out of the house in California, I— . . . Dad wasn't around, I just gave up. . . . I didn't have much to lose, I figured. . . .

(SLIDE: "I'd rather go to hell.")

I'd rather go to hell. . . .

(getting a bit angry)

My life is far better than it was. I've got a place to live and no big problems or worries. I don't worry about where I'm going to sleep or about food. I've got a bike, got some pot. . . . I don't think of myself as a pothead. A pothead is somebody who's totally stoned all day long. I don't do it enough to make it a problem. . . . Off and on, there doesn't have to be any big reason, it's no big deal. . .

.

(calming down)

I'm still mostly the same. . . .

(SLIDE: "Getting my life together.")

Getting my life together.

(BRAD hangs up, takes one of HARRY's notepads and pens; goes to his radio and turns it on; music: "Time" {Alan Parsons Project}; he sits on the blanket and writes a letter)

HARRY

When Brad introduced me to his mother, after proudly showing her the cabin during a brief but long-anticipated visit, I asked whether she felt she could exert a guiding influence over him living one thousand miles away in Southern California.

(reading from one of his index cards)

"We've always been a thousand miles apart," she replied, "even when we were under the same roof."

(SLIDE: Voices)

BRAD

(looks up suddenly, turns off the radio, stares at it, then shouts)

I'm not gonna get caught! I'm not that rotten of a kid!

(sound of distant thunder; HARRY stares at BRAD; BRAD stares back, turns on the radio, sits and wraps himself in the blanket, continues writing)

HARRY

(SLIDE: "emotional problems")

Toward the end of the second year, Brad started to reveal and, somewhat reluctantly, to discuss some deep-seated emotional problems. More and more he kept to himself, a low profile that served double duty. He had a strong aversion to being looked at in settings where he felt he didn't blend in, and his somewhat remote cabin protected him from the eyes of all strangers, including the law.

(SLIDE: "His cabin became his fortress")

In his view and experience, to get in trouble with the police was the worst thing that could happen. He had a shifty manner about him that aroused suspicion, and a police record poised to turn the slightest problem into something more serious. Brad became more hesitant about making trips into town. His cabin became his fortress, and the security of it offered a sense of protection, a place where he could keep out of trouble by keeping to himself.

(HARRY walks slowly to BRAD and touches him on the shoulder; BRAD reacts by pulling away cautiously and staring suspiciously at HARRY)

(SLIDE: There's Always a "Dark and Stormy Night" Somewhere)

(HARRY returns to his desk, puts a rubber band around the second deck of index cards, lays them down and exits, staring worriedly at BRAD)

BRAD

(reading aloud what he's written)

(SLIDE: {the letter as written below in BRAD's shaky handwriting})

Hi

if I sit hear and stair

at this pieac of paper

eny longer ill go crazy

I dont think im scaird

of witing just don't like

to remind myself I

need improvment. its

raining alot past

few days but its warm

'n dry inside

(SLIDE: Stay Put)

(music up; lights fade and sounds of rain and distant thunder continue and segue out; BRAD exits, taking the bike offstage)

SCENE THREE: INTERPRETATION

(SLIDE: Scene Three: Interpretation)

HARRY

(enters carrying a second stool with a small boxed cake on it, sets it stage left; music fades out)

Interpretation is sense-making—to reach out for understanding or explanation beyond the limits of analysis. A researcher transcends data and probes into what's to be made of them through past experience, intuition, and emotion. Both the reach and the risks constitute more of a dare.

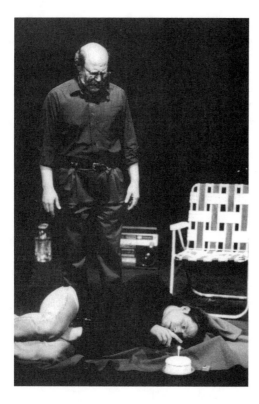

HARRY: He exhibited moods of depression and described relentlessly distracting thoughts.

(SLIDE: Proceed with Caution)

(HARRY returns to his desk, picks up the third deck of index cards)

Fieldwork itself is unquestionably that part of qualitative inquiry in which you have the least control. The more successful you are as a fieldworker, the more you'll learn things that you didn't intend—and possibly didn't want—to learn.

(SLIDE: Paying a Price for Living the Ethnographic Life)

(BRAD enters wearing a black T-shirt under a parka, smoking a joint; he turns on his radio, "Sailing" {Christopher Cross} plays softly under; he sits on the blanket, huddled within himself, fetal-like)

Things had begun going downhill for Brad. He'd come to the conclusion that his life wasn't going anywhere. He exhibited moods of depression and described relentlessly distracting thoughts. He seemed to be living at the edge—not just the edge of town, but the edge of the law, the edge of any sense of community. For once, he wasn't in trouble with anyone else; this time the trouble was within.

(HARRY brings a small birthday cake out of the box and lights its single candle, sets it in front of BRAD; BRAD stares at the candle, moves his finger through the flame)

(SLIDE: "emotional stress")

A once eagerly anticipated 21st birthday that would mark the end of two full years on the mountain became a time of emotional stress and increasing personal anguish for Brad. For failing to seek employment, his food stamps had been cut off and he was penniless. Activities at the cabin often appeared aimless and repetitive. On dreary, rainy days he sometimes sat for hours gazing into the flames of his wood stove, brooding over his hard life and things that seemed forever beyond his reach:

BRAD

A job, a car, friends. A girlfriend.

(HARRY massages BRAD's temples)

HARRY

Along with increasingly frequent headaches, I found him growing preoccupied with events and people largely the creation of his own imagination. Brad described distant voices, usually approving and just within his hearing.

(first voice-over: "Boy, look at that guy—how strong he is—I wouldn't want to mess with him"; BRAD stands suddenly, turns off radio, looks around; second voice-over: "He could be a movie star"; BRAD winces in pain)

Brad, what is it? What's going on in your mind?

(SLIDE: "A sledgehammer to the brain.")

BRAD

A sledgehammer to the brain.

(sound effect of plane taking off, increases in volume as BRAD speaks)

One of my friend's older brothers in Southern California was a crazy fucker. One time they decided to go out to the runways where the jets were coming in. They'd go out there laying right underneath the skid marks, just right under the planes. I never would get that close. Just being out there, after jumping the fence and walking clear out to the runway, is close enough. I never did lie on the runway.

(plane effect becomes a deafening roar then fades out)

(BRAD crosses to his backpack and starts putting personal items into it)

HARRY

(takes cake to his desk, puts it in wastebasket)

Though I note this now in hindsight, Brad, as a young male in his early 20s, was statistically right on schedule as a candidate for a diagnosis of

"I never would get that close."

BRAD: *I never would get that close. . . . I never did lie on the runway.*

(SLIDE: "paranoid schizophrenia")

paranoid schizophrenia. In time—or, not quite in time—before he sank unexpectedly into a mood of utter despair a few days after celebrating his birthday, Brad abruptly announced:

(SLIDE: Now or Never)

BRAD

I'm hitting the road.

(growing agitated)

Something's gotta happen, there's nothing for me here.

HARRY

(crossing to BRAD)

Brad, take a few days to—

BRAD

There's nothing for me here!

(HARRY goes to BRAD and hugs him tightly; BRAD is close to crying)

I thought of pulling myself up by a rope, and when you came up here looking for me you'd be staring at my feet swinging from a tree.

(SLIDE: {office building})

HARRY

(to audience)

I contacted the county mental-health office to learn what resources were available, and I approached Brad with the idea that we should find someone for him to talk with (HARRY helps BRAD out of his parka; he sits BRAD down on the second stool), someone who might provide more help than I could offer. I was able to get him to a counselor, although he insisted that it wouldn't really help. If something specific was bothering him, I hoped he'd be able to talk about it.

BRAD

(to HARRY)

My dad took me to a counseling center at the university; they told me I was "winning the battles but losing the war."

(he turns away and mimes talking to a counselor)

HARRY

(crosses right and caresses the parka)

Although there was little doubt that someday Brad would leave, I felt grave reluctance about seeing him depart in his present mental state. He happened along at a time in my life when I needed someone like him, a strange combination of son and lover. But I happened along in his life when he needed someone desperately, too. I suddenly realized that I would greatly miss this unexpected intruder in my life and thought.

(BRAD rises; HARRY crosses to him)

After a short consultation, Brad was asked to return the following morning to meet with a staff doctor. And what had been the outcome of his visit to the mental-health office?

(SLIDE: "They wouldn't help me.")

BRAD

Counselors don't do anything but talk. Dumb questions. "Do you know what day of the week it is? Today's date? Who's president?" They wouldn't help me.

HARRY

(helps BRAD into his parka)

The two options offered him were to receive outpatient attention or to commit himself to a mental institution until he could

BRAD

get things straightened out.

HARRY

He was adamantly opposed to medication and outpatient care, but he seemed intrigued with going to a mental hospital where he would be clean, comfortable, and cared for.

BRAD

(as if an idea dawns on him)

Hmm. Crazy Brad. OK, if that's what they want me to be, that's what I'll be. I'll tell them whatever I have to tell them to make them think I'm crazy.

(he exits quickly, taking the lawn chair and blanket with him)

(SLIDE: "out of options")

HARRY

They had never intended to commit him. He tried joining the military, but that alternative was blocked because he hadn't graduated from high school. He was out of options, and Brad's pattern was to run rather than give up.

(BRAD reenters with a cardboard box, hurriedly packs his personal belongings in it, and sets it under HARRY's desk)

He wasn't free of society but he had become disconnected from it. Once adrift, nothing seemed to beckon or guide him back. A young man in a hurry to be on his way but with no particular place to go. Brad rummaged through his assortment of belongings and packed valued items in cartons that he stored safely in my basement. I reminded him that the cabin would still be standing, and that he could return there—

(HARRY looks at BRAD, almost pleading)

or to my home.

(BRAD gets his backpack, both men standing awkwardly)

(SLIDE: "I know you like me.")

(to BRAD)

Once you get to the freeway, you have to decide whether you'll head north or south.

BRAD

South. Yeah. See what happens and not worry too much about it.

HARRY

Things usually end up OK.

(BRAD turns to HARRY, looks at him, then hugs HARRY tightly)

BRAD

(tearfully)

I'm sorry. I know you like me.

(HARRY hugs tighter and BRAD struggles loose, rushes to the carton and rummages through it, pulls his toolbox out)

HARRY

Moments before his departure he suddenly changed his mind and began sorting through his possessions, looking for anything that might bring a few dollars at a pawnshop.

BRAD

(defiantly, to HARRY)

These are my things; I can do whatever I want with them!

(he rushes to the radio, grabs it, and runs offstage)

HARRY

Then he was off. He was gone. For a while, I thought he might return to the cabin. Eventually, I resigned myself to the idea that I would probably never see him again.

(as HARRY speaks, he looks through the items in the carton left behind, then goes to his third deck of index cards, takes the rubber bands off the first two sets, shuffles through them as if looking for answers)

(SLIDE: "dysfunctional paranoia")

More than two months after he left, I received a telephone call from his mother in Southern California. A customary wariness that had served him well on the streets seemed to have escalated into dysfunctional paranoia. He hitchhiked a thousand miles and cast about for several weeks, broke, hungry, and lost. After hustling on Santa Monica Boulevard and spending several days in jail in a suburb of Los Angeles on a shoplifting charge, Brad telephoned his mother and confided that he was being followed and that the "Hollywood Mafia" was after him. The streets had become too dangerous. It was time to go home.

(SLIDE: Going Home)

Shortly after arriving at his mother's, Brad voluntarily committed himself to the county mental institution for 16 days. In response to a letter I sent to him in care of his mother, Brad telephoned me once from the institution. The conversation seemed forced and aimless; he concluded it by saying, "Send me money."

(SLIDE: Be Crazy)

After he was released, he started taking prescribed antidepressants and, in his mother's words, eventually became "mellow." As soon as he was formally diagnosed as a mental-health patient, she resigned herself to the fact that he was "insane"—her term—and to the likelihood that she would have to look after him the rest of his life. She said he occasionally rode his bicycle, mostly sat in the little trailer house she rented for him listening to rock music, and was leading what she described as a "very boring life."

(SLIDE: "I always seem to screw things up at the end.")

(beat; HARRY picks up his books from the desk, rises, crosses upstage center)

Brad had been prophetic years earlier when he reflected on what had been and what was yet to be: "I always seem to screw things up at the end." Brad did come back, two and a half years after he had left, unexpectedly and unannounced.

(sound effect of a chain saw continues through the next scene)

(SLIDE: "his deadly ambush")

(BRAD enters wearing his parka and carrying a large gasoline can; he sets it down, goes through HARRY's desk drawers, reads a few index cards)

Hours before either Norman or I returned home one November evening, Brad broke into the house, siphoned 500 gallons of stove oil onto the floors from a storage tank, took my chain saw to cut holes in the ceilings and roof, and trashed the house,

(BRAD flings the index cards through the air and they scatter across the stage, then hides under HARRY's desk)

so that the instant he poured on gasoline and ignited it, the place would become an inferno. Then he waited until either Norman or I came home and walked into his deadly ambush. As usual, I arrived first.

(SLIDE: "You hate me!")

(chain saw sound effect increases in volume; HARRY crosses right as if to reenter his house, stops when he sees the mess)

BRAD

(whispering at first, then building to hysteria; shouts repeatedly)

You hate me. You hate me!

(BRAD grabs HARRY from behind, wrestles him to the floor, sits on his chest, and beats him violently)

HARRY

(pleads then shouts over BRAD's shouting as he's beaten, tries to fend off BRAD's attack)

Brad! What are you doing this for? I don't hate you—I love you!

BRAD

You fucker! I'm gonna kill you! You don't love me! You hate me! You hate me!

(the sound of an automobile driving up, stopping, and car door opening and closing is heard; BRAD is momentarily distracted, HARRY wrestles away from BRAD, runs toward the exit and shouts)

HARRY

Norman! Don't come in! Run!

BRAD

(BRAD rushes to HARRY, grabs and holds him from behind)

Fucker!

HARRY

Go get help—Brad's back—call the police!

BRAD

No!

(BRAD panics; HARRY wrenches away from BRAD and runs offstage; BRAD rushes to the gasoline can and douses the floor; repeats breathlessly)

You hate me. You hate me.

(BRAD crosses to side of stage, reaches into pocket, pulls a match and lights it, throws it and runs off)

HARRY

(shouting offstage)

Norman!

(SLIDE: {a burning house})

(sound of the chain saw is accompanied by the sound of approaching sirens, fire engines; the stage is bathed in red flashing siren lights, fog; HARRY reenters and looks on, dazed; sound of chain saw fades slowly)

The arson inspector described it as the hottest fire he'd ever investigated.

(SLIDE: {HARRY's home after the fire})

(HARRY loses his balance slightly)

The destruction was total.

(light and sound effects fade as HARRY sits)

In the emergency room, being stitched back together, I realized that my worldly possessions now numbered three: an old Chevy Impala and

(pulls the pens from pocket)

two Bic pens.

(he drops them onto the floor)

Losses included my entire professional library—a devastating loss to me—field notes from my previous studies, my lecture and reading notes, a lifetime accumulation of family memorabilia, our household goods, slide photography, recorded music, art and artifacts from all over the world.

(SLIDE: "guilty but insane")

Brad was quickly apprehended and voluntarily confessed to arson and assault. He told the police I had ruined his delusional "Hollywood career," and insisted that everything about our relationship was "detestable" to him.

(BRAD enters in dress shirt and slacks, both men move a stool to center stage)

Initially, Brad had been charged with attempted murder, but the district attorney's office decided on a lesser charge, one that would stick. He changed his plea to "guilty but insane," and the case headed into court for a jury vote as to Brad's sanity.

(SLIDE: {courtroom})

(sound of gavel; HARRY and BRAD stand and mime being sworn in)

Brad had found my place; now it was society's turn, through the courts, to make sure that people like me knew my own.

(both men sit; BRAD tries to control his nervous twitching)

The trial was a professional as well as personal nightmare. Although I was allegedly the victim, for the first four days I became the defendant while a carping public defender built a case to suggest I had gotten exactly what I deserved. Psychiatric testimony argued that although Brad exhibited classic paranoid schizophrenic symptoms, the crime he committed was rooted in a pattern of anti-social behavior he had been demonstrating most of his life. Under oath, Brad's mother insisted he had made up most of his story—the story I felt I had finally gotten right. A further implication was that I extracted the interviews to enhance my career and thus

(they stare at each other)

exploited Brad not only sexually but professionally as well.

(sound of gavel; BRAD and HARRY rise)

(SLIDE: Getting Locked Up)

Three weeks after the jury was convened, they returned their verdict: guilty. They rejected the insanity plea since the state had produced records and counselor reports as far back as when Brad was 11 showing traces of anti-social behavior years before his delusions began. At his sentencing hearing two months after the trial, Brad was asked if he wanted to make a statement. He made one last plea to be sent to the state mental hospital rather than to prison.

(SLIDE: "famous")

BRAD

(looks toward the audience, as if speaking to the judge; he shakes slightly, seems distracted and hyper)

Your Honor, when I was 19 I cut down Professor Wolcott's precious trees. I didn't know I did anything wrong. I could have cleaned up the place, I could have said I was sorry, but he didn't want me to become famous. There's not a doubt in my mind Professor Wolcott hated me for ruining his property, and he broke me so I couldn't become famous.

(stepping forward)

Your Honor, in being famous it's good looks or good luck, and I have good looks. I know I could be a movie star or model or dancer, and have a big house and a swimming pool and a Corvette with my name on the license plate. Professor Wolcott screwed with my head, my ass, and my life. He knew there was something wrong with me and he thought it was funny.

(SLIDE: "I couldn't control myself")

What that man did to me was a crime and I couldn't let him get away with it. I couldn't live the rest of my life thinking that that house, where my career was ruined, was still standing. Your honor, I think I should have been found guilty except for insanity. I couldn't control myself, I was obsessed with hate for that man!

(beat)

I'm, I'm not that bad. I couldn't control myself.

(pantomimes getting handcuffed)

HARRY

The judge imposed a 20-year sentence, and urged that Brad be considered for psychiatric assessment and assistance in prison. However, he imposed no *minimum* sentence.

BRAD

(spoken towards HARRY, menacingly)

Besides, they've got to let you out sometime.

(BRAD turns to exit but stops before completely off)

HARRY

I had hoped—and even formally requested—that Brad be sentenced to a mental institution rather than prison, but I didn't relish the idea of his ever again being without supervision. For most of the time he was assigned to a special voluntary program for emotionally disturbed inmates. At his parole hearing, I assume Brad had been well coached as to appropriate responses, because he stated, in my presence,

BRAD

(to the judge, trying to appear sane)

I don't even think about Harry Wolcott any more.

(exits)

HARRY

(visibly hurt by Brad's remark)

(SLIDE: "he was eventually released")

When he was eventually released, Brad was rearrested for a parole violation that increased the total time he served to almost five years. When paroled the second time, he was sent to California in the custody of his mother.

(crosses to his desk)

During one brief period Brad started making telephone calls—long distance, collect—but I was overseas at the time. His calls terrified Norman. Then he stopped.

(SLIDE: "I don't even think about Harry Wolcott any more.")

Has Brad forgotten about me, as he insisted so appropriately? What was the genesis of his hate? And why did it get transformed into his insistence that *I* hated *him* in the last words he ever spoke to me?

(sorting through notepads)

Years later, rereading materials and looking through old notes, I discovered that I had Brad's Social Security number.

(picks up phone, dials)

On a whim, I called the agency to see if anyone would at least tell me whether he's still alive.

(holds receiver to ear; beat)

He is. They said they could tell me that, but nothing more.

(hangs up)

Somehow the news excites me, as though there's hope of someday learning what went wrong. If we were back at square one, I'd still exchange rib-crushing hugs with him. But a confrontation might be fatal. A court psychiatrist once suggested that the critical unknown is: "What triggered Brad's violent response, and could a similar reaction be precipitated again?"

HARRY: Well. Quantitative *studies* have *always been safer.*

(pause)

Well. *Quantitative* studies *have* always been safer.

EPILOGUE

(SLIDE: Epilogue)

(HARRY picks up some of the index cards, sets the stage aright as best as he can, puts away things in his desk)

HARRY

In a professional lifetime devoted to teaching, research, and writing, I know little and understand even less about this case, the one that's affected me the most, and the one that continues to haunt me for answers I doubt I'll ever find.

(SLIDE: Getting It Right)

I felt I knew Brad so well, so intimately, that I would get a straight story—and get the story straight. I was reeling then, and continue to do so to this day, from realizing how little we ever know, heightened in this instance by the feeling that this time, in my own cultural milieu, my own language, and even in my own backyard, I had finally *gotten it right.*

(getting angry, he slams the desk drawer shut)

I just wish that it all might have turned out differently.

(SLIDE: Meaning)

What is this *really* a study of? The meaning of the story isn't precisely clear because meanings themselves aren't all that apparent or clear. We don't have neat findings, tidy hypotheses, conclusions that can be summarized or reduced to tables and charts. There are no guarantees, no umbrellas or safety nets, no fool-proof scientific method to follow.

(SLIDE: Validity)

Fieldwork consists of more than collecting data, something that catapults it beyond simply being there. And whatever constitutes that elusive "more" makes all the difference. Regardless of outcome, I think the critical test is how deeply you've felt involved and affected personally. *Provocative*, not *persuasive*.

(SLIDE: Understanding)

(HARRY is close to tears)

After years of attending so singularly to the sanctity of methods, I finally realize that only *understanding* matters. We must not only transform our data, we must *transcend* them. *Insight* is our forte! The whole purpose of the enterprise is *revelation*! When you emphasize description, you want your audience to see what you saw. When you emphasize analysis, you want your audience to know what you know. When you emphasize interpretation, you want your audience to . . . understand what you think you yourself have understood.

(pause)

(SLIDE: Last Words)

(he walks to the projection screen)

In the end, we only abandon our studies; we never really complete them. The human condition doesn't remain static long enough for the work to be completed, even for an instant. You need to recognize when to keep reaching, when to focus, and when to stop.

(SLIDE: {face shot of BRAD})

So. How *do* you "conclude" a qualitative study?

(music up: "Father Figure" by George Michael; HARRY looks at slide of BRAD)

You don't.

(lights fade to black; SLIDE of BRAD fades to black as music rises)

(CURTAIN CALL: HARRY and BRAD in tableau, both staring intensely at each other; SLIDE: {the woods}; lights out; both men exit as music continues and house lights rise)

References and Select Bibliography

Atkinson, Paul, Amanda Coffey, Sara Delamont, John Lofland, and Lyn Lofland, eds.
2001 Handbook of Ethnography. London: Sage.

Barone, Thomas
2002 From Genre Blurring to Audience Blending: Thoughts Inspired by the Ethnodrama, "Finding My Place: The Brad Trilogy." Anthropology and Education Quarterly 33(2).

Bernard, H. Russell
1988 Research Methods in Cultural Anthropology. Newbury Park, CA: Sage.

Bourdieu, Pierre
1986 L'illusion Biographique. Actes de la Recherches en Sciences Sociales 62/63 (translated as The Biographical Illusion. Working Papers and Proceedings of the Center for Psychosocial Studies 14, 1987).

Brandes, Stanley
1982 Ethnographic Autobiographies in American Anthropology. *In* Crisis in Anthropology: View from Spring Hill, 1980. E. A. Hoebel, R. Currier, and S. Kaiser, eds. Pp. 187–202. New York: Garland Publishing Company.

Brettell, Caroline B., ed.
1993 When They Read What We Write: The Politics of Ethnography. Westport, CT: Bergin and Garvey.

Busier, Holly-Lynn, Kelly Clark, Rebecca Esch, Corrine Glesne, Yvette Pigeon, and Jill Tarule
1997 Intimacy in Research. Qualitative Studies in Education 10(2):165–70.

Cesara, Manda [Karla Poewe]
1982 Reflections of a Woman Anthropologist: No Hiding Place. New York: Academic Press.

Coffey, Amanda
1999 The Ethnographic Self: Fieldwork and the Representation of Identity. London: Sage.

Cole, Ardra L., and J. Gary Knowles, eds.
2001 Lives in Context: The Art of Life History Research. Walnut Creek, CA: AltaMira Press.

Cole, Sally Cooper
  1995 Ruth Landes and the Early Ethnography of Race and Gender. *In* Women
     Writing Culture. Ruth Behar and Deborah A. Gordon, eds. Pp. 166–85.
     Berkeley: University of California Press.

Cousins, Norman
  1961 Confrontation. Saturday Review of Literature, March 25.

de Laine, Marlene
  2000 Fieldwork, Participation and Practice: Ethics and Dilemmas in Qualitative
     Research. London: Sage.

Denzin, Norman K.
  1997 Interpretive Ethnography. Thousand Oaks, CA: Sage.

Ditton, Jason
  1977 Part Time Crime. London: Macmillan.

Edgerton, Robert
  1978 The Study of Deviance—Marginal Man or Everyman? *In* The Making of
     Psychological Anthropology. G. D. Spindler, ed. Pp. 442–76. Berkeley: Univer-
     sity of California Press.

Edson, C. H.
  1982 Schooling for Work and Working at School. Perspectives on Immigrant and
     Working-class Education in Urban America, 1880–1920. *In* The Public School
     Monopoly. Robert B. Everhart, ed. Pp. 145–87. Cambridge, MA: Ballinger.

Eisner, Elliot W., and Alan Peshkin, eds.
  1990 Qualitative Inquiry in Education: The Continuing Debate. New York:
     Teachers College Press.

Estroff, Sue E.
  1981 Making It Crazy: An Ethnography of Psychiatric Clients in an American
     Community. Berkeley: University of California Press. [Reissued in paperback
     1985 with a new epilogue.]

Fortes, Meyer
  1938 Social and Psychological Aspects of Education in Taleland. Supplement to
     Africa 11(4):1–64.

Geertz, Clifford
  1973 The Interpretation of Cultures. New York: Basic Books.

Ginzberg, Eli
  1980 The School/Work Nexus: Transition of Youth from School to Work.
     Bloomington, IN: Phi Delta Kappa Educational Foundation.

Grinker, Richard Roy
  2000 In the Arms of Africa: The Life of Colin M. Turnbull. New York: St. Mar-
     tin's Press.

Herskovits, Melville J.
1948   Man and His Works: The Science of Cultural Anthropology. New York: Alfred A. Knopf.

Hobbs, Dick
2001   Ethnography and the Study of Deviance. *In* Handbook of Ethnography. Paul Atkinson, et al., eds. Pp. 201–19. London: Sage.

Jaeger, Richard M., ed.
1988   Complementary Methods for Research in Education. Washington, DC: American Educational Research Association.
1997   Complementary Methods for Research in Education. 2nd edition. Washington, DC: American Educational Research Association.

Järvinen, Margaretha
2000   The Biographical Illusion: Constructing Meaning in Qualitative Interviews. Qualitative Inquiry 6(3):370–91.

Kirk, Stuart A., and Herb Kutchings
1992   The Selling of DSM: The Rhetoric of Science in Psychiatry. New York: Aldine de Gruyter.

Kleinman, Arthur
1995   Writing at the Margins: Discourse between Anthropology and Medicine. Berkeley: University of Calfornia Press.

Kulick, Don, and Margaret Willson, eds.
1995   Taboo: Sex, Identity and Erotic Subjectivity in Anthropological Fieldwork. New York: Routledge.

Levin, Henry M.
1982   Education and Work. Program Report No. 82-B8. Palo Alto, CA: Institute for Research on Educational Finance and Governance, Stanford University.
1983   Youth Unemployment and its Educational Consequences. Educational Evaluation and Policy Analysis, 5(2):231–47.

Lewin, Ellen, and William L. Leap, eds.
1996   Out in the Field: Reflections of Lesbian and Gay Anthropologists. Urbana, IL: University of Illinois Press.

Lewis, Oscar
1961   Children of Sanchez: Autobiography of a Mexican Family. New York: Random House.

Luhrmann, Tanya M.
2000   Of Two Minds: An Anthropologist Looks at American Psychiatry. New York: Random House.

MacNeil, Ian., and G. Glover, producers
1959   Four Families. Film narrated by Ian MacNeil and Margaret Mead. National Film Board of Canada.

Maguire, Patricia
1987 Doing Participatory Research: A Feminist Approach. Amherst: Center for International Education, University of Massachusetts.

Mailer, Norman
1979 The Executioner's Song. New York: Warner Books.

Mann, Dale
1982 Chasing the American Dream: Jobs, Schools, and Employment Training Programs in New York State. Teachers College Record 83(3):341–76.

Markowitz, Fran, and Michael Ashkenazi, eds.
1999 Sex, Sexuality and the Anthropologist. Urbana: University of Illinois Press.

Mead, Margaret
1953 National Character. In Anthropology Today. A. L. Kroeber, ed. Pp. 642–67. Chicago: University of Chicago Press.

Miles, Matthew B., and A. Michael Huberman
1984 Qualitative Data Analysis: A Sourcebook of New Methods. Beverly Hills, CA: Sage.
1994 Qualitative Data Analysis: An Expanded Sourcebook. 2nd edition. Thousand Oaks, CA: Sage.

National Commission on Excellence in Education
1983 A Nation at Risk: The Imperative for Educational Reform. Washington, DC: Department of Education.

Noblit, George W., and William T. Pink, eds.
1987 Schooling in Social Context: Qualitative Studies. Norwood, NJ: Ablex Publishing Company.

Oregon Department of Education
1980 Oregon Early School Leavers Study. Salem: Oregon Department of Education.

Page, Reba
1997 Teaching About Validity. International Journal of Qualitative Studies in Education 10(2):145–55.

Peacock, James L., and Dorothy C. Holland
1993 The Narrated Self: Life Stories in Process. Ethos 21(4):367–83.

Plummer, Ken
2001 The Call of Life Stories in Ethnographic Research. In Handbook of Ethnography. Paul Atkinson, et al., eds. Pp. 395–406. London: Sage.

Punch, Maurice
1986 The Politics and Ethics of Fieldwork. Sage University Paper on Qualitative Research Methods, Volume 3. Beverly Hills, CA: Sage.

Reed-Danahay, Deborah
  2001   Autobiography, Intimacy and Ethnography. *In* Handbook of Ethnography. Paul Atkinson, et al., eds. Pp. 407–25. London: Sage.

Saldaña, Johnny
  1998a Ethical Issues in an Ethnographic Performance Text: The "Dramatic Impact" of "Juicy Stuff." Research in Drama Education 3(2):181–96.
  1998b "Maybe Someday, If I'm Famous . . .": An Ethnographic Performance Text. *In* Drama and Theatre in Education. Juliana Saxton and Carole Miller, eds. Pp. 89–109. Brisbane, Australia: IDEA Publishers.
  1999   Playwriting with Data: Ethnographic Performance Texts. Youth Theatre Journal 13:60–71.

Shaw, Clifford R.
  1930   The Jack-Roller: A Delinquent Boy's Own Story. Chicago: University of Chicago Press.

Simmons, Leo, ed.
  1942   Sun Chief: The Autobiography of a Hopi Indian. New Haven: Yale University Press.

Singleton, John
  1983   On Editorial Succession and Academic Orthodoxy. Anthropology and Education Quarterly 14(1):2.

Snodgrass, Jon, ed.
  1982   The Jack-Roller at Seventy: A Fifty-Year Follow-Up. Lexington, MA: D.C. Heath & Company.

Tengström, Anders, Sheilagh Hodgins, and Gunnar Kullgren
  2001   Men with Schizophrenia Who Behave Violently: The Usefulness of an Early-Versus-Late-Start Offender Typology. Schizophrenia Bulletin 27(2):205–18.

Tron, Esther, ed.
  1982   Adequate Education: Issues in Its Definition and Implementation. School Finance Project, Working Papers. Washington, DC: Department of Education, National Institute of Education.

Wallace, A. F. C.
  1961a The Psychic Unity of Human Groups. *In* Studying Personality Cross-culturally. Bert Kaplan, ed. Evanston, IL: Row Peterson and Company.
  1961b Schools in Revolutionary and Conservative Societies. *In* Anthropology and Education. F. C. Gruber, ed. Pp. 25–54. Philadelphia: University of Pennsylvania Press.

Werth, Barry
  2001   The Scarlet Professor: Newton Arvin: A Literary Life Shattered by Scandal. New York: Doubleday/Random House.

Willis, Paul H.
  1977   Learning to Labour: How Working Class Kids Get Working Class Jobs. Hampshire, England: Gower Publishing Co.

Wolcott, Harry F.

1964 A Kwakiutl Village and Its School. Unpublished doctoral dissertation, Stanford University.

1967 A Kwakiutl Village and School. New York: Holt, Rinehart and Winston. [Reissued 1989 by Waveland Press with a new afterword.]

1973 The Man in the Principal's Office: An Ethnography. New York: Holt, Rinehart and Winston. [Reissued 1984 by Waveland Press with a new introduction.]

1974 The Teacher as an Enemy. *In* Education and Cultural Process: Toward an Anthropology of Education. George D. Spindler, ed. Pp. 411–25. New York: Holt, Rinehart and Winston. [Reissued 1987, 1997 by Waveland Press.]

1982 The Anthropology of Learning. Anthropology and Education Quarterly 13(2):83–108.

1983 Adequate Schools and Inadequate Education: The Life History of a Sneaky Kid. Anthropology and Education Quarterly 14(1):3–32. (Reprinted in Wolcott 1994.)

1987 Life's Not Working: Cultural Alternatives to Career Alternatives. *In* Schooling in Social Context: Qualitative Studies. George W. Noblit and William T. Pink, eds. Pp. 303–24. Norwood, NJ: Ablex. (Reprinted in Wolcott 1994.)

1990a On Seeking—and Rejecting—Validity in Qualitative Research. *In* Qualitative Inquiry in Education: The Continuing Debate. Elliot Eisner and Alan Peshkin, eds. Pp. 121–52. New York: Teachers College Press. (Reprinted in Wolcott 1994.)

1990b Writing Up Qualitative Research. Newbury Park, CA: Sage.

1994 Transforming Qualitative Data: Description, Analysis, and Interpretation. Thousand Oaks, CA: Sage.

1995 The Art of Fieldwork. Walnut Creek, CA: AltaMira Press.

1997 Validating Reba: A Commentary on "Teaching About Validity." International Journal of Qualitative Studies in Education 10(2):157–59.

1999 Ethnography: A Way of Seeing. Walnut Creek, CA: AltaMira Press.

2001 Writing Up Qualitative Research. 2nd edition. Thousand Oaks, CA: Sage.

Index

Acknowledgments

THREE people are directly responsible for my writing this book and for the form it has taken. John Singleton has voiced encouragement ever since he wrote a foreword to the original Sneaky Kid piece in 1983. He jumped at the chance to write again this time, still affirming his support for what he calls a "morally significant ethnography." Mitch Allen first let me draw the three separate Brad articles into the trilogy in 1994 and recently suggested it was time to write the book. With a deft editorial hand, he then suggested the arrangement of material you have here, reducing five chapters I originally proposed at the end into the one succinct chapter with which I conclude the account. Johnny Saldaña reinvigorated the whole story by asking if he could write an ethnodrama about it. He has generously allowed me to reproduce the play's script here.

Others lent help and encouragement, especially Sakre Edson, whose notes from the trial were superb, Rachel Fudge, Barbara Harrison, and Arden Munkres. Norman wasn't especially enthused about the project but understood that this was a book I had to write someday, and now it is done.

About the Authors

HARRY F. WOLCOTT is professor emeritus in the Department of Anthropology at the University of Oregon. He has been at the university since completing a Ph.D. at Stanford in 1964 and has served on the faculties of the College of Education and the Department of Anthropology.

JOHNNY SALDAÑA is a professor of theatre at Arizona State University, and his studies in qualitative research range from ethnography to ethnotheatre. He has written several articles on theatre teachers' perceptions of their practice and young people's development as audiences and artists. One of these studies includes the ethnodrama *Maybe Someday, If I'm Famous . . .*, a one-act case study of an adolescent actor.